# An Introduction to Christian Apologetics

# An Introduction to Christian Apologetics

## Exploring, Explaining, and Establishing the Gospel in Light of Its Organic Character

DAVID P. SMITH

WIPF & STOCK · Eugene, Oregon

AN INTRODUCTION TO CHRISTIAN APOLOGETICS
Exploring, Explaining, and Establishing the Gospel in Light of Its Organic Character



Wipf & Stock
An Imprint of Wipf and Stock Publishers
199 W. 8th Ave., Suite 3
Eugene, OR 97401

www.wipfandstock.com

PAPERBACK ISBN: 979-8-3852-7531-1
HARDCOVER ISBN: 979-8-3852-7532-8
EBOOK ISBN: 979-8-3852-7533-5

VERSION NUMBER 05/15/26

*Dedicated to Gresham, Isaac, and Katherine—*
*blessings beyond my ability to express.*

“But ‘Systematic Theology’ does not exist by itself or for itself. It is a member of an organism, and it exists for the organism of which it is a part and in which it plays its part for the benefit of the whole.”

B. B. Warfield, “The Idea of Systematic Theology”

# Contents

# Introduction

Christian apologetics can be broadly defined as the defense of the Christian faith. Apologetics has always been a part of the life of God's people, because of who God's people are—those who have been called by God out of the darkness of their own sin into the light of God's way, truth, and life, and thereby equipped with the gospel in order to propagate it. But while Christian apologetics has always been a part of the church's existence, the church's clarity regarding how apologetics fits within her total life and doctrine has not always been very clear. How exactly does apologetics relate to evangelism? Is there a difference? If so, what is the difference? And how precisely does apologetics fit with being a disciple of the Lord Jesus? Is it necessary for it? It is these and other questions that the present volume seeks to answer—at least in some provisional way.

Within American Christianity, apologetics began to emerge in a serious way during the nineteenth century, particularly because of the rise of Protestant Liberal theology.[1] Of course, this in itself may come as a surprise to some today, whose familiarity with apologetics doesn't seem to stretch any further past the date of their initial profession of Christian faith, if it even goes back that far. Over the past 150 years, in the Reformed and Presbyterian world the discipline of apologetics has been led by men such as Abraham Kuyper (1837–1920), Herman Bavinck (1854–1921), Benjamin Breckinridge Warfield (1851–1921), J. Gresham Machen (1881–1937), Cornelius Van Til (1895–1987), and Francis Schaeffer (1912–84), to name a few. Most of what has transpired in the discipline of apologetics since Schaeffer and Van Til went to their eternal rewards has been a debate on the most biblically faithful method

1. For a sketch of the history of apologetics and the defining of it near the beginning of the twentieth century see Warfield, "Apologetics," in *Works* 9:3–21. For a history of Protestant Liberal theology see Dorrien, *Making of American Liberal Theology*.

for doing apologetics. For the most part, that debate has been set up as a contrast between presuppositionalism and evidentialism.

Typically, the debates surrounding apologetics revolve around whether one is a presuppositionalist—believing that Christian unbelief is best attacked by challenging the controlling beliefs (presuppositions) by which the non-Christian interprets the evidences for Christian faith—or one is an evidentialist—believing that Christian unbelief is best attacked by stockpiling evidence that shows the compelling reasons why one should believe in Jesus as one's Savior. Each approach generally aligns with one of two views of truth: coherence or correspondence. Presuppositionalism addresses whether a person's reasoning coheres, is self-consistent or valid, whereas evidentialism addresses whether a person's reasoning corresponds to the objective reality outside of one's self. At a certain point, the debate can get to be a bit silly. After all, attacking a non-Christian's presuppositions can only be done by addressing how they handle or interpret evidences. As my late friend, Gary Davis, used to say: "My presupposition is that you need some evidence!" Neither camp actually engages in apologetics without acting in concert with principles stressed in the other camp. While I recognize that this is a bit of an over-simplification of their differences, nonetheless there is too much truth to this to allow the debate to have more credibility than it should. Having studied and written on these matters for over thirty years, I have concluded that if more attention had been paid to Warfield the intensity of this debate, and a few others, would not have given as much shape to the apologetical literature as it has. In my estimation there seems to be generally two reasons for this.

First, it is the result of some men misrepresenting other men's positions on these matters, and second, it is the result of misconceiving the nature of apologetics. The two are not unrelated. In particular, the *organic union* of the two can be seen in the treatment, or the lack thereof, received by Warfield.

While Warfield is well known among those steeped in American church history and especially the history of Reformed and Presbyterian theology, the history written about him, and in particular his view and practice of apologetics, has needed correction.[2] Some of this correction has taken place over the last few decades and, of course, is unavoidably

2. For some of these corrections see Calhoun, *Princeton Seminary;* Helseth, *"Right Reason" and the Princeton Mind*; Smith, *B. B. Warfield's*; Zaspel, *Theology of B. B. Warfield*.

connected to needed corrections on the history of Old Princeton (1812–1929) in general.[3] Still, questions remain as to the degree to which these corrections have gained traction or bore much fruit, especially in the area of apologetics.

I chose the term *organic union* above because Warfield identified the Christian faith and life as a living organism and applied the organic motif or theme in his analysis of all aspects of Christian theology.[4] Herein lies a window into understanding Warfield's thought and written work. Warfield took seriously the Bible's emphasis on the Triune personal God as truth. According to him, God is truth and so is his written word. Jesus, the Second Person of the Trinity said, "I am the way, and the truth, and the life. No one comes to the Father except through me" (John 14:6). Truth is a *living being*, an *organism*. Furthermore, God equates himself with his written word (Gen 12:3/Gal 3:6–8; Exod 9:16/Rom 9:17; Gen 2:24/Matt 19:5; John 1:1–5) so that we only rightly understand the Scriptures of the Old and New Testament when we understand them as a living organism (Heb 4:12–13). Still further, this living organism that is the Christian Scriptures entails the sound doctrine that Christians are to believe and propagate. This is why the gospel of the Lord Jesus Christ, which those same Scriptures communicate, is the *power* of God for salvation to all those who believe those Scriptures. This salvation is eternal *life* and *knowledge of God* (John 3:16; 17:3). Warfield's view of theology in general and apologetics in particular expresses what he believed were at least some of the unavoidable implications of these truths. Sadly, his views were misunderstood and misrepresented by many, even by some

3. For a recent foray into these broader corrections see DeYoung et al., *New Perspectives on Old Princeton.*

4. The organic theme pervades Warfield's writings so there is not simply one essay to which we would go to discover it. For a few representative examples see Warfield, "Apologetics," in *Works* 9, op. cit. fn. 1; "Biblical Idea of Revelation," in *Works* 1:3–34; "Christianity and Revelation," in *Selected Shorter Writings* 1:3–30; "Idea of Systematic Theology," in *Works* 9:49–87; "Task and Method of Theology," in *Works* 9:91–109; "Right of Systematic Theology," in *Selected Shorter Writings* 2:219–79; "Spiritual Culture in the Theological Seminary," in *Selected Shorter Writings* 2:468–96. Warfield was not alone in stressing the organic nature of the Christian faith and life and Christian theology. During the late nineteenth and early twentieth centuries Abraham Kuyper and Herman Bavinck did the same. Warfield, however, faulted both in various ways for failing to be fully consistent with Scripture's organic theme. Warfield, "Introduction to Francis R. Beattie's *Apologetics*," in *Selected Shorter Writings* 2:93–105; "Review of *De Zekerheid des Geloofs*," in *Selected Shorter Writings* 2:106–23; Bavinck, *Reformed Dogmatics*; Kuyper, *Principles of Sacred Theology*; Kuyper, *Lectures on Calvinism*; Brock and Sutanto, *Neo-Calvinism*; Eglinton, *Trinity as Organism.*

who have largely been sympathetic to his general commitment to the inerrancy of Scripture, Reformed theology, and the Westminster Confession of Faith.[5]

What follows in these pages is a treatment of apologetics that seeks to be consistent with Warfield's conception of it. By stating things in this way I recognize that there are ways in which I may have failed to do full justice to Warfield's conception of apologetics and how it relates to theology more broadly, and Christian evangelism and discipleship in particular. Obviously, I don't think that I have failed in that regard, but I am open to correction. At any rate, what follows is not, by any stretch of the imagination, a full treatment of Warfield's views on these matters. Instead, it is *a Warfieldian* perspective. But it is a perspective that I believe is not only consistent with what Warfield affirmed, but also, and more importantly, faithful to Scripture, and has the potential to help those already well versed in these matters to rethink their understanding of not merely Christian apologetics, evangelism, and discipleship, but also Christian theology in general.[6]

Some of us are accustomed to speaking about and affirming the need for paradigm shifts, or simply a change in thinking, a changing of the lens, so to speak, through which something is viewed. What Warfield gave to me was nothing less than a paradigm shift regarding theology and the whole Christian faith and life. It all revolves the organic motif.

I have been a professing Christian nearly all my life. I was taught that in order to become a Christian I would need to repent of my sin and trust Jesus as my Lord and Savior. Pretty basic. In other words, to be a Christian meant you believed particular things to be true, other things to be false, and in order to mature or grow as a Christian one had to learn the Bible and act in accordance with it. Still pretty basic, and all

5. For a more in-depth look at these misunderstandings and misrepresentations see Smith, *B. B. Warfield's*.

6. I would concur with Mathison, *Toward a Reformed Apologetic*, 230–32, regarding what a faithfully Reformed apologetic must strive to be, and would add that Warfield's scholarship meets the requirements that Mathison lays out. His criteria is: (1) "a solid understanding of real historical Reformed theology" by using the Reformed confessions as "the base line standard in the development of a Reformed apologetic" while interpreting them "within their own historical, ecclesiastical, theological and philosophical context"; (2) "an apologetic that conforms to what we find in Scripture" rather than "presuppose our apologetic and then read Scripture through that lens"; (3) uprooting "any unbiblical philosophical elements that have been planted in Reformed soil"; and (4) "an apologetic that can be understood by any intelligent Christian, and it will be one that can be put into practice."

completely true. What this inevitably entailed was a stress on getting one's doctrine correct and one's behavior in line with what Scripture reveals. All this lays a heavy stress on thinking, on getting one's thinking in line with how one is living. This is all basic to Protestantism, nor is it, in itself, contrary to Scripture.[7] And because it is not, the most faithful pastors and theologians in the Christian tradition have always stressed right doctrine. In fact, this is reflective of both the Protestant view of the Bible, in general, and the Reformed and Presbyterian view of apologetics and evangelism and discipleship, in particular. But only to a point. This only describes the relationships between these things in one way. That way is not incorrect, but what Warfield can help us see is that it is not sufficient in itself to express the full truth regarding that relationship. As a result, while the descriptions are true, they are also somewhat reductionistic. In short, they can easily mislead us to the fuller truth that their *organic* union reveals.[8]

Imagine that you are in a room full of people and among them are two individuals, one man and one woman. Obviously, because they are in the room they bear some relationship to each other. I ask you to tell me about their relationship. You don't know them, so, you ask them some questions and you come back and tell me that what also defines their relationship to each other is that they both like chocolate ice cream and classical music, have known each other for thirty-two years, live in the same town, and both like baseball. We both conclude that these two people have a somewhat significant relationship. Should we go away thinking that we know enough about them so that we can accurately interpret

7. For a recent treatment of spiritual formation that stresses this point see Bingham, *Heart Aflame for God*.

8. While Bingham, *Heart Aflame for God*, rightly faults Roman Catholic and Greek Orthodox treatments of spiritual formation for their reductionistic sacramentalism and mysticism, and certain Protestant denigrations of a word-centered piety, he fails to understand that there is some merit to the critique of an overly intellectualized or cognitivist approach to spiritual formation within the Reformed tradition. This can be seen in his own failure to do full justice to the organic nature of spiritual formation. This is demonstrated in his somewhat shriveled analysis of the individual Christian in relationship to the church. Ironically, while he has an appendix, "A Brief Note on Spiritual Formation, Individualism, and the Church," 337–41, that warns against an "unhealthy *individualism*" (italics his), it is this appendix that actually serves to reveal why one simply cannot do full justice to the Christian faith and life and its view of spiritual formation by failing to thoroughly integrate one's treatment of the individual with the life of the church in one's Bible reading, prayer, and meditation. To put it simply, the Bible does not allow us to regard the individual Christian in any way apart from their place within God's covenant community.

their interactions with each other? If we did, we would be foolish. It is not that any of these truths are inconsequential regarding how we should think about them, but that by themselves these truths are not sufficient. After all, they have known each other for thirty-two years. There is more to their relationship that demands further investigation. What if they are actually brother and sister? What if they are husband and wife? Those are two very different kinds of relationships and if either one is true of them, then that truth ought to seriously condition how we think about everything that we know of those individuals. This one truth about what exactly characterizes their relationship can dictate our entire interpretation of the rest of our knowledge of them. This is what Warfield's organic motif has the potential to do for us with respect to theology and the Christian faith and life—lead us to reexamine and reinterpret what we thought we knew of it.

Warfield's stress on the organic motif in his treatment of Christian theology can challenge our previously held assumptions. How should we think about human thinking? Are our thoughts merely rational connections? Is what we or anyone else believes best understood as an intellectual exercise involving the pursuit of understanding logically coherent thoughts? Is Christian doctrine merely a set of beliefs that are supremely expressed in grammatically correct statements? How exactly does Christian living that involves our affections or desires relate to Christian thinking? If I just get my thinking straight as reflected in my assent to particular grammatically correct statements, does this, by itself, make me a Christian? My understanding of the answers to these questions was revolutionized once I read Warfield. It has everything to do with his stress on the organic.

According to Warfield, God's revelation, and therefore Christian theology that is an intellectual reflection on that revelation, is best understood along organic lines. According to him, God's revelation, which can be identified according to two species—either as natural and supernatural, or general and special or natural and soteriological[9]—is most accurately understood as an organism, because this revelation is alive—literally! Warfield referred to these two couplets that describe God's revelation as forming "one organic whole."[10] What they both reveal is God

9. The term "soteriological" comes from the New Testament Greek word *sotēr* which means "savior." *Sōzō* is the New Testament Greek verb which means "I save." That which is soteriological pertains to matters of salvation.

10. Warfield, "Christianity and Revelation," in *Selected Shorter Writings* 1:27.

himself, and because they do, one is only correct in one's understanding of God's revelation when one affirms that it is an organism, a living reality. As Warfield put it:

> Revelation is, therefore, never an unconscious emanation or an involuntary reflection of God in his works: it is always a conscious, free, intentional making of himself known, a purposed self-expression. That God may be known at all from his works, is due, therefore, to his designed expression of himself in his works, with the end of giving knowledge of himself and so of awaking and nourishing religion in his creatures.[11]

In this same essay, Warfield referred to God's special revelation as a "historic process, an organic system, a continuous divine activity directed to destroying the power of sin," which "is the redemptive process itself conceived as a manifestation of God's nature and character."[12] Since God is the *living* God, his revelation of himself could not be anything less than living. This has profound implications for how we think about the entire Christian faith and life, and in particular not only what we ought to mean by Christian doctrine in general, but how we conceive of the relationships that hold between the doctrines that comprise the Christian faith and life.

Throughout his four decades of teaching, preaching, and writing, Warfield gave expression to what he believed were implications that followed from these truths. Among other things, this stress on God's revelation and Christian doctrine as organisms affirms that human thinking cannot *merely* be analyzed and evaluated as rational propositions but rather as a living organism. Warfield would have us understand that the Christian church as a whole and every expression of it, every individual Christian, and every theological or doctrinal affirmation are all living organisms in various stages of health and growth. In turn, they are all part of the living organism of God's revelation. This means that each can and should be evaluated and treated according to what marks their health and quality of organic growth. And what is true of organisms is that every individually distinct part of them is unavoidably united to every other part of them.

Living organisms are the expression of a living system. Some, of course, are more complex than others. One can safely say that since God is Triune—the Father, the Son, and the Holy Spirit—he is the most

11. Warfield, "Christianity and Revelation," in *Selected Shorter Writings* 1:28.

12. Warfield, "Christianity and Revelation," in *Selected Shorter Writings* 1:29.

complex organism of all organisms. He is an utterly unique organism and the source and definer of all other organisms, since he is the creator. Since creation reveals God, then in some sense we can say that there is a fundamental organic, relational, and divine nature to reality. Psalm 19 and Rom 1 make the same point. This is the fundamental reason why individual Christians cannot be rightly analyzed apart from their relationship to the whole body of Christ, the church. According to Warfield, all of the organic character to these realities has profound implications for how we view the gospel, the Christian faith and life, and defend and commend the gospel.

When we go to Scripture to consider the nature of the Christian faith and life, we find that nature in all its organic character plays a vital role in Jesus explaining the Christian faith and life. Jesus constantly drew people's attention to the creation and how it displayed numerous truths central to the Christian faith and life. Salt and light, trees and fruit, seed and its production, vines, weeds and thorns, sheep, the flowers, rocks and sand, the moon, sun and stars, and bread and water were all used by Jesus to teach truths that reveal the nature of the Christian faith and life. One of my favorites is in Matt 7 when Jesus teaches about false prophets and compares them to a tree that produces bad fruit. Good trees produce good fruit. What the tree *is* determines what the tree *does*. So too with people. It is a profound theological and metaphysical truth. But at a time when it is believed by so many that we can't have true knowledge of what *is* and humans must manufacture their own reality, it is easy not to work at discerning what is and living in harmony with it, but instead trying to manufacture reality on your own, and merely deciding how things are related.[13] The biblical conception, however, is that the entire creation has a living character to it given by God, and that the Christian life is just that—a life, with Jesus as the vine, apart from whom we can do nothing (John 15:1–8). Warfield can help us return to and accurately understand this perspective.

By operating with an organic perspective we will learn how to *distinguish* two or more realities (often doctrines or ideas) from each other without *disconnecting* them from each other so that they have no meaningful relation to each other, or *dissolving* them into each other so that their distinct identity is lost. Like a flower petal that is unavoidably united organically to the stem and root system while still maintaining its own

13. For an analysis of how many in Christian education circles have fallen prey to this pattern of thought see Hoch and Smith, *Old School, New Clothes*.

distinct character, Warfield's organic motif helps us see the organic union between doctrines and theological concepts that enables us to identify them for what they are in themselves, while also distinguishing them from and relating them to other doctrines and concepts to which they are unavoidably united. Indeed, we will see how particular distortions of the Christian faith and life are all about either disconnecting particular doctrines and realities from each other so that they are set off against each other, or by dissolving them into each other so that their distinct identity and character is lost, and distorted into something that Scripture reveals that they aren't.

What follows is an exploration of Christian apologetics that seeks to do justice to the organic nature of the gospel and the Christian faith and life. Warfield's perspective commends to us that our beliefs and reasoning processes are not first and foremost intellectual or rational enterprises, though they are intellectual and rational. Rather, they are, above all, aspects of an organism that is inherently moral and exists in a particular relationship to the living, Triune God. This organism of which we are a part determines how we ought to think about everything. Herein lies the key to understanding the organic union between Christian apologetics, discipleship, and evangelism. But bear in mind that this is an introduction, and it is an introduction from this organic perspective. We will not cover every conceivable matter in Christian apologetics, at least not in detail, although, in a sense, we will indirectly touch on every matter of Christian apologetics, precisely because everything is organically related!

In chapter 1, we utilize the emphasis found in Warfield's writings that the Christian faith and life is a living organism. We explore and explain how the gospel of the Lord Jesus Christ is the DNA of Christianity. The DNA of every living organism makes that organism what it is, and is expressed in every facet of that organism. We see this truth expressed in Christianity in that the gospel produces in the Christian three simultaneous activities—evangelism, discipleship, and apologetics. These three activities by the Christian have often been regarded as three different activities that occur in somewhat of a temporal sequence, and have even been considered by some as optional. This chapter explains how the three activities ought to be regarded as organically produced by Jesus in the Christian and integrated so that we should regard them as mutually defining each other so that one cannot do any one of them without doing the other two.

In chapter 2, we focus on the nature and function of apologetics. Even as Warfield leads us to think of the gospel of Jesus as the DNA of Christianity that produces evangelism, discipleship, and apologetics, he also regarded apologetics as the DNA of Christian theology. Consistent with Warfield's definition of apologetics, we identify it as the discipline within Christian theology that explores, explains, and establishes the basis for the knowledge of God that is the hope of every Christian. The definition of apologetics is explained and sets the stage for how the remainder of the book unfolds. Apologetics is shown as something that is not added to the Christian's discipleship or merely one aspect of evangelism, but a constituent part of both. This chapter highlights the unitary and systematic nature of the Christian faith, and, therefore, the organic union between all of Christian doctrine. In addition, we will see that apologetics should be thought of as not only addressing the non-Christian, but also the Christian, who always remains a sinner in this lifetime, and whose salvation is wrapped up in their learning (discipleship) and believing more faithfully in who Jesus is and what he does (evangelism).

In chapter 3, we explore and explain the organic union between apologetics, discipleship, and evangelism in relation to God's sovereign regeneration that produces repentance in particular sinners, not merely once, but continuously throughout their life so that they are renewed by the Holy Spirit. The Christian's fitness for apologetics is revealed as dependent on (1) God regenerating or resurrecting them from the spiritual dead, (2) their lifelong learning from God's word (discipleship), and (3) the conviction of their sin by the Holy Spirit so that they are enabled to more faithfully trust in Jesus (evangelism) rather than themselves and effectively defend the actual gospel of the Lord Jesus Christ. Questions regarding the biblical doctrine of sin are explored and the answers explained from Scripture through some illustrations given in Scripture of God regenerating deadened sinners and then renewing them as they repent. Thus, we look at God's word's explanation of regeneration, repentance, and renewal, while noting their relationship to apologetics.

Beginning with chapter 4, we explore how the explanation of the gospel is actually part of the gospel, because the establishment of the gospel is organically united to the right explanation of it. If Christians are going to explain the gospel accurately to others, they need to pay attention to how Jesus, and the apostles he established, explained it. We explore three conversations that Jesus had with three very different people under three very different circumstances—the Samaritan woman in John 4, the wealthy young man in Matt 19, and the thief on the cross in Luke 23. Through these conversations we explore principles that emerged, and ought to guide our own explanations of the gospel to others. We explore the differences between the Christian and Jesus that need to inform how we think about our explanations of the gospel and what we should and should not expect to see established as we explain it.

In chapter 5, we continue the exploration of various ways of explaining the gospel by exploring some of the preaching done by Jesus's apostles. In particular, we focus on sermons by Peter and Paul, and explain how they were sent to two fundamentally different groups: Jews and gentiles. We explain how these two groups are not primarily identifying people according to their ethnic character but according to their exposure to and knowledge of God's written word. Explanation is given regarding how we must stress certain aspects of the gospel more than others depending on how much of the Scriptures the person knows to whom we are explaining the gospel. The unique role of the apostles, as the authoritative interpreters of Jesus life, death, resurrection, and ascension, is explored and explained. Thus, we see from chapters 4 and 5 that Scripture directs us on how we are to explain the gospel.

In chapter 6 we conclude our exploration of the gospel's explanation by explaining more precisely the authority and power that Jesus alone had to explain the gospel and the unique place that he gave his apostles in this proclamation. Since Jesus explained that he fulfilled the old covenant, we explore how the authority and power of apostolic preaching established by Jesus, and seen in the New Testament, actually fulfills the Old Testament. Thus, we explore and explain how God's word brought first in the old covenant era through God's Spirit is fulfilled by Jesus, and how his fulfillment is applied through the apostles he chose. Through this, we see how the Old Testament offices of prophet, priest, and king given to Old Testament Israel are not only fulfilled by Jesus, but also through Jesus's apostles in their preaching of the gospel, and then their writing of the New Testament. We explore, then, the organic union between Old Testament Israel and the New Testament church as well as the organic union between the Christian doctrines of the church, salvation, and Scripture.

While in the previous chapter we explained an interpretation of Scripture that is organically related to Scripture's view of apologetics, discipleship, and evangelism, in chapter 7 we explore and explain that people unavoidably interpret reality, and how the worldview concept can serve as a helpful tool to analyze people's interpretations. After a brief historical sketch of the worldview concept, and some observations about its history that should serve as a caution about how we use it, we explore a biblically faithful use of it through a definition of it given by the late Christian philosopher Ronald Nash. We explore, in general, what every person's worldview entails, and observe how the worldview concept is able to help Christians compare and contrast a Christian worldview with any and all non-Christian ones. We conclude by explaining how, according to Scripture, there are ultimately only two worldviews—a Christian one that expresses the right worship of God and a non-Christian one expressing false worship, or idolatry.

In chapter 8, we explore more precisely what constitutes a Christian worldview. We do this by exploring the intellectual content that comprises biblically faithful thinking on the five subjects that are an unavoidable part of everyone's worldview: metaphysics (the study of reality), epistemology (the study of knowledge), theology (the study of God), ethics (the study of right and wrong), and anthropology (the study of humans). Yet, this invariably raises two vitally important questions: (1) How do we, or can we, know that the Bible is giving us knowledge of the truth regarding these matters? and (2) How is it that we are able to know any truth at all? This chapter introduces the foundational truths that explain the answers to both questions, while chapter 9 explains the answers in greater detail.

In chapter 9, we explore and explain how the Scriptures of the Old and New Testament provide the only credible basis upon which we can affirm that anyone knows anything at all. We identify the seven aspects that are part of everyone's epistemology, or theory of knowledge, and show that while all non-Christian worldviews can partially account for six of the seven aspects, only Christianity can fully account for all seven. An explanation is provided for how the Triune personal God, who is both creator and redeemer, is alone able to reveal knowledge and cause his creatures to know truth, because he has united them to himself by not merely creating them, but creating them in his image. The biblical explanation is therefore given for the basis for the knowledge of God so that we see that the gospel and the Scriptures that reveal it are their own apologetic. Common questions about and challenges to actual knowledge of truth are provided as we address the "Fact/Value Divide," the relationship of scientific knowledge to religious knowledge, the relationship of faith to reason, the distinction between true and exhaustive knowledge, and the human quest for certainty.

We conclude with a summary of our previous nine chapters, and provide a brief bibliographical essay on Warfield's writings that particularly focus on the nature of apologetics and present a clear Christian apologetic. We highlight the truth that Christian belief and apologetics is rooted in our trust of the Scriptures of the Old and New Testament, and particularly rests on why we can trust the New Testament as a reliable source of truth on who Jesus is and what he does. This in turn points the reader to the appendix: "Why We Can Trust the New Testament."

May you enjoy the exploration and find the explanations fruitful.

# 1

# Christianity's DNA

"But alas! alas! dead things are not led! Of course, the Christian is led by the Holy Spirit—and let us see to it that we heartily acknowledge it and fully recognize this directive supernaturalism throughout the Christian life. But that it may become Christian, and so come under the leading of the Spirit, the dead soul needs something more than leading. It needs reanimation, resurrection, regeneration, re-creation."[1]

B. B. Warfield

"According to the Scriptures, therefore, special revelation is a historic process, an organic system, a continuous divine activity directed to destroying the power of sin, to the building up of the Kingdom of God, to the restoration of the Cosmos, to the summing up of all things in Christ. In this historic process, God makes himself known as the God of Grace: and every element that enters into it is a substantial constituent of this special revelation. Properly taken, therefore, special revelation is the redemptive process itself conceived as a manifestation of God's nature and character."[2]

B. B. Warfield

1. Warfield, "Christian Supernaturalism," in *Works* 9:44.
2. Warfield, "Christianity and Revelation," in *Selected Shorter Writings* 1:29.

## INTRODUCTION: THE GOSPEL IS AN ORGANISM

The Bible is about the gospel of the Lord Jesus Christ. As simple and as direct as that statement is, it nonetheless is true and too often either missed, forgotten, or to one degree or another misunderstood. There is a profound simplicity and unity to the Bible, even with all its great diversity of stories, places, people, events, and doctrines. Since the gospel is about who Jesus is, what he did, is doing, and will do, the gospel is about a living being. Among other things, this means that the gospel can be thought of as an organism. After all, this is what living beings are. Furthermore, in Rom 1:15–16 we read the apostle Paul telling us that he was eager to *preach* the gospel because he was not ashamed of it, because it is the power of God for salvation that reveals God's righteousness. In other words, God reveals his power of eternal life in, by, and through the proclamation of Jesus's life, death, resurrection, and ascension. These four aspects of Jesus—his life, death, resurrection, and ascension—are the essential experiences that mark Jesus as the Savior of sinners and Lord of creation. These are the central features of the biblical gospel. Thus, the biblical gospel is about the Second Person of the Trinity dispensing his eternal life to sinners who would otherwise be headed for the pains of hell forever. Among other things, this means that the gospel, like other living organisms, has its own DNA.

## CHRISTIANITY'S DNA: THE GOSPEL THAT GENERATES AND GROWS EVANGELISM, DISCIPLESHIP, AND APOLOGETICS

DNA, or deoxyribonucleic acid, is a molecule that exists in all living organisms. It contains the information that results in living organisms reproducing, developing, and functioning as *that* organism. There is a uniqueness to the DNA of each living organism that makes that organism what it is. A good way to think of the Christian faith and life is that it has its own DNA. The DNA of Christianity is the gospel, or the "good news" of who Jesus is and what he does. Because of who Jesus is and what he does, three simultaneous actions are accomplished by those who have salvation in and from him, or who have his life bearing fruit in them. These three actions are apologetics, discipleship, and evangelism.

While perhaps many have thought that these three are referring to three different topics and perhaps even optional actions within the

Christian faith and life, it is more accurate to identify them as three interrelated and inseparable aspects of the gospel that mutually determine and define each other. The three names emphasize a particular result generated by the gospel that are an indispensable part of the living organism that is the Christian faith and life.

We therefore improve our understanding of the Christian faith and life by looking at each of these three—apologetics, evangelism, and discipleship—and yet only understand any one of them rightly to the degree that we understand it in relation to the other two. Moreover, because they are part of a living system, they need nourishment to grow. This nourishment is first and foremost God's word applied by God's Holy Spirit. This is not to discount how our behavior helps shape and assist us in our own growth, but to merely state that the only behaviors that shape and assist the Christian for evangelism, discipleship, and apologetics are taught and empowered by God through his word written, preached, and taught in conjunction with baptism and the Lord's Supper as applied by God's Spirit. After all, Jesus made clear in John 15 that he is the vine and those whom he saves from sin are the branches. Apart from Jesus, who is God's Word made flesh, Christians can do nothing. Only by abiding in Jesus, or God's Word, are sinners able to bear fruit that nourishes others, help build up Christ's church, and advance his kingdom. This is what it means to be a faithful disciple of the Lord Jesus Christ and glorify God the Father (John 15:1–8).

To say that Christians need to abide in Jesus is to say that they need to abide in God's Word, which is also to say that they need to continuously receive the gospel, because the gospel is both about who Jesus is and what he does. This is why the apostle Paul affirms that the gospel is the power of God for salvation to those who keep on believing it (Rom 1:16–17).[3] As it turns out, then, to be a disciple of the Lord Jesus is to continuously receive and believe in the gospel of the Lord Jesus. We could say that there is a sense in which the Christian is continuously being evangelized. After all, the word *evangel* refers to the gospel. The true disciple of Jesus, then, grows by continuously receiving the gospel. Still further, this reception of the gospel that marks true disciples of Jesus is organically united to apologetics.

The apostle Peter, in writing to Christian disciples, stated, "But in your hearts honor Christ the Lord as holy, always being prepared to make

3. "Who keep on believing" is the proper translation of the participle Paul uses in Rom 1:16.

a defense to anyone who asks you for a reason for the hope that is in you; yet do it with gentleness and respect" (1 Pet 3:15). The term for *defense* in this verse is the Greek term *apologia* from which we derive our English term *apologetics.* In other words, the Christian view of apologetics requires us to see it as organically joined to Christian discipleship. And, thus, to the degree that Christian evangelism is joined to Christian discipleship, then that evangelism is joined to apologetics.

We ought not, then, to think of evangelism, discipleship, and apologetics as (1) isolated from each other, or (2) as existing in a relationship to each other that sees them as following each other simply in a sequentially temporal progression, or (3) as optional extras in which the Christian chooses whether they want to participate in them, or (4) as either addressing only the non-Christian or only the Christian. These matters become clearer to us as we learn what God's word teaches regarding salvation as God's eternal life given to deadened sinners (John 3:16; 17:3).

Christian evangelism, discipleship, and apologetics are the expression of God's eternal life in a previously deadened sinner. By the very nature of the case, then, they are united and ongoing in those whom God is saving from sin and are unavoidably united to Christ's body or bride, the church. Since the gospel of the Lord Jesus Christ is the power of God for salvation and reveals God's righteousness, as Rom 1:16–17 indicates, it is proper for us to conclude that *God produces* evangelism, discipleship, and apologetics. By God giving spiritual life, causing deadened sinners to be born again to a living hope through the resurrection of Jesus from the bodily dead, he creates his church. While evangelism, discipleship, and apologetics are practices that the true Christian does, it is more accurate to say that these are practices that God produces and nurtures in the Christian by his Word and Spirit. Since God has always been at work in human history saving a community of people to himself, his covenant community—the church—we must not view apologetics, discipleship, or evangelism from primarily an individualistic lens that would cause us to view the individual Christian as either remotely or, less still, isolated from the church, but instead we must regard the individual and the practices of apologetics, discipleship, and evangelism as an organic aspect of the church's life.

Through the remainder of this chapter, we will look more closely at evangelism and discipleship, and in chapter 2 zero in on apologetics.

## EVANGELISM, GOSPEL AND GOD'S COVENANT

The English words *evangelism*, *evangelist*, and *evangelization* are derived from the New Testament Greek term *euangelion* (and its various grammatical forms) that is generally translated *gospel*. Our English term *gospel* means *good news*. This term first appears in the English translation of the Bible in Isa 40:9 as an expression of God's work of saving sinners from sin. It is summarized as "Behold your God," who tends "his flock like a shepherd" (Isa 40:11). The Greek terms for *gospel* and *evangelism* are so similar that we could perhaps refer to evangelism as *gospelism*, an evangelist as a *gospelist*, and evangelization as *gospelization*. The good news or gospel is about salvation from sin that can also be described as the Triune God reigning or ruling over all creation so that he applies his eternal life, or covenant blessing, to his chosen covenant people and the physical creation, while he simultaneously applies his covenant curse, or death, to particular aspects of creation, including those who are not his covenant people.

God's covenant can be defined as his love-life bond with all creation, sovereignly administered by him, in which he sets forth commands to be obeyed, promising blessing upon obedience, curse upon disobedience, and sealed in his blood. The whole Bible is about God establishing and fulfilling his covenant, which is why the entire Bible is divided according to God's old and new covenant. As Jesus said in Matt 5:17, he came not to abolish the law and the prophets (that is, the old covenant) but to fulfill them. In doing so, Jesus has brought, is bringing, and will bring his, the Father's, and the Spirit's kingdom. Notice that from our human perspective there is always a past, present, and future aspect to God's work of salvation. Jesus's physical life, physical death, physical resurrection, and physical ascension into heaven brought and continue to bring God's kingdom to earth, and thus fulfill God's covenant.

Since the biblical gospel is the good news regarding Jesus, what we are first and foremost commanded to do with the gospel is to believe it. We believe it in order that we might be changed by it, and thereby proclaim it through what we say and do. The majority of time, when the gospel is referred to in Matthew, Mark, and Luke, its verbal proclamation is highlighted along with the obligation of the listener to believe it (Matt 4:23; 9:35; 24:14; 26:13; Mark 1:14; 13:10; 14:9; 16:15; Luke 3:18; 4:18; 7:22; 9:6; 16:16; 20:1). Repeatedly in the Gospel accounts, people are commanded to repent and believe the gospel. This same emphasis continues in the book of Acts (8:25, 40; 14:7, 15, 21; 15:7; 16:10; 20:24).

Interestingly enough, the term *gospel* never appears in the Gospel of John. This helps us see that we must be careful not to attach too much importance to simply particular words when trying to understand or communicate a concept or idea. Which is not to say that the Christian gospel is exclusively or even primarily an idea or concept. While the biblical gospel is not merely a concept it is at least that, and what is true of other concepts or ideas is also true of the biblical gospel; it can be expressed using a variety of communicative devices through words, phrases, events, and objects. Human thinking, including our verbal explanations of the gospel, as well as our theology or doctrine, is done using words but for the purpose of understanding and expressing concepts. In this regard, we want to be careful not to commit a *word-concept fallacy*.

This fallacy occurs when we confuse a word with a concept, or, to put it another way, we think that only a particular group of words, or perhaps even just one particular word, can communicate a particular concept. For example, if I said that I was angry it would be silly for someone to try and correct me by saying, "No, you were mad." The words can mean the exact same thing. Multiple words can communicate the same concept. God's entire written revelation in the Old and New Testament reveals this.

While John never uses the word *gospel* in his account of the gospel, he is still communicating the gospel of the Lord Jesus Christ. Matthew, Mark, Luke, and John all wrote Holy Spirit-inspired accounts of the gospel that differed in various ways, and yet were all true.

## THE GOSPEL AND THE WHOLE BIBLE

Since the whole Bible is about the gospel regarding the Lord Jesus Christ, we only rightly understand this gospel when we learn how the entire content of the Bible reveals it. One could get rather detailed in all this. After all, there are thirty-nine books in the Old Testament filled with many stories regarding a lot of history. Yet, in all its detail, the Old Testament reveals the one gospel of the Lord Jesus. Jesus made this point in his words in Matt 5:17 that I referred to earlier. We also see it in John 5:39–47, where he stressed that Moses wrote about him. Years ago, I was taught a simple and yet, I believe, a very helpful way to understand the whole

Bible as it relates to the gospel. As with all summaries it simplifies, but is nonetheless accurate. It is as follows:

I. The Old Testament: The Picture of and Preparation for the Gospel

II. Matthew, Mark, Luke, John: The Manifestation of the Gospel

III. Acts and the Pastoral Letters: The Expansion and Explanation of the Gospel

IV. Revelation: The Consummation of the Gospel

Each of these four could be further subdivided many times depending on how one wanted to analyze the content in them. Still, from beginning to end, the Bible is all about the gospel of the Lord Jesus Christ. By identifying the Old Testament in this way I am not denying that Christ and the gospel is truly present during the old covenant era. But, since the Son of God came in the flesh at a particular point in history, we must affirm that while the gospel is present in the old covenant era it is present in a way that is different from the way it is present in the new covenant era. In keeping with an organic view, and one of Jesus's own parables about God's kingdom (Matt 13:31–32), we can liken the gospel to a tree whose seed eventually sprouts and grows. The Old Testament is the seed and sapling, and the New Testament gives us the fully grown tree. The fully grown tree looks very different from the sapling and seed, and yet they are, fundamentally, the same.

## THE GOSPEL, DISCIPLESHIP, AND APOLOGETICS ARE FOR CHRISTIANS, NOT JUST THOSE WHO NEED TO BECOME ONE

The New Testament, of course, begins with four accounts of the gospel. They tell us about Jesus, and that Jesus preached the gospel of the kingdom (Matt 4:23; 9:35; 24:14; Luke 16:16). This gospel is also called the gospel of Jesus Christ, of Christ, or of God (Mark 1:1, 14; Rom 1:1). In Acts 20:24 the apostle Paul refers to it as *the gospel of the grace of God*. In Rom 1:9 Paul refers to it as *the gospel of his Son*, that is, God's Son, and in Rom 1:16 he refers to it as *the power of God for salvation to everyone who believes it*. Paul wrote the Letter to the Romans because he was eager to preach the gospel to all those in Rome who are loved by God and called to be saints (Rom 1:7). In other words, the book of Romans is Paul's presentation of the gospel, and yet it is to Christians, or those who were already believing the gospel (Rom 1:15). While those to whom Paul desired to preach the gospel were already believers in it, he regarded them as needing to understand it better, more fully, and to obey it more faithfully. The gospel of Jesus Christ is not simply for those who have never heard it or believed it. Instead, the gospel must be continuously explored, explained, received, and believed even to those who genuinely believe it, and because of what the gospel is (the message of the eternal kingship of Jesus) and does (the power of God for salvation or the means by which the Holy Spirit applies Jesus's eternal life to people). To the degree that we identify evangelism with the gospel, then it would seem to that same degree that we must identify those who are already believers of the gospel as needing to continue to be evangelized. This fits with who Jesus is and does, and this helps us see the unbreakable union between biblical discipleship and biblical evangelism.

## THE GOSPEL AND DISCIPLESHIP ARE ABOUT WHO JESUS IS AND WHAT HE CONTINUES TO DO

Mark 1:15 tells us that "after John the Baptist was arrested Jesus came into Galilee, proclaiming the gospel of God, and saying, 'The time is fulfilled, and the kingdom of God is at hand; repent and believe in the gospel.'" Notice that what Jesus proclaimed is called the *gospel of God* (cf. Rom 1:1; 15:16; 1 Thess 2:2, 9). The preposition *of* is an elastic term; it can cover a lot of territory! For Jesus to proclaim the gospel *of* God is to say that the good news he proclaimed is *from*, *through*, and *about* God (Rom 11:33–36). Part of what this reveals is that the gospel possesses the same attributes that God possesses. Paul summarizes these points when he concludes his presentation of the gospel that extends from Rom 1:1 to 11:35. He wrote in Rom 11:36 regarding God and the gospel, "For from him and through him and to him are all things. To him be the glory forever. Amen." The biblical gospel *reveals* God. God is the source, means, and goal of the gospel.

We can and should, therefore, think of the biblical gospel, and the Christian faith and life joined to it, as a living organism. After all, God is life, and not merely life but *eternal* life (John 3:16). The Triune God is the *living* God (Deut 5:26; Ps 42:2; 84:2; Rom 9:26; 2 Cor 3:3; 1 Tim 3:15; Heb 12:22). To believe, proclaim, and explore the gospel is to believe, proclaim, and explore eternal life. In other words, there is no end to believing, proclaiming, and exploring the gospel of the Lord Jesus Christ. The view of evangelism given to us by Jesus and his apostles is one of perpetual discipleship. This fits with the eternality of the gospel. Christian discipleship and Christian evangelism possess an ongoing character, and thereby so does Christian apologetics. Central to all three is a question that particularly plagues people living in Western culture: Can we have true knowledge of God?

## ANSWERING A CRITICAL AND NECESSARY QUESTION: CAN WE HAVE TRUE KNOWLEDGE OF GOD?

Since the biblical gospel is from, through, and about God—the infinite and eternal God revealed in the Scriptures of the Old and New Testament—we can never totally or exhaustively understand, explore, or explain the gospel. This, however, does not mean that we cannot accurately or truthfully understand it. This is the way it is with knowing a person, even those who are not both God and human at the same time, as Jesus is!

I am married and have three children. I know many things about my wife and children. While I have accurate or truthful knowledge about them, I still do not know everything that could possibly be known about them. My limitations in knowing my wife and children does not stop me from talking to other people about my wife and children, or my relationship to them. Frankly, this is true for us all regarding everything we talk about or ever could talk about. It touches on a very important truth: *Just because we cannot know everything does not mean we cannot know anything.* So, by saying that the gospel is about the one and only infinite and eternal Triune God, one should not then conclude that one is confined to statements that are totally inaccurate.

According to the Bible, all humans know some truth because God causes us to know truth because he created us in his image (Gen 1:26–28; Rom 1:19–21; Jas 3:9). The Bible does not explain how humans go through the process of knowing; it simply reveals that we know truly. In part this is revealed in Jesus and his disciples simply proclaiming the gospel. They operated with the assumption that their words were understandable. They spoke truth that they knew, and they knew that what they said made some sense to their listeners. All that they said can be summarized as being about God—who he is and what he does.

Central to understanding these foundational issues regarding human knowledge is the truth that as humans we have two basic challenges to overcome, at least to some degree, in order that we might know truly. These challenges are our finitude, or our natural limitations as finite humans, and our fallenness, or our sinful condition. As the quote from Warfield indicates that is at the beginning of this chapter, God has given his special revelation of himself in order to destroy the power of sin (1 John 3:8; Heb 2:14; Rom 6:1–14). Christian theologians have for centuries distinguished God's creation as his general revelation, and the Scriptures of the Old and New Testaments, along with Jesus, himself, as God's special revelation. General revelation is given to all humans by virtue of their being alive in God's creation (Ps 19; Rom 1:18–25). God's general revelation merely leaves every human without an excuse for their sin, but it cannot save people from their sin, which is why God gave his special revelation—for the salvation of sinners. We will have more to say about these two kinds of revelation later. Thus, the gospel of the Lord Jesus Christ is God's special revelation. Understanding its most fundamental character is crucial to our defending and commending it to others.

## THE PAST, PRESENT, AND FUTURE NATURE OF THE BIBLICAL GOSPEL

As previously mentioned, the gospel of God is also called the gospel of Jesus Christ (Mark 1:1; Rom 15:19; 1 Cor 9:12; 2 Thess 1:8). Not only does this reveal that the Bible presents Jesus as God, but also means that the biblical gospel is about who Jesus is and what he does. Over and over again we will come back to this profound and glorious truth. We could even say that we will never get beyond this truth. Yet, because as Rev 14:6 tells us, this gospel is *eternal*, those who believe it, or entrust themselves to it, will explore its dimensions for all eternity. Indeed, it is the Lord Jesus himself who defines eternal life as knowledge of God (John 17:3).

Perhaps you noticed that I have referred to Jesus in the present tense. I did not say that the gospel is about who Jesus was and what he did, although I could have. I phrased all this in the present tense precisely because Jesus lives and is working. Jesus rose from the dead and ascended into heaven and currently has all authority in heaven and on earth (Matt 28:18–20). Still, it perhaps helps clarify matters to state that since the gospel is about who Jesus is and what he does, it is about who Jesus *has always been* and *always will be*, along with what Jesus *has done* and *will continue to do*. In part, this is what it means that the whole Bible reveals the *eternal* gospel.

While Matthew, Mark, Luke, and John tell us about some of the historical events of Jesus's life, only John begins by addressing Jesus's past prior to his coming to earth. He declared that Jesus is God and that he was with God prior to his taking human flesh (John 1:1–5). John calls Jesus *the Word*. These are not easy things to understand! This is one of the reasons why the Bible is as large as it is! It is also one of the reasons why the gospel is called *glorious* (1 Tim 1:11) and why Jesus is called *glorious* or *the Lord of glory* (Jas 1:1). When we believe and proclaim the gospel we are believing and proclaiming something about the past, our present, and the future that is beyond our ability to *fully* understand, even though we can have true or accurate knowledge of it, or him. What it means to evangelize someone to the gospel, disciple them in it, and engage in gospel apologetics is governed by Jesus's eternal and glorious character.

## THE TERM DISCIPLE

In the first-century world in which Jesus lived and the New Testament was written, the Greek term *mathētēs* meant disciple. The term *disciple* means *learner*, *student*, or *follower*.[4] A disciple implies a master or teacher to whom the disciple was devoted. Such a relationship between a teacher and a disciple was present in the ancient Greek culture hundreds of years before Jesus's earthly life, but is ultimately rooted in the demand for fathers to teach their children the Scriptures (Deut 6:4–9; Prov 1:1–7; 2:1—7:27). The exact relationship that a disciple had to his master (in the ancient world) was almost exclusively a relationship between an older, wiser, or more knowledgeable male with a younger and less knowledgeable one, and defined by the master and his particular expertise. During Jesus's life, the Pharisees, many of whom opposed Jesus, had their disciples; so too did John the Baptist. Jesus's disciples, then, were not in a relationship with him that was completely unknown to people of that time period. Still, Jesus, as the master of his disciples, defined what his relationship to his disciples entailed. Because Jesus is the unique God-Man,

4. Wilkins, "Disciples," in *Dictionary of Jesus and the Gospels*, 176–82.

the eternal Son of God, the Second Person of the Trinity, discipleship to him possesses some unique qualities.

## THE UNIQUENESS OF JESUS'S APOSTLES AND ALL FUTURE DISCIPLES OF JESUS

In Matt 28:16–20 we read: "But the eleven disciples proceeded to Galilee, to the mountain which Jesus had designated. When they saw him, they worshiped, but some were doubtful. And Jesus came up and spoke to them saying, 'All authority in heaven and on earth has been given to me. Go, therefore and make disciples of all nations, baptizing them in the name of the Father, and of the Son and of the Holy Spirit, teaching them to observe all that I have commanded you. And behold, I am with you always, to the end of the age.'" There are a number of features that were true of this conversation of which we need to take note.

First, Jesus spoke this to his specially chosen disciples who were also known as Jesus's apostles. It is vital that we understand the unique role that Jesus gave them in his founding and establishment of the church in the new covenant era (and we will devote more attention to this later). Our discipleship to Jesus and discipling others starts with how Jesus created, maintained, and perfected his relationship with his first disciples.

While Jesus certainly taught great crowds of people and had many disciples through this, he had twelve specially chosen disciples. The twelve grew to thirteen when Judas betrayed Jesus, was replaced by Matthias (Acts 1), and later Paul was added. These men had a special relationship to Jesus that Jesus created through the work of the Holy Spirit. These men came to be known as Jesus's *apostles*. The term *apostle* means "sent one." The word is a form of the Greek term *apostellō* which means "I send" (Matt 10:16). The relationship that Jesus had to these men was not identical to the relationship that he had with all men and women, boys and girls who came to be his disciples during his earthly ministry. These were men specially chosen by Jesus in conjunction with the work of the Holy Spirit to have a special authority and role in the church (Luke 24:44–49; Acts 1:2). Each man had to have been an eyewitness of Jesus's earthly ministry, his death and resurrection (Acts 1:21–22), and were given by Jesus the authoritative interpretation of his life, death, resurrection, and ascension. These were the men who first preached and taught the gospel and later either wrote the Gospels and Letters that became the New

Testament, or they superintended their writing. Their authority and work lie at the root of Jesus's work of establishing and building his church so that the gates of hell do not prevail against it (Matt 16:13–28). Thus, it is necessary and proper to make a distinction between Jesus's chosen apostles and all other disciples in the history of the church, while also recognizing how the work Jesus gave his apostles relates to the discipleship of all other Christians. Biblical disciple-making and discipleship is rooted in the relationship Jesus created and completes through his apostles in his giving them the authoritative and powerful life-giving revelation (the New Testament) regarding himself through the Holy Spirit.

The second thing we should notice about Matt 28:16–20 is that in order for Jesus's disciples to make disciples they had to involve themselves with others in a way similar, although not identical, to how Jesus related to them. As previously mentioned, for Jesus's disciples to make disciples was Jesus's continued work of making disciples through his initial disciples, because Jesus told them that he would be present with them. This is why some have observed that the book of Acts in the New Testament might be better titled "the book of Jesus's Acts Through His Apostles." We see this in Jesus's initial statement that all authority had been given to him in heaven and on earth, and that the logical consequence of this was for the disciples to go and make other disciples of Jesus. "Go, therefore" follows Jesus's declaration of his authority. In other words, Jesus begins and ends this statement to his disciples with the emphasis on who he is (Lord of heaven and earth) and what he does (order all things in heaven and on earth so that he remains with his disciples in their earthly work; cf. Luke 24:44–49). As Christopher J. H. Wright has stated, "It is not so much that God has a mission for his church in the world, but that God has a church for his mission in the world."[5]

Furthermore, because Jesus is the eternal Son of God, who promised to always be with his disciples in their making of disciples, there is an unavoidably perpetual character to what it means to be his disciple. This harmonizes with the point that the apostles preached, taught, and wrote the gospel to those who already believed it. The two clauses explaining what the disciples were to continue doing in order to make disciples of Jesus are "baptizing them in the name of the Father, Son, and Holy Spirit" and "teaching them to observe all that I have commanded you."

5. Wright, *Mission of God*, 62.

## CHRISTIAN DISCIPLE MAKING: BAPTIZING IN AND TEACHING ABOUT WHO THE TRIUNE GOD IS AND WHAT HE DOES

It is far beyond the goal of this work to give a complete doctrine of Christian baptism. Instead, we need to see two very important aspects of Christian baptism that are joined to making Christian disciples. First, notice that this baptism is in the *name* of the Father, the Son, and the Holy Spirit. When the *name* or *names* of God are emphasized in the Bible, stress is placed on God's character and conduct, that is, who God is and what God does. So, in order to make disciples *of Jesus* one has to rely upon and reveal the character and conduct of the Triune God. Strictly speaking, this is what *Jesus does* through the work of his Holy Spirit.

In its broadest sense the term *baptism*, as it is used in the New Testament, refers to being brought into an involvement with what someone is doing. For example, the apostle Paul wrote in 1 Cor 10:2–4 regarding the old covenant people of God that they were all "baptized into Moses, in the cloud and in the sea, and all ate the same spiritual food and drank the same spiritual drink; for they were drinking from a spiritual rock that followed them; and the rock was Christ." Paul's point was that those old covenant people of God who were led by Moses were involved in what God was doing with Moses. God led Moses by the cloud, through the sea, and out of Egypt. But notice that by itself this involvement or baptism into Moses did not automatically mean the people physically following Moses had salvation. After all, the very next thing Paul wrote in 1 Cor 10:5–10 tells us that God destroyed many of them because of their idolatrous disobedience to him. This is one of the many places from Scripture that reveals that the act of Christian baptism does not, by itself, save from sin the one baptized, nor does it necessarily mean that the one who receives it has been saved. Christian baptism signals that the baptized person has been brought into what the Father, the Son, and the Holy Spirit are doing so that the person baptized is *taught* about who the Triune God is and what he does that *requires us to believe and obey him.*

From this we should see that Matt 28:16–20, Luke 24:44–49, and Acts 1 and 2 reveal the unique authority and duty that Jesus gave to his apostles to be his first disciple-makers. They were to bring others into what God the Father, the Son, and the Holy Spirit were still doing because of who the Father, the Son, and the Holy Spirit are. This required teaching others all that Jesus had commanded them to believe and do. This did not mean that the people they did this with would automatically be saved from their sins or that they already were saved (1 Cor 10:1–13). Nonetheless, it was still the necessary way in which the Triune God would save many from their sins. Just as the gospel is the power of God for salvation, so too is Christian discipleship the expression of God's power to make his disciples. God saves and God makes his disciples. Gospel evangelism and disciple-making are one and the same. Indeed, we see this perhaps most clearly in Jesus's apostles.

Jesus's apostles were sinful men who needed to hear, believe, and obey the gospel. Jesus's apostles did not stop being sinners when they became Jesus's apostles; rather they became a certain kind of sinner: they became sinners who lived by faith in Jesus and repentance from their sin, yet with a unique authority and role in the church. This faith in Jesus and repentance from their sin is another way of describing believing and obeying Jesus. It is what it means to be Jesus's disciple. This is simply another way of describing what we are commanded to do with the gospel: believe and obey it. And, finally, this is also what we are told to do with the *sound doctrine* that was taught and preached by the apostles. The sound doctrine or sound teaching is what Jesus gave his apostles to proclaim and live by so that they grew in their discipleship to him and were enabled to make disciples of him. To make disciples of Jesus his apostles had to rely upon and reveal the power and authority of the Triune God by learning about him and living in obedience to him. Christian disciple-making is Jesus's ongoing work of bringing people into his kingdom through the ongoing presence and power of his Holy Spirit as the Holy Spirit applies the authoritative apostolic teaching or doctrine to the souls of sinners (John 14:26; 15:26–27; 16:13–15).

## JESUS, THE SCRIPTURES, THE HOLY SPIRIT, AND MAKING DISCIPLES

Jesus did not turn over to his disciples his unique authority as the incarnate Word, who alone is able to reveal God the Father. Rather, he exercised his authority regarding these things *through* them, and this took place through the giving and work of the Holy Spirit. Even after he ascended into heaven Jesus continued making disciples through his initial disciples by his and God the Father's sending the Holy Spirit (John 14:26; 15:26–27; 16:13–15; Acts 1:1–2:47). Christian baptism highlights not merely an act with water but what that act represents—the involving of the person in what the Triune God does to save his covenant people from their sins (Matt 28:18–20; 1 Cor 10). Thus, the presence and power of God is on display when true disciples of Jesus are made. God's presence and power marked not only Jesus's apostles through whom he wrote the New Testament (2 Tim 3:16; 2 Pet 1:16–21), but all other disciples of Jesus who came to believe and obey the teaching that Jesus brought through his first disciples or apostles (2 Cor 3:18—4:18; Phil 2:12–13; Col 1:24–29). The baptism of which Jesus spoke was unavoidably united to teaching or doctrine that came from Jesus, and to and through a particular group of men—Jesus's initial disciples, or apostles—and according to Jesus this all meant obedience to him (Rom 6:1–17).

## "SOUND" DOCTRINE IS THE GOSPEL; CHRISTIAN DISCIPLESHIP IS CHRISTIAN EVANGELISM

This twin emphasis on learning from and obeying Jesus is seen in the preaching and teaching of Jesus's disciples as revealed from Acts to Revelation. It is why when Paul wrote Romans, he was presenting the gospel and yet also presenting the sum and substance of Christian doctrine. Throughout Paul's New Testament Letters the term *sound doctrine* is a synonym for the gospel—they are both used to refer to what is to be believed, proclaimed, and obeyed by individual Christians and the church corporately. This is why we cannot think of evangelism *to* the gospel and discipleship *in* the gospel as two different pursuits, but instead one and the same.

While the apostle Paul wrote that he "decided to know nothing among you except Jesus Christ and him crucified" (1 Cor 2:2), he obviously did not see this contradicting the requirement to preach and teach sound doctrine, or the pattern of sound words that he emphasized in his Letters to Timothy and Titus. Paul regarded himself as having been appointed to preach and teach these sound words because Christ Jesus "abolished death and brought life and immortality to light through the gospel" (1 Tim 1:10; cf. 1 Tim 6:3; 2 Tim 1:8–14). Preaching the fullness of God's word, according to Paul, meant doing the work of an evangelist. For Paul, there was not evangelism over on one side of Christian ministry and on the other engaging in preaching and teaching the whole counsel of God in order to make disciples (2 Tim 3:16–4:5). Paul uses the same description for both the gospel and the sound doctrine he preached. While the gospel, strictly speaking, should be regarded as the good news regarding the life, death, resurrection, and ascension of Jesus, the sound doctrine of the Christian faith is nothing less than the necessary organic expression, implications, or results of Jesus's life, death, resurrection, and ascension. We could perhaps state it this way: The Christian gospel and Christian sound doctrine exist in a relationship to one another that is like that of a root system to its plant. All that is present with the root system reveals itself in the entire plant.

The gospel is the power and grace of God for salvation. The sound doctrine is also the manifestation of God's grace which "has appeared, bringing salvation for all people, training us to renounce ungodliness and worldly passions, and to live self-controlled, upright and godly lives in the present age" (Titus 2:11–12). For Paul, as for the rest of the apostles, believing in Jesus for salvation harmonized with obedience to God in every aspect of life so that what it means to be evangelized to the gospel is what it means to be made a disciple of the Lord Jesus. Both required learning and obeying the sound doctrine of the Christian faith, just as Jesus had stated in Matt 28:16–20. When we pay attention to what the apostles wrote in the New Testament regarding Christian apologetics, we see that what marks Christian evangelism and discipleship is also expressed in Christian apologetics.

## CONCLUSION AND SUMMARY

According to the Scriptures of the Old and New Testament, sinners are evangelized and discipled in and with the gospel of the Lord Jesus Christ. Jesus, through the Holy Spirit, involves his disciples in the work he is doing to build his church so that the gates of hell do not prevail against it. He does call his disciples to make disciples, but he is with them always. It is Jesus who empowers his disciples to make disciples, and their disciple-making is part of their discipleship. Further, it is Jesus who evangelizes, who makes his gospel known through his Holy Spirit revealing the truth regarding his gospel. Thus, disciple-making and evangelism are by Jesus through his people. We will see in the next chapter that it is also the gospel of the Lord Jesus Christ that is defended in Christian apologetics and that this gospel is its own defense. Thus, while God's people are to engage in apologetics, they too, because they have the residue of unbelief in them, must still have a defense of the gospel presented to their own hearts so that they are convinced more and more regarding the truth of the gospel. Christian evangelism, discipleship, and apologetics are organically united in, by, and through the Lord Jesus Christ.

# 2

# The Nature and Function of Apologetics

"But apologetics does not derive its content or take its form or borrow its value from the prevailing opposition; but preserves through all varying circumstances its essential character as a positive and constructive science. . . . It is the function of apologetics to investigate, explicate, and establish the grounds on which a theology—a science or systematized knowledge of God—is possible; and on the basis of which every science which has God for its object must rest, if it be a true science with claims to a place within the circle of the sciences."[1]

B. B. Warfield

Apologetics "has for its object the laying of the foundations on which the temple of theology is built, and by which the whole structure of theology is determined. It is the department of theology which establishes the constitutive and regulative principles of theology as a science; and in establishing these it establishes all the details which are derived from them by the succeeding departments, in their sound explication and systematization."[2]

B. B. Warfield

1. Warfield, "Apologetics," in *Works* 9:4.
2. Warfield, "Apologetics," in *Works* 9:9.

## GOSPEL APOLOGETICS IS BY THE CHRISTIAN AND FOR BOTH THE CHRISTIAN AND NON-CHRISTIAN

The term *apologetics* comes from the Greek term *apologia*, which can be translated "defense," "reason," "vindication," or "explanation." The primary text from which the church has identified the need for apologetics is 1 Pet 3:15. There we read: "But sanctify [or 'set apart'] Christ as Lord in your hearts, always being ready to make a defense to everyone who asks you to give an account of the hope that is in you, yet with gentleness and reverence." Christian apologetics is about defending the gospel, or giving a reason for why one has faith in Jesus for salvation. But we must be careful of how we conceive of apologetics. Because the gospel is an organism, all the aspects of it are organically related. If we are to rightly conceive of apologetics we must think of it in such a way that is consistent with the gospel itself, which in turn means we must think of both the gospel and apologetics in a way that is consistent with human beings and their relationship to the gospel. One of the things this means is that we must recognize how the gospel and apologetics relate to the point we observed in our previous chapter, namely, that we possess two fundamental challenges in our pursuit of knowledge—we are finite and fallen creatures. That is, all people do not merely stand in a relationship to the gospel as fallen sinners, but as finite creatures. Thus, our understanding of the gospel and apologetics must factor this truth into our conceptions of them both. Among other things, this means that Christian apologetics is not merely or even primarily "the application of biblical truth to unbelief."[3] Instead, as Warfield points out in our quote above, the very character of apologetics is that it has a positive and constructive character to it that reflects the fundamental needs of who we are as creatures created in God's image who have rational capacities that thirst for understanding truth. While it is true that after the fall into sin humans were saddled with this additional challenge to their knowing truth, we dare not think that our rational capacities and needs for understanding God's revelation were merely given to us through our fall into sin. Adam and Eve were born rational creatures who would have still needed to rationally understand their relationship to God, one another, and their earthly duty even if they had never sinned. However, since they did sin, human rationality since the fall has not only been corrupted by sin, but this corruption was unavoidably united to our finite character. So, while there is truth to

3. Oliphint, *Covenantal Apologetics*, 29.

the point that apologetics is about the application of truth to unbelief, it is not only that, although this is perhaps the only way many Christians think of it. Let's see if we can unpack this further.

There are two terms that generally appear in most definitions and explanations of apologetics. Those terms are *defending* and *unbelief*. It is likely safe to say that many, if not most, Christians think of apologetics as defending the Christian faith against accusations and assaults from non-Christians. If we think this way, then we would think of the "application of biblical truth to unbelief" primarily, if not exclusively, as the Christian answering or refuting the non-Christian's arguments or accusations against the Christian faith. While Christian apologetics can include this, it is not confined to it, and at least according to nineteenth- and twentieth-century theologian B. B. Warfield, this does not do full justice to the true nature and function of apologetics. This is where it is important to understand one of the great principles in sports—sometimes your best offense is a good defense.

In some sports, like baseball, you can't score while playing defense—you can only prevent the other team from scoring. But, other sports, like football (the American kind!), allow for the defense to actually score points. An interception or fumble return for a touchdown, or tackling the opposing team's ball carrier in his own end zone for a safety, are ways that the defense can score in football. Christian apologetic's conception of defense is like football's. When done properly or well, a defense of the Christian faith actually asserts its truthfulness and validity, and thus implements an offensive move against unbelief. Faithful Christian apologetics will answer an objection to Christian faith by demonstrating a truth that exposes the illegitimacy of unbelief. Yet, we need to be careful that we do not immediately conclude that this unbelief only resides with the non-Christian.

## THE TRUE CHRISTIAN HAS UNBELIEF THAT MUST BE OVERCOME

The apostle Paul preached and wrote the gospel to those who believed it, and had salvation (Rom 1:14–15). Even those who truly believe the gospel have some lack of belief in it. Any time and to any degree that we fail to obey our Lord, we fail to believe the gospel, because we are failing to trust Jesus with our life. According to God's word, belief and obedience are united—it is why the writer of Hebrews affirms that the vast majority of the first generation of Israelites were not able to enter the promised land: their failure to believe in God was demonstrated by their disobedience (Heb 3:17–19). Every true Christian remains a sinner in this lifetime, even while sin no longer reigns over them (Rom 6:5–14). The call for Christians to consider themselves dead to sin, to not let sin reign in them, but to grow and to work out their salvation, to perfect holiness in the fear of the Lord, and to confess their sin (Rom 6:11–12; 2 Pet 3:18; Phil 2:12–13; 2 Cor 7:1; 1 John 1:6–8) all testify to the truth that there are ways in which genuine Christians do not fully understand, believe, and obey the gospel. Christian apologetics, then, is not merely for the non-Christian, but even for the Christian, because genuine faith in Jesus grows or matures, and this is because what God gives in salvation is a *life*, an *eternal life*.

## CHRISTIANS WILL MATURE: APOLOGETICS AS GOSPEL DISCIPLESHIP AND EVANGELISM

We have to make a distinction that the Scriptures make between the *presence of true or genuine* saving belief in the Lord Jesus and the *health*, or *maturation*, of that belief. Saving faith in the Lord Jesus is truly a life—eternal life. There are plenty of plants and animals that look very different in their early stages of growth than they do in their more mature stages. Sometimes the difference is so stark that one has difficulty believing that the organism in its immature stage of growth really is the same organism in its later mature stage. This ought to encourage and caution the Christian. It ought to encourage Christians to recognize that both they and their fellow Christians can make great advances in wisdom and holiness—and, indeed, should. But it also ought to caution us about making hasty judgments about professing Christians who are not demonstrating a great deal of maturity. Just because a professing Christian shows signs of immaturity in their behavior does not mean they are not genuinely Christian. The glaring and devastating sins of King David alone alert us to the truth that one can truly have salvation and yet fall prey to rather obvious sins. It is all the more reason that if we profess to be disciples of the Lord Jesus Christ, we need to be concerned about our growth, or putting away sin and living obediently to our Lord.

God's word tells us that this eternal life *grows* within the one who possesses it. Furthermore, the one who possesses it is commanded to do things that aid growth, which amounts to *their* growth. The apostle Peter at the end of his second letter in the New Testament wrote: "You, therefore, beloved, knowing this beforehand, be on your guard so that you are not carried away by the error of unprincipled men and fall from your own steadfastness, but *grow* in the grace and knowledge of our Lord and Savior Jesus Christ" (2 Pet 3:17–18, italics mine). Peter commands the Christian to be on guard and to grow. The context is one in which he addresses believing and obeying the true doctrine of the Christian faith, while on guard against false teaching and false teachers. The faithful Christian life is marked by growth or changes, advancements, and developments as the Christian receives the true doctrine of the Christian faith. This is because the true Christian has the Holy Spirit residing with them, enabling them to understand the truth of God's word, to love it, and to put it into practice (Rom 8:4–16, 23–27; 1 Cor 2:10–16; 3:16; 12:1–11; 2 Cor 1:21–22; 5:5; 13:14; Gal 3:1–6; Eph 4:30; Titus 3:5). This true doctrine, which the Holy Spirit enables the Christian to understand, love, and obey, is what the Christian defends and commends. This is what apologetics is all about. This doctrine is inherently reasonable and this reasonableness meets the deepest needs of the human spirit.

One of the most important and faithful biblical and theological scholars over the past several hundred years, B. B. Warfield, said the following regarding Christian apologetics:

> It finds its deepest ground . . . in the deepest needs of the human spirit. If it is incumbent on the believer to be able to give a reason for the faith that is in him, it is impossible to be a believer without a reason for the faith that is in him, and it is the task of apologetics to bring this reason clearly out in his consciousness and make its validity plain.[4]

Notice that Warfield affirmed that Christian apologetics is necessary to, and a defining feature of, Christian faith, and it is about revealing the rational validity of Christian faith. Thus, apologetics is not an optional activity simply for those Christians who decide they would like to engage in it. This fits with the truth that Peter's statement in 1 Pet 3:15 is a *command* to the church and therefore involves in some way all Christians. Put another way, all Christians are to learn the rational character of the

4. Warfield, "Apologetics," in *Works* 9:4.

Christian faith, or hope in Jesus, which, of course, is also to say that failing to believe the gospel or rebelling against God is irrational.

## WHAT DOES APOLOGETICS ADDRESS?

Since Jesus is Lord of heaven and earth, his lordship covers everything. Among other things, this means the rational validity of the Christian faith and life relates to all things; there is no subject matter, no event, no reality that is unrelated to Christian faith and living. Christian faith and living are not private spiritual phenomena; they are both public and historical realities. Jesus is not merely Lord of our internal life of thoughts, beliefs, and feelings, or of our behavior that is isolated to merely us and our fellow Christians. Christianity is a public, indeed cosmic, matter. Consequently, the rational validity of the Christian faith and life is not confined to the Christian's thinking and living. The rational validity of the Christian faith and life is a public issue, and is the very basis upon which Christians are to call non-Christians to repent of their sin. John the Baptist publicly called Herod to repent of his sin. The apostle Paul publicly called Agrippa, Felix, and Festus to repent of their sin. No one's sin is merely a private matter. Part of what this means is that as we grow in our understanding of the rational validity of Christian belief and living, we will also grow both in our repentance and our willingness and ability to call others to repentance.

We should also note that the rational validity of our hope in the Lord Jesus has an eternal character to it. After all, Jesus is the eternal Son of God, the Second Person of the Trinity. We have an eternal hope and faith in Jesus that has to do with all things in heaven and on earth. While it is popular to isolate religious or spiritual matters to an individual's private, emotional, subjective experience, and to regard the individual Christian and the church as practically disconnected from the public and physically verifiable realm of human life, the Bible warrants no such thinking. This kind of separation is called the "Fact/Value" Divide or Split, and we will have more to say about this later. For now, it is sufficient to state that Christian apologetics is about everything and everyone all the time, because Jesus is Lord of everything and everyone all the time. So, we can never completely learn all that can be learned about the rational validity of the Christian hope. Our exploration of such things could never come to an end.

## THE UNITARY, SYSTEMATIC, AND ORGANIC NATURE OF APOLOGETICS

Since Jesus is Lord of heaven and earth, and apologetics requires giving reasons for our hope in him, Christian apologetics recognizes a unity to all human knowledge. This means we can and should think within a system of truth that includes all subject matters. And, as we have already highlighted, this unitary system of truth is *organic*. It is *through* Christ Jesus that all things have been created, and they have been created *for him*, and *in him* all things hold together (Col 1:17). This means at least two important things for apologetics. First, there is no subject matter of human knowledge that is not theological in nature. Secondly, systematic theology ought to be regarded as the "Queen of the Sciences." Or as B. B. Warfield stated:

> Over against the world and all that is in the world . . . stands God; and He—He Himself, not our thought about Him or our beliefs concerning Him, but He Himself—is the object of our highest knowledge. And to know Him is not merely the highest exercise of the human intellect; it is the indispensable complement of the circle of human science, which, without the knowledge of God, is fatally incomplete.[5]

God has actually revealed himself in his works (Ps 19:1–2; Rom 1:18–20). The view that knowledge of God was necessary for right knowledge in every branch of human learning was a common belief in the Western world, prior to the attack on Christianity in the seventeenth and eighteenth centuries in Europe by scholars in several fields of learning (often, ironically, called "the Enlightenment"). This theological view of all knowledge is certainly the biblical view. God is the creator and his creation reveals him (Ps 19:1–2; Rom 1:20–21). Yet, because of sin, as Paul says in Rom 1:18, we suppress the truth in our unrighteousness, and we literally handicap ourselves intellectually. We even deny that we know some things that we actually do know. The text says of us that we profess to be wise, but in so doing become fools (Rom 1:22). This does not mean that the unrepentant sinner knows absolutely nothing at all, but rather what they do know they twist and distort so that their interpretation of it

5. Warfield, "Task and Method of Systematic Theology," in *Works* 9:97. Consider also Warfield, "Idea of Systematic Theology," in *Works* 9:69: "All science without God is mutilated science, and no account of a single branch of knowledge can ever be complete until it is pushed back to find its completion and ground in Him."

leads them to a variety of faulty intellectual conclusions that warps their reasoning and produces a life of rebellion against God. We need another revelation from God to overcome the effects of sin on our reasoning, affections, and actions. Christian theologians have often referred to it as "special revelation," and God has given this in the Scriptures of the Old and New Testaments and supremely in his Son, the Lord Jesus Christ (John 1:1–4; Col 1:15–20; Heb 1:1–4). As Warfield put it:

> It is not to meet any failure in general revelation that special revelation is introduced, but to meet failure in man to whom the revelation is addressed. It is not the power of nature that it seeks to break, but the power of sin: nature it is its end rather to restore and fulfill. The great organism of revelation thus includes the totality of his operations, in nature and history and grace.[6]

Or, to put it another way:

> One of the most grievous of the effects of sin is the deformation of the image of God reflected in the human mind, and there can be no recovery from sin which does not bring with it the correction of this deformation and the reflection in the soul of man of the whole glory of the Lord God Almighty. Man is an intelligent being; his superiority over the brute is found, among other things, precisely in the direction of all his life by his intelligence; and his blessedness is rooted in the true knowledge of his God—for this is life eternal, that we should know the only true God and Him whom He has sent.[7]

God had to intervene in human history and overcome the effects of Adam's sin, and this he did. But in so doing, his revelation, by the very nature of the case, addresses everything, because there is no reality outside of God that God did not either bring into being or allowed to come about. This is all centered, so to speak, on the Lord Jesus Christ, as Paul reveals in Col 1:15–20. Thus, there is a unity to all truth, and to all knowledge because it all holds together in Christ. This is why true Christians are both able to know, and that all we know rightly can be rationally understood and explained, although this does not mean that anyone has the capacity to rationally understand or explain all of reality. Moreover, this rationality is best understood within the broader context of a living relationship to God the Father through Jesus the Son by way of the Holy

6. Warfield, "Christianity and Revelation," in *Selected Shorter Writings* 1:28.

7. Warfield, "Biblical Idea of Revelation," in *Works* 1:13.

Spirit. Human knowledge, then, is moral, theological, systematic, and organic. Human rationality can only be rightly understood as governed by an organic theological system, because all knowledge truly reveals God, has its origin in God, and ultimately leads us to God (Gen 1:1—2:3; Rom 11:33–36; Col 1:13–20). This is why we are correct to affirm that "all science without God is mutilated science, and no account of a single branch of knowledge can ever be complete until it is pushed back to find its completion and ground in Him."[8]

## RESTATING AND CLARIFYING WARFIELD'S DEFINITION OF APOLOGETICS

Recall the quote from Warfield at the beginning of the chapter in which he affirmed that "the function of apologetic is to investigate, explicate, and establish the grounds on which a theology—a science or systematized knowledge of God—is possible" (cf. 1n). By substituting a few words in place of the ones Warfield used and summarizing his basic point, I believe we can arrive at a definition of apologetics that is faithful to Warfield's perspective, but above all else, is faithful to Scripture, and perhaps easier to remember and grasp. Let's substitute the term *explore* for *investigate*, the term *explains* for *explicate*, and retain *establish*. Then let's draw upon Peter's words in 1 Pet 3:15 and use the word *hope* in relation to knowledge of God. Our definition for apologetics is: *The discipline in Christian theology that explores, explains, and establishes the basis for the knowledge of God that is the hope of every true Christian.* Now, we are hopefully ready to unpack this a little bit. Or, if you will, explore and explain it!

## EXPLORING THE BASIS FOR THE KNOWLEDGE OF GOD OR THE BIBLICAL GOSPEL

Our exploration of the basis for the knowledge of God is endless because the God who is known had no beginning, has no end, and anything we could possibly know is related to him. We could never come to a fully complete knowledge of God, nor completely understand the rational validity of faith in him. As we covered in chapter 1, some draw the wrong conclusion from this and think that it means we cannot know anything about God at all. But let us remind ourselves that just because we cannot

8. Warfield, "Idea of Systematic Theology," in *Works* 9:69.

know everything about God, the world, and our experience in it does not mean that we cannot know anything rightly at all. Still, Scripture presents God as Triune, infinite, eternal, holy, just, wise, righteous, good, and truth itself. Furthermore, God's creation fundamentally reveals him and so our exploration of the basis for the knowledge of God can reach as far as our intellects can understand both the experience we have of God within his creation and his written word.

You can perhaps also see from this that attacks or accusations against Christianity can come from any subject matter. This also is likely why many Christians can feel intimidated about engaging in apologetics, or at least explaining the biblical gospel. Perhaps you have thought: Who are you to try and respond to the truth claims of someone like Stephen Hawking, or countless men and women who have a PhD in their academic field? It is good for us to have humility and recognize that there are many things that we need to learn before we are equipped to explain the rational validity of Christian faith. Yet, we also need to bear in mind at least two very important truths about the Christian faith and our knowledge of it.

## SCRIPTURE IS CLEAR AND REPENTANCE FROM SIN CLARIFIES

First, Scripture doesn't present us with an intellectually complicated view of the Christian faith as a whole, or the doctrine of sin in particular. One actually does not have to be extremely intelligent or have extensive life experience to understand either the character of Christian belief or human sin. After all, Jesus revealed that his heavenly Father reveals himself to children and he commanded that his disciples should not prevent children from coming to him (Matt 11:25–27; 19:14; Mark 10:13–14; Luke 18:15–17). There is both a simplicity to God's truth that can be understood by the simplest of minds and yet there is a breadth and depth to it that can be explored beyond anyone's ability to completely comprehend. Yet, as we busy ourselves with exploring what Scripture teaches, we can learn how to think about all the truth claims that deny the truth of Christianity. In other words, the attacks from men like Stephen Hawking aren't nearly as complicated as they might otherwise seem. This is not to oversimplify some of the questions that highly intelligent people have regarding the Christian faith, but rather to affirm that because God has made truth known that relates to all things, submitting to God's truth will equip you to learn how to navigate any and all questions that could be raised up against the knowledge of God.

One of the doctrines of Scripture that is about Scripture itself is the *perspicuity* of Scripture. The term is somewhat ironic, because it is not one people use much and so its meaning is often unclear. But this is just exactly what it does mean—that Scripture is clear! While the original texts of the Old and New Testaments were written in Hebrew and Greek respectively, for some two thousand years the church has been at work translating these texts into numerous other languages. Of course, we no longer have the original texts, but rather thousands of copies of the original. We have Jesus's own verification of the Old Testament, his own veracity throughout his life, death, and resurrection, and thousands of manuscripts of the Greek New Testament. Indeed, the Greek New Testament is the most well-attested document from the ancient world. In fact, throughout the history of the church, rarely does anyone seek to *credibly* refute the Christian faith on the basis of challenging the church's possession of the Old and New Testaments, but rather they challenge the interpretation of the documents. No one seeks to challenge the idea that Jesus believed that the Old Testament is God's word, or that the New Testament apostles believed they possessed the authority to speak in Jesus's name; instead they challenge Jesus's interpretation of the Old Testament and the apostles' interpretation of Jesus.[9] One thing is certain in all this: If Jesus did bodily rise from the dead, as the apostles claim (Matt 16:21; 28:1–20; Mark 16:1–8; Luke 24:1–53; John 20:1–21:25; Acts 17:22–31; 22:3–21; 24:21; 25:12–18; Rom 1:1–6; 4:24–25; 6:4–5, 9–11; 10:9; 1 Cor 15:1–58; Phil 3:10–11; Heb 1:1–4; 4:14; 1 Pet 1:3; 3:18 [Notice how close this is to the classic text for Christian apologetics!]; 1 John 2:23–25; 5:1, 11–12, 20–21; 2 John 9–11; Jude 20–21; Rev 1:8; 4:1—5:14; 7:9–12; 11:15–18; 15:1–4; 19:1–6; 20:4–6, 11–15; 21:1–8, 22–27; 22:12–13, 16, 20), then this reality and truth changes everything—and I do mean *everything*! Not the least of which is how we think about salvation, how we are *able* to obey the Lord, and what it means to defend and commend the biblical gospel.

The second vital truth we should keep in mind as we explore the biblical gospel is that because sin is moral blindness that corrupts our reasoning, those who daily repent of their sin and continue exploring

9. McDowell, *New Evidence That Demands a Verdict*, 34. Included with this interpretation is denial of the "authenticity of much of what the gospels record Jesus as saying." See Linnemann, *Historical Criticism of the Bible*, and *Is There a Synoptic Problem?*

the Christian faith and life will inevitably mature in their knowledge and wisdom. Thus, it is not intelligence itself that is the key to knowledge of God, but rather repentance from sin. Scripture presents those who refuse to repent as spiraling further downward into intellectual confusion, degenerate practices, and unholy affections (Rom 1:18–32; 3:9–18). The result is that no matter how many academic degrees you amass, you simply cannot possess rational thinking that actually passes for "rational," or can match that of the faithful Christian, who has been exploring and learning what Scripture teaches and been faithful to obey the Lord Jesus. In fact, there is a kind of disadvantage that the intelligent non-Christian possesses precisely because of their intelligence—in their pride they are apt to place great confidence in their own thinking. None of this is to say that the faithful Christian's arguments will always conform to biblical truth, or that they will automatically be received as credible by the non-Christian. But it also does not mean that the Christian's arguments are automatically not credible merely because the non-Christian doesn't understand them. What has to be clearly kept in mind is that denying that Christianity is the truth is an irrational assertion and based on irrational thinking. Scripture itself makes the point. Let's explore it a little.

In Rom 1:20, when Paul tells us that those who suppress the truth in their unrighteousness are "without excuse," the Greek term he uses is *anapologetos*. It is actually a form of the word *apologia*, or our term from which we derive "apologetics." The two letters "a" and "n" at the beginning of the term form what is called the alpha privative. They effectively negate what comes after them. In other words, it is tantamount to Paul saying that, ultimately speaking, there is no rational defense or explanation for sin; sinful thoughts, desires, and actions have no apologetic. The more we explore the truth about the basis for the knowledge of God that is the hope of every true Christian, the more equipped we will be to rationally defend it and expose the irrationality of those who oppose it. The rest of this work seeks to explore and explain these issues.

## EXPLAINING THE BASIS FOR THE KNOWLEDGE OF GOD OR THE BIBLICAL GOSPEL

The whole idea of explaining the basis for the knowledge of God confronts us with a delicate, if not difficult, challenge. After all, since God is infinite, eternal, and holy, the creator, sustainer, and redeemer of the creation, the one for whom all things exist and to whom all things are related, how is it that we can provide adequate and believable explanations regarding the basis for the knowledge of him? Can what we are to believe and do as Christians be rationally explained? Can it be reduced to rational explanations?

The term *explains* in my definition may lead to a particular misunderstanding. So let me try and clarify what I mean and don't mean by my use of this term.

## CHRISTIAN DOCTRINE: WHAT THE CHRISTIAN IS TO BELIEVE

The doctrines Christians are commanded to believe ought *not* to be thought of as simply providing us *explanations* of what we believe. Though the doctrines that a Christian is commanded to believe are providing some explanations of what the Christian believes, such doctrine, if it is true to Scripture, accomplishes much more than simply providing an explanation. If we think of Christian doctrine as simply providing an explanation, then we have reduced the Bible to simply providing concepts and information. This is to think as a rationalist. A theological rationalist "gives undue weight to reason at the expense of something else."[10] It is rationalistic to believe that all one can know or needs to know can be apprehended (taken hold of) and comprehended (understood) by one's reason. If what we are commanded to believe is equated with, or made equal to, an explanation, then I presumably cannot believe it until I understand the explanation. Explanations are given precisely to provide understanding; they explain. The explanation does not accomplish its goal until the person who is receiving it understands it. But God does not simply or primarily require that we *understand* him, but rather that we *believe* him. This is not to set our trust of God off against our intellect, reasoning, and understanding, but to simply stress their actual relationship to each other. The distinction between our belief in God and our understanding of him may appear small. It is not. The history of Christian theology and the church testifies to the truth that it isn't.

If we reduce Christian doctrine to merely the explanations of what we are to believe, then there are many doctrines crucial to the Christian faith that we simply could not believe. The doctrine of the Trinity,

10. Curley, "Rationalism," in *Companion to Epistemology*, 411.

of the virgin birth of Christ, of the supernatural miracles of Jesus, of the supernatural power present in the preached word of God and the administration of the Lord's Supper and baptism are just a few of the doctrines that defy a complete and credible rational explanation. By "complete" explanation I mean one that answers all possible questions regarding the doctrines; ones that leave us with no ignorance or unknowns regarding the doctrines. But the doctrines which are at the very heart of the Christian faith and life cannot be fully understood by the human intellect by itself. Moreover, even with God's revelation in Scripture and the illuminating work of the Holy Spirit, there are aspects to these doctrines that we simply cannot fully comprehend. Thankfully, though, we do not have to completely understand them in order to believe what Scripture says about them and trust our lives to them. However, none of this means that these doctrines *completely defy* rational explanation. They are not what we would call *ineffable* or utterly unknowable. There is much about them that we *can* know and that we can explain, and we dare not pretend otherwise. After all, what do we think the preaching and teaching of Jesus's apostles entailed? We can know truly, not just exhaustively. We can explain rationally, not just exhaustively.

In chapter 4 we will devote ourselves to exploring several examples from Scripture of faithful explanations of the gospel, and we will see that while they are rational and convicting, they were never meant to be explanations that addressed every conceivable topic; they were explanations given to particular people at a particular time and place, and to address particular issues or questions. Part of what this means is that having preplanned statements or ways of presenting the gospel to all people fails to do justice to what Scripture reveals as the way the gospel was presented by Jesus, his apostles, and their co-laborers.

## ESTABLISHING THE BASIS FOR THE KNOWLEDGE OF GOD OR THE BIBLICAL GOSPEL

Apologetics not only means exploring and explaining the gospel but also establishing it. So, what ought we to mean by this? After all, what *could* we mean by this, if indeed we are speaking about the biblical gospel? Do sinners saved by God's grace have the ability within themselves to *establish* the gospel? Can the Christian determine who does or does not turn to Jesus in repentance in order to be saved?

Scripture is clear: *Jesus saves*. This is the shortest and clearest way I know to articulate the biblical gospel. Still, the truth that Jesus saves does not contradict Jesus's use of his own disciples to carry the gospel message to others through which others are saved from sin. So, there are at least three ways in which we ought to understand what it means for the gospel to be established.

First, we establish the gospel by accurately explaining the gospel. By this I mean that as long as we have accurately stated the truth of the gospel, or affirmed what the Bible affirms regarding the life, death, resurrection, and ascension of Jesus, of his having accomplished eternal redemption and his subsequent application of the benefits of this accomplishment through the work of the Holy Spirit, then we have, in some sense, established the gospel or the truth about it. This is no guarantee that the people to whom we speak these things will accept the truthfulness of them or believe them, but their lack of belief does not render our accurate explanation false. Thus, one of the things we mean by establishing the gospel is clarifying through our explanation what God has done, is doing, and will do through the Lord Jesus Christ and the Holy Spirit to accomplish and apply eternal redemption.

Secondly, we establish the biblical gospel to the degree that the Holy Spirit blesses our presentation of it by using it to regenerate the souls of sinners so that they place their trust in the Lord Jesus for salvation. This covers the experience of a person's conversion to Christianity. It is vital that we understand, however, that we, by our powers, cannot cause the unregenerate sinner to be regenerated; we cannot cause people to repent and believe the gospel. Yet, this does not mean that our explanations of the gospel are irrelevant or unimportant to the non-Christian's conversion. God uses his people to bear testimony to who he is and what he has done, is doing, and will do. This is part of the great privilege and even responsibility of being a Christian—to explain to others why he or she should trust in the Lord Jesus Christ for their whole life. But perhaps you are thinking that while you confess faith in the Lord Jesus for salvation, you still have many questions yourself about what the Bible teaches, and about the Christian faith and life. You're just not sure you are very well equipped to try and answer many questions non-Christians might have. This is precisely why it is important to understand the third sense in which we can establish the gospel through apologetics.

Thirdly, establishing the gospel is not merely about some sinners trusting in the Lord Jesus Christ for the first time for their salvation.

Instead, it is also about Christians exploring the gospel and explaining it in accordance with what Scripture reveals so that they come to a better understanding of it and have the gospel *further* established in them. This is what we should mean by the ongoing evangelization of believers. Repeatedly, in the letters that the apostles wrote to the church that are part of Scripture, we read them praying for and exhorting church members to do things such as "grow in the grace and knowledge of our Lord and Savior Jesus Christ" (2 Pet 3:18), or to "perfect holiness in the fear of God" (2 Cor 7:1), or to "work out your salvation with fear and trembling, for it is God who is at work in you both to will and work for his good pleasure" (Phil 2:12–13), or to "go on to maturity" (Heb 6:1). Earlier in his second letter, Peter calls Christians to supplement their "faith with virtue, and virtue with knowledge, and knowledge with self-control, and self-control with steadfastness, and steadfastness with godliness, and godliness with brotherly affection, and brotherly affection with love" (2 Pet 1:5–7). All this is to prevent us from becoming "ineffective or unfruitful in the knowledge of our Lord Jesus Christ" (2 Pet 1:8). Furthermore, Peter goes on to say that if the professing Christian is not working at this process of growth or maturation, then they are blinded and don't remember that they have been cleansed from sin. In other words, they are not remembering the purpose for which Christ lived, died, rose again, and ascended into heaven.

This third sense in which the gospel is established through exploring and explaining it is so clearly addressed throughout the New Testament that it becomes almost impossible to list all the passages that speak to it. One can easily argue that the whole text of the New Testament is consumed with it! After all, the whole Bible is addressed and given to God's covenant people. Jesus summarized the point in Matt 4:4 when he responded to Satan's temptation in the wilderness by stating, "It is written, 'Man shall not live by bread alone but by every word that comes from the mouth of God.'" As Paul would state later in Rom 10:17, "So, faith comes from hearing and hearing by the word of Christ." His point was not merely that saving faith comes only initially or one time through hearing Christ's word, but rather that as Christ's word continues to come, saving faith continues to grow or be further established in those who believe the gospel through the work of the Holy Spirit. All of this shaped the prayers that Paul communicated that he offered on behalf of the church.

In Col 1:9–12 Paul told the Christians at Colossae, one of the ancient Mediterranean cities where the gospel had taken root, what and why he and his co-laborer in the gospel prayed for them.

> And so, from the day we heard of it, we have not ceased to pray for you, asking that you be filled with the knowledge of his will in all spiritual wisdom and understanding, so as to walk in a manner worthy of the Lord, fully pleasing to him, bearing fruit in every good work and increasing in the knowledge of God; being strengthened with all power, according to his glorious might, for all endurance and patience with joy; giving thanks to the Father who has qualified you to share in the inheritance of the saints in light.

So, as Christians explore the gospel, which is eternal and, when believed, results in eternal life, they have the truth of God's word applied to them by the Holy Spirit so that they increase in the knowledge of God and are more energized and equipped to explain the gospel. Through the work of the Holy Spirit, this results in the gospel being further established in the one who is exploring and explaining it, and even established in others, who receive their explanation of it and trust in the Lord Jesus for salvation.

It is this salvation, which is the eternal hope of every true Christian, that we need to explore further, so that we know how to faithfully explain it, so that it might be further established in us, and by God's grace and mercy established in others. This is the nature and function of apologetics. It is the way of Christian discipleship. It is what results in some being evangelized for the first time, because the gospel takes root in them, or it results in the bearing of further gospel fruit and further belief in the gospel. What, then, does it look like for the gospel to be established in a person? Let's explore the answer to that question.

# 3

# Exploring and Explaining the Three R's of the Gospel

"The redemption of Christ is therefore no more central to the Christian hope than the creative operations of the Holy Spirit upon the heart: and the supernatural redemption itself would remain a mere name outside of us and beyond our reach, were it not realized in the subjective life by an equally supernatural application."[1]

B. B. Warfield

"Christianity is the cross; and he who makes the cross of Christ of none effect eviscerates Christianity. What Christianity brings to the world is not the bare command to love God and our neighbor. The world needs no such command; nature itself teaches the duty. What the world needs is the power to perform this duty, with respect to which it is impotent. And this power Christianity brings it in the redemption of the Son of God and the renewal of the Holy Ghost. Christianity is not merely a program of conduct: it is the power of a new life."[2]

B. B. Warfield

"Salvation in Christ involves a radical and complete transformation wrought in the soul (Rom. xii. 2, Eph. iv. 23) by God the Holy Spirit (Tit. iii. 5, Eph. iv.

1. Warfield, "Christian Supernaturalism," in *Works* 9:44.
2. Warfield, "Christianity and Our Times," in *Selected Shorter Works* 1:47.

24) by virtue of which we become 'new men' (Eph. iv. 24, Col. iii. 10), no longer conformed to this world (Rom. xii. 2, Eph. iv. 22, Col. iii. 9), but in knowledge and holiness of the truth created after the image of God (Eph. iv. 24, Col. iii. 10, Rom. xii. 2). The conception, it will be seen, is a wide one, inclusive of all that is comprehended in what we now technically speak of as a regeneration, renovation, and sanctification. It embraces, in fact, the entire subjective side of salvation, which it represents as a work of God, issuing in a wholly new creation (II Cor. v. 17, Gal. vi. 15, Eph. ii. 10)."[3]

B. B. Warfield

## INTRODUCTION

If we are to evangelize people to the Christian faith, or defend and commend the gospel that is the Christian's hope, or be faithful disciples of the Lord Jesus who disciple others, we must know the gospel well. The biblical gospel includes all biblical doctrine. It is about the Triune God as our hope. We are not our own hope. Perhaps this is even the most appropriate way to summarize the doctrine of salvation revealed in the Bible. The Bible describes the Christian's salvation, or hope, as God *regenerating* a sinner, or causing a person to be "born again" so that he or she *repents* of sin that leads to their *renewal* in holiness through God's grace by his word and Spirit. Thus, one way of summarizing our salvation is that it is our *regeneration* (out of spiritual death or sin), *repentance* (from sin, which is perhaps the chief act of saving faith), and *renewal* (in holiness by God's word of truth, a holiness given in "seed form" in our regeneration).

3. Warfield, "On the Biblical Notion of 'Renewal,'" in *Works* 2:439. Perhaps Warfield's most significant student, Machen, *What Is Faith?*, 208, stated the following: "At the beginning of the Christian life there is an act of God and of God alone. It is called in the New Testament the new birth or (as Paul calls it) the new creation. In that act no part whatever is contributed by the man who is born again. And no wonder! A man who is dead—either dead in physical death or "dead in trespasses and sins"—can do nothing whatever, at least in the sphere in which he is dead. If he could do anything in that sphere, he would not be dead. Such a man who is dead in trespasses and sins is raised to new life in the new birth or the new creation. . . . Thus [*sic*] the Christian life is begun by an act of God alone; but it is continued by co-operation between God and man. The possibility of co-operation is due indeed only to God; it has not been achieved in the slightest measure by us; it is the supreme wonder of God's grace. But once given by God it is not withdrawn." Cf. Warfield, "Regeneration," in *Selected Shorter Writings* 2:321–24.

There are numerous Scriptures that reveals these truths, and by better understanding them we are equipped to accurately and compassionately call others to saving faith, or Christian discipleship in the Lord Jesus, and give reasons for our hope in Jesus.

## DEFINING THE TERMS

Recognizing the importance of regeneration, repentance, and renewal for the Christian faith and life requires understanding the meaning of these terms. Let's first look at their definitions, and then focus on each one separately. *Regeneration* is the act of God causing a spiritually dead sinner to be brought back from their spiritual death to spiritual life. *Repentance* is the act of sinners grieving and hating their sin so that they confess it, reject it, or turn from it and live more obediently to Jesus. *Renewal* is the act of receiving spiritual strength from God so that we mature and become more like Jesus.

All three of these are part of each other; they exist in a living, organic union with each other. Thus, we only understand each of them in relation to the other two, and we never have one without the other two. Repentance and renewal, however, begin with regeneration. Furthermore, none of them can be rightly understood unless one understands the biblical doctrine of sin, because they are each about the conquering of sin.

## REGENERATION AND THE REALITY OF SIN

The first thing that we are told about humans in the Bible is that the Triune God created them in his image for the purpose of them being fruitful, multiplying, filling the earth, and subduing it (Gen 1:26–28). But the first male and female humans sinned against God, or rebelled against him by disobeying his command to not eat of the tree of the knowledge of good and evil (Gen 2:17). Just as God promised, Adam and Eve died when they ate what they were commanded not to eat. While they did not immediately or fully die physically, they did *begin* to die physically and they also died spiritually, and this can be seen in how they began to think about God and relate to him after they sinned (Gen 3:7–13). After Gen 3:13, the remainder of the Bible is the account of how God has acted in his creation to overcome sin and all its deadly consequences.

To *be* a sinner means that we are spiritually dead (Eph 2:1). "For the wages of sin is death," Paul wrote in Rom 6:23, "but the free gift of God is eternal life in Jesus Christ our Lord." Notice that when Paul proclaimed the gospel through the Letter to the Romans, he began by emphasizing sin and its consequence—God's judgment against it: death. Only by understanding that we are spiritually dead (Eph 2:1, 5)—or as Jesus expressed it, spiritually enslaved (John 8:31–36)—can we understand that God and God alone can and must cause us to be "born again to a living hope" (1 Pet 1:3), and thereby make "us alive together with Christ" (Eph 2:5), if we are to have spiritual life or freedom. Or as B. B. Warfield stated:

> What Christianity brings to the world is not the bare command to love God and our neighbor. The world needs no such command; nature itself teaches the duty. What the world needs is the power to perform this duty, with respect to which it is impotent. And this power Christianity brings it in the redemption of the Son of God and the renewal of the Holy Ghost. Christianity is not merely a program of conduct: it is the power of a new life.[4]

## QUESTIONS REGARDING SIN

The Bible does not give or explain answers to some of the questions that we might have about sin. It does not even give us a formal definition of sin, although in numerous places it gives us descriptions of it, and from the words and actions of the men and women mentioned in Scripture we are given a vivid picture of sin. Sin is, above all, the failure to conform to who God intended for us to be as his image-bearers and the failure to accomplish what he commanded us to do. This is why one of the confessions of the church answered the question, "What is sin?" with these words: "Sin is any want of conformity unto, or transgression of, the law of God" (Shorter Catechism of the Westminster Confession of Faith 14). Sin is not simply what we do, but a condition that corrupts or pollutes who we are. In other words, we sin because we are sinners.

Perhaps you have questions about how Adam was even able to sin, since he was part of God's good creation. After all, didn't God create all things "perfectly"? Many people have tried to give what they believe is a good and right answer to that question. But one of the most important things we will ever learn to do is to submit our thinking to God's word.

4. Warfield, "Christianity and Our Times," in *Selected Shorter Writings* 1:47.

We should not try and go beyond what Scripture has revealed. God even specifically tells his people that he rescues from sin that there are limits placed by him on their knowledge. In Deut 29:29 we read, "The secret things belong to the LORD our God, but the things that are revealed belong to us and to our children forever, that we may do all the words of this law." Notice the purpose for which God reveals his word of truth—so that those to whom he reveals it would obey it. If God's word does not answer a particular question, then it is God's way of telling us that we do not need an answer to that question in order to faithfully obey him. Precisely how Adam was even able to sin is never addressed in Scripture. What is addressed is (1) *that* he sinned, and (2) what his sin consisted of, and (3) who he sinned with, and (4) what the consequences of his sin were, and (5) how God acted to both judge and conquer Adam's and Eve's sin. When we explain the gospel to others, we want to be careful to emphasize what the Bible emphasizes and not get distracted with trying to answer questions that the Bible does not answer.

## THE NECESSITY FOR REGENERATION

Regeneration or resurrection from the spiritual dead is necessary because the wages of our sin is death. Every human needs to be resurrected or regenerated from this spiritual death if they are going to regard Jesus as worthy to be trusted and obeyed. Apart from God regenerating sinners by the power of his life-giving Word and Spirit, deadened sinners will remain spiritually dead. God must make a sinner "alive together with Christ" (Eph 2:5); a sinner, Jesus said, "must be born again" (John 3:3), or they simply cannot see the kingdom of God. Residing in spiritual death means that one is unable and thereby unwilling to repent of or from their sin and turn to Jesus for salvation. Jesus said, "No one can come to me unless the Father who sent me draws him" (John 6:44). We must pray to God for people's salvation. Recall that it is the gospel that is "the power of God for salvation" (Rom 1:16). All people need God's power of and for life, both physically and spiritually.

This, of course, does not mean that we refrain from speaking with others about the Christian faith, or fail to persuade them of its truthfulness. It means the exact opposite. The New Testament abundantly testifies to the truth that the apostles reasoned with people and sought to persuade them of the gospel's truthfulness. Indeed, it is God's Spirit that uses God's word of truth spoken by others to regenerate deadened sinners. That sin and its deathly condition plagues all humans is consistently taught throughout the whole Bible, and it means regeneration is necessary for salvation. Let's look at just a few examples that make this point.

## ISRAEL WAS SET FREE FROM EGYPT BY WHAT GOD DID

We could mention God coming and calling to Adam and Eve while they were hiding from God (Gen 3:8–9), and we could cite Noah receiving favor from God before we are told of Noah's good character, but let's focus on another example of God's giving new birth to the spiritually dead as seen in how he freed his covenant people from Egypt.

The Old Testament book of Exodus reveals that all that God did in protecting, preserving, and preparing Moses was because he remembered his covenant promise to Abraham, Isaac, and Jacob (Exod 2:23–25). And, yes, Abraham, we are told at the end of Gen 11, was descended from Noah and Noah from Adam. Paul would later mention in Gal 3:6–8 that Abraham had the gospel preached to him by God giving his covenant promise to him (Gen 12:1–3). The clear message from Exodus is that God was personally involved in freeing Israel from Egypt because he remembered his covenant promise or his gospel to Abraham, Isaac, and Jacob.

God, not Moses, is the hero of the exodus of Israel from Egypt because God brought the plagues that concluded in the death of the firstborn male of all the Egyptian households, and even of their livestock. God set Israel free from Egypt (Exod 12–14). All this was a physical demonstration of the spiritual reality of regeneration. Israel was enslaved to the Egyptians and incapable of freeing herself from this bondage. Of course, we have to be careful how far we take this point regarding how regeneration is pictured in God setting Israel free from Egypt. After all, most of that first generation of Israelites died in the wilderness because they did not exercise faith in God or believe him (Heb 3:7—4:11). Perhaps it is more accurate to say that Israel being set free from Egypt is not only a picture of regeneration, but also a picture of how some who are involved with God's covenant community and experience to some degree the blessings of God's covenant never actually believe the promises of God and end up receiving God's covenant curse. Judas, who betrayed Christ while being part of Jesus's inner circle of twelve disciples, is the most vivid example of this. Thus, if someone is to have salvation, they need to be fully freed from their sin by God. Jesus made this and a few other points about this in John 8.

## REGENERATION, REPENTANCE, AND RENEWAL IN GOD'S WORD OF TRUTH

In John 8:31–36 we read the following:

> So Jesus said to the Jews who had believed him, "If you abide in my word, you are truly my disciples, and you will know the truth, and the truth will set you free." They answered him, "We are offspring of Abraham and have never been enslaved to anyone. How is it that you say, 'You will become free'?" Jesus answered them, "Truly, truly, I say to you, everyone who practices sin is a slave to sin. The slave does not remain in the house forever; the son remains forever. So if the Son sets you free, you will be free indeed."

There are several truths mentioned here by Jesus that are critical for a right understanding of regeneration, repentance, and renewal that help explain gospel evangelism, apologetics, and discipleship. First, John tells us that Jesus spoke these words to some "Jews who had believed in" Jesus. More of this conversation is recorded in John 8:37–59. We might say that things did not end very well. At the end of this conversation, the group to whom Jesus was speaking picked up stones to throw at him. Speaking God's truth sometimes can have severe consequences. Truly, many of Jesus's conversations did not end like this one recorded in John 8, and hopefully many, if not most, of ours will not end like this either, but we need to see that one of the results of speaking to spiritually dead people is that sometimes they react quite harshly to God's word of truth. We always need to ask the Lord to make us alert to whom we should speak, make us courageous in our speaking, but also sensitive to when a conversation regarding the gospel needs to end. While Jesus and his disciples were quite bold in speaking God's word to people it was also Jesus who commanded his disciples: "Do not give dogs what is holy, and do not throw your pearls before pigs, lest they trample them underfoot and turn to attack you" (Matt 7:6). Seeking to make disciples, evangelize, or to engage in apologetics means, among other things, that we make wise and discerning judgments regarding not only what to say, but also to whom we say it. All this is another way we see how prayer is vital to our lives.

Secondly, notice that discipleship, and therefore apologetics and evangelism, require remaining in Jesus's word—both the Old and New Testament. Jesus said that he came to fulfill the Old Testament, not do away with it (Matt 5:17). The Old and New Testament do fit together; they harmonize. Indeed, it is the New Testament that reveals to us the way in which it fits with the Old Testament. If we are thinking of God's word as living, as Heb 4:12 says that it is, then we will identify the Old and New Testament as having an organic union, much the way we would identify a flower as having an organic union to the whole plant of which it is a part. We should think of the Old Testament as the root and stem and the New Testament as the flower. Still further, this organic union of the parts of Scripture results in an organic sustenance given to those who abide in that written word, because this abiding in the text is abiding in Jesus himself. John identifies Jesus as the Word who became flesh (John 1:1–14). Jesus himself said that if we abide in his word, we are truly his disciples, and we will know the truth, and the truth will set us free (John 8:31–32)—that is, free from sin. Furthermore, he commands his disciples to abide in him in order to bear fruit, because apart from him, his disciples can do nothing (John 15:1–5). So, to remain in God's written word is, in some sense, to remain in and with Jesus, or to be Jesus's disciple.

Thirdly, Jesus credits his word of truth with setting sinners free from their sin, or regenerating them. This does not discount the role of the Holy Spirit, but simply that God's word of truth is what the Holy Spirit uses in regeneration. The fact that Jesus highlights God's word does not automatically mean he is negating or diminishing the role of Holy Spirit. Even Jesus did not explain everything that could be explained all at once. Jesus's emphasis in John 8 was on God's word of truth. Emphasizing it did not automatically mean diminishing the role of the Holy Spirit.

The apostle James (1:18) tells us that Christians are "brought forth by the word of truth." James's point has to do with our regeneration or our initial freedom from spiritual death. Peter likewise expressed this same truth: "You have been born again, not of perishable seed but of imperishable, through the living and abiding word of God" (1 Pet 1:23). True disciples of Jesus are able to abide in God's word because God's word abides in them, and this word of God is life.

Fourthly, observe how Jesus presents discipleship to him as an ongoing process in which we are continuously freed from sin. In other words, the true disciple of Jesus is initially freed from sin and then, throughout their life, must be continuously freed from sin. Jesus said, "If you abide [present active indicative verb] in my word, you are truly my disciples, and you will know [future active indicative verb] the truth and the truth will set you free [future active indicative verb]" (John 8:32). The verb forms mandate that we recognize that abiding or remaining in Jesus's word on an ongoing basis is a characteristic of Jesus's disciples. Doing this has an ongoing result. In other words, the regeneration of a sinner has an ongoing effect in them. As the apostle Paul described it, the Christian's salvation is God saving "according to his own mercy, by the washing of regeneration and renewal of the Holy Spirit, whom he poured out on us richly through Jesus Christ our Savior, so that being justified by his grace we might become heirs according to the hope of eternal life" (Titus 3:5–7). This is consistent with Jesus's statement that his Spirit, the Spirit of Truth, would take what belonged to Jesus and apply it to Jesus's disciples (John 14:15–17; 15:26–27; 16:13–15).

Finally, it is actually Jesus who operates through his word and by his Spirit to regenerate and renew a sinner. Jesus said, "If the son shall set you free, you will be free indeed." The ESV translators rightly capitalize the word "Son" in John 8:36, because Jesus is referring to himself in that statement. Even today, Jesus still regenerates sinners and continues to renew them in conjunction with his Spirit of Truth (John 14–16). Jesus had stated the necessity for this regeneration earlier to a man named Nicodemus and then he demonstrated it with another man named Lazarus. In both situations Jesus revealed that regeneration and renewal are united and that he performs each work.

## ILLUSTRATIONS FROM JESUS

In John 3 we are told of the encounter Jesus had with a Jewish religious teacher: a Pharisee named Nicodemus. Nicodemus came to Jesus at night—a way that suggests he was concerned about whether others saw him speaking with Jesus. Nicodemus began his conversation with Jesus declaring what he and other Pharisees knew about Jesus. This is particularly important because knowledge of or about God is an important theme in John's Gospel. John tells his readers that he wrote his Gospel so that they might believe that Jesus is the Christ and that by believing would have life in Jesus's name (John 20:31). The eternal life that comes from believing in Jesus is identified by Jesus in John 17:3 as knowledge of God or himself.

John tells us prior to John 3 that Jesus knew all men and that he did not need anyone's testimony concerning man. This is quite revealing since Nicodemus announced to Jesus what he and the other Pharisees knew about Jesus. Yet, as the conversation develops, it is apparent that Nicodemus did not know about the things of which Jesus spoke. Jesus spoke to him concerning being "born again," or regenerated, and who causes this to happen.

Jesus told Nicodemus that one must be born again or born from above. John regularly tells us that Jesus taught that he and his kingdom were "from above" or "not of this world." The point is that Jesus has a kingdom that he brought with him. It is rightly called *supernatural*. It cannot be acquired or achieved by people simply using the powers or abilities they have available to them on earth. This point is seen in John 18:36 and 19:11, when Jesus explains about (1) the character of his kingdom and (2) the origin of Pilate's own authority, both of which are "from above." The point is that the origin and character of Jesus's kingdom, and therefore knowledge of it, is not simply or only from the natural material realm, but from the supernatural realm that controls the natural. Because Jesus is the creator of the physical world, he controls it; he came into it from outside of it, and he brought his kingdom to it.

While Nicodemus is confused in John 3, Jesus continues to explain that being born "again" or "from above" is the act of the Spirit of God. Jesus says that the Spirit's work is like the wind. The wind blows and we hear it, but we do not know where it comes from or where it goes. Jesus said that this is what it is like with those born of the Spirit.

What is Jesus's point? The wind is like God's Spirit and our knowledge of the Spirit of God is like our knowledge of the wind. Both God's Spirit and the wind have an effect that can be seen, but we do not actually see them, and we do not know (recall the theme of knowledge of God) where they came from (that is, besides from God) and where they go next. Whatever else we might conclude from this encounter, one thing is clear—it is the Spirit of God that causes a person to be "born again," or *regenerated*, and the Spirit of God is not someone we control. Furthermore, it helps us see that it is God's Spirit that works by and with God's word in the regeneration of a sinner.

By Jesus giving a person spiritual rebirth, that person is able to place their faith in Jesus. Just as Jesus healed blind people causing them to see, healed deaf people causing them to hear, or healed the lame causing them to walk, so too he heals some people spiritually, bringing them back from spiritual death. It is not our faith in Jesus that causes our spiritual rebirth; it is the other way around. If our faith in Jesus gave us our regeneration, then we could claim that we were the cause of our regeneration, at least we could if we thought our faith in Jesus came from us. But any person who places their faith in Jesus for salvation has a faith that the Bible tells us is from God's grace and not from them.

## THE EXPLANATION FROM THE APOSTLE PAUL ABOUT SAVING FAITH

"For by grace you have been saved through faith. And this is not your own doing; it is the gift of God, not a result of works, so that no one may boast" (Eph 2:8–9). No one who repents of their sin, believes the gospel, and becomes a disciple of the Lord Jesus can take credit for their salvation—not a single part of it. Put another way, at no point in the whole process of regeneration, repentance, and renewal are we the cause of them. *We are active* in all them. But we are active precisely because *we are acted upon by God* and continue to be acted upon by him through his Spirit. In Eph 2:10, Paul goes on to describe the true disciple of Jesus as being God's work: "For we are his workmanship, created in Christ Jesus for good works, which God prepared beforehand that we should walk in them." Such a description credits God with making "us alive together with Christ" (Eph 2:5) and of our need for him to do so because "we were dead in our trespasses" (Eph 2:5). God, not us, is the one who saves from sin. God is the creator, not us. We can be given life, but we cannot create life where there is no life. Even as humans reproduce, they are not creating life out of no life. The ability to reproduce is part of a life that has been given by God. In part, it shows us that while we can be active in helping produce life, we are not the Author of Life and therefore we cannot ultimately determine whether life is present—either physically or spiritually.

We need to have clearly fixed in our mind what the Bible teaches concerning the relationship between faith in Jesus and *regeneration*. There are only two possible options. Either we exercise faith in Jesus and this causes us to be regenerated, or the Spirit of God regenerates us and this causes us to exercise faith in Jesus. We might pose the following question that strikes at the heart of the matter: Ultimately, is God in control of his creatures, and determining that his kingdom comes, or do God's creatures control him, and determine whether his kingdom comes?

## REGENERATION AND THE DOCTRINE OF GOD AS CREATOR AND REDEEMER

John 1:13 makes clear that the person who believes in Jesus (this is what it means to believe in "his name") has been given the right to become a child of God, and such a person is "born of God." It is not coincidental that Jesus uses the concept of a birth to communicate salvation. The terms "born again," or "born from above," and "regeneration" are creational concepts. In other words, when a person comes to have salvation something new is created in that person. This is precisely what the apostle Paul describes in 2 Cor 5:17–18: "Therefore, if anyone is in Christ, he is a new creation. The old has passed away; behold, the new has come. *All this is from God*, who through Christ reconciled us to himself and gave us the ministry of reconciliation" (italics mine). To say we are new creatures if we believe in Jesus is not to foolishly say that we never existed prior to our believing in Jesus for salvation. The term *new* refers to the *re*newing of something that was already present but lay dead, much the way Lazarus's body lay dead before Jesus resurrected it.

## CREATOR, CREATION, REGENERATION, AND RENEWAL

In 2 Cor 5 and elsewhere Paul explains about the relationship between God as creator and God as redeemer. To put it succinctly, God is the only redeemer from sin because God alone creates life. God is life itself. As Paul stated in Acts 17:28, "For in him we live and move, and have our being." What may be especially interesting about these words is that Paul not only affirmed that they accurately described the relationship all people have to God, but also that non-Christian poets had affirmed them. Paul was quoting one of the non-Christian Greek poets of his day when he spoke those words. This is a testimony to the truth that even non-Christians know some true things about God. It is a reminder of what Paul wrote in Rom 1:19–20—that God has revealed himself to all people. Even though sin causes people to distort and suppress the truth about God, no one can go on living and get rid of all knowledge of God from themselves. To be a living human is to have some knowledge of God, because humans are created in the image of God and all the objects of our knowledge are, in some sense, a part of God's creation that reveals him. Even as the sinner's regeneration and renewal are from God, the creator and redeemer, this new life and its growth are united to existing realities brought into being and sustained by God. All of what this includes does not remain wholly unknown to the one who has not yet trusted in Jesus for salvation.

## LEARN FROM THE OBJECT LESSON JESUS PERFORMED

In John 11 we read of Jesus resurrecting Lazarus, who was the brother of two women, Mary and Martha. Mary was a common name among God's people and there are several "Marys" mentioned in the New Testament. The "Mary" of John 11 was the sister of Martha and they were both from Bethany, and disciples of Jesus. While no women were a part of the group of the twelve men Jesus chose as his closest disciples, numerous women were regarded as Jesus's disciples, and treated by Jesus in a remarkably different way than they were treated by the majority of men within the Jewish community during Jesus's life. Mary and Martha had come to trust Jesus for their salvation, as Luke 7:36–50 and 10:38–42 indicate. Jesus's raising Lazarus from the dead is an object lesson regarding salvation. In this event we have salvation demonstrated, and more specifically, regeneration demonstrated.

John 11:17 tells us that by the time Jesus arrived on the scene Lazarus had been in the grave for four days. In the early part of the chapter, we learn that Jesus had delayed his arrival, and that when Jesus finally arrived, Martha said to Jesus, "Lord, if you had been here, my brother would not have died." In John 11:23 Jesus said to Martha, "Your brother shall rise again." But Martha's response demonstrates that she takes this as no more than the normal devout Jewish way of consoling those who lost loved ones by reminding them of the resurrection at the end of history.[5] Martha said to Jesus, "I know that he will rise again in the resurrection on the last day." It is upon these words that Jesus responds by redirecting

5. Carson, *Gospel According to John*, 412.

Martha's belief from simply a reality far off in the future to her need to believe in *him*. This belief in *him* is believing in something Jesus does.

Jesus responded to Martha, "I am the resurrection and the life; he who believes in me shall live even if he dies, and everyone who lives and believes in me shall never die. Do you believe this?" The question challenged Martha regarding whether she believed Jesus could and would give her, and her brother, both spiritual and physical life.

At Lazarus's tomb, Jesus cried out in a loud voice, "Lazarus, come out!" and Lazarus came out of the tomb. Jesus gave Lazarus life. When Lazarus was dead, he did not cooperate with Jesus. He could only cooperate after he was made alive by Jesus. Jesus gave Lazarus life. In doing this, Jesus demonstrated that he alone, through the power of the Holy Spirit, in accordance with the will of God the Father, overcomes the just penalty for sin—death. Only the Triune God can reverse the effects of sin. Only God can bring life where there is none. Only the creator can regenerate.

Sin affected Lazarus completely, just as it does every person. Jesus had to resurrect Lazarus's mind and will before Lazarus could use them again. This is a picture of salvation. In particular, then, with respects to the human will we must affirm that *it is a person's will that is dependent on God's will*. If we are to exercise our will in a way that honors God, God must enable us to do so through a special act of his mercy and grace whereby he resurrects our will, along with the rest of us, or regenerates us, from spiritual death. When God regenerates us by his word and Spirit, this enables us to repent and believe the gospel.

## REPENTANCE: THE SIGN OF REGENERATION, THE WAY TO RENEWAL

In other words, a sinner's repentance from sin is another way of describing their believing in the gospel. Repentance describes the act in negative terms or what one negates, opposes, or renounces—sin. *Believing the gospel* describes *repentance* in positive terms or what one affirms, endorses, or embraces—the good news about the Lord Jesus. Thus, Jesus summarized his preaching about his kingdom this way: "The time is fulfilled, and the kingdom of God is at hand; repent and believe in the gospel" (Mark 1:15). Such repentance and belief are not simply a one-time action but a continuous way of living.

## HOW YOU GOT GOING IS HOW YOU KEEP GOING

The way we get going in the Christian life is the way we keep going in it. Paul summarized the point this way in his Letter to the Galatians: "Having begun by the Spirit, are you now being perfected by the flesh?" (Gal 3:3). Paul's question could be reworded: Having begun spiritually by God choosing to give you what you did not have—spiritual life—are you now going to persevere and mature in the Christian faith and reach the goal God has for you by looking to what is only from and of you? Since it is eternal life that Jesus gives, this life remains with, and in, the one to whom it is given. This is because Jesus remains with that person. As Paul would later write, "He who began a good work in you will bring it to completion at the day of Christ Jesus" (Phil 1:6). Since the Triune God is alone eternal, he is the one who sustains this life that he gives to the objects of his mercy (Luke 1:46, 54, 72; Rom 9:15–16; 12:1–2; 2 Cor 4:1; Eph 2:4; 1 Tim 1:13–16; Titus 3:5; Jas 3:17; 1 Pet 1:3; 2 John 1:3). To defend and commend the gospel of the Lord Jesus is to stress that Jesus through the Holy Spirit for the glory of God the Father must *regenerate* deadened sinners so that they *repent*. If Jesus resurrects someone from spiritual death, they remain spiritually alive. But this spiritual life needs nourishment or spiritual food so that it is *renewed* or strengthened and reaches the goal God has for it. All this takes place as the truth of God's word goes forth, because it is by this word of truth that sinners are spiritually birthed or regenerated (Jas 1:18; 1 Pet 1:23), and by this same word that sinners are renewed so that they change to be like Jesus (Rom 8:29; 12:2; Eph 4:7–16).

## REGENERATION PRODUCES REPENTANCE THAT RENEWS US IN JESUS'S LIFE

At the beginning of Rom 12:1–2, the apostle Paul makes clear what Christians must do because of what God has accomplished, is accomplishing, and will accomplish through the Lord Jesus. Paul wrote, "I appeal to you therefore, brothers, by the mercies of God, to present your bodies as a living sacrifice, holy and acceptable to God, which is your spiritual worship. Do not be conformed to this world, but be transformed by the renewal of your mind, that by testing you may discern what is the will of God, what is good and acceptable and perfect."[6] In these words, we have a summary of the entire Christian life. This is not to say that this is the only way to summarize the Christian life, but it is certainly a divinely inspired way of doing so, because it is God's word. Just as Jesus stated both negatively and positively what it meant to be his disciple or be evangelized to the gospel—"Repent and believe in the gospel" (Mark 1:15)—so too did the apostle Paul. Paul's "do not be conformed to this world" equals what Jesus meant by "repent." Paul's "be transformed by the renewal of your mind" equals what Jesus meant by "believe in the gospel." If we are Jesus's disciples, these will be ongoing activities in our lives, since God's eternal Spirit has regenerated us, giving us eternal life, and giving us the power to submit ourselves to being transformed by the renewal of our mind.

Recall what we have already seen from Jesus's words in John 8:31–32. There we saw that Jesus said, "If you abide in my word, you are truly my disciples, and you will know the truth, and the truth will set you free." This is the same point that Paul makes in Rom 12:2; although Paul does not specifically use the terms *God's word* or *gospel* or *word of truth* for what our minds are renewed in and by, this is what he implies. After all, as Paul had previously stated in Rom 1:16, the gospel is the power of God for salvation for everyone who believes it (the statement affirms the *necessity* of the sinner believing the gospel, but does not affirm the *origin* of this belief). Paul's point in his commands in Rom 12:2 is that our fulfillment of them is a demonstration of our salvation. The same point can be seen when we see that in Rom 10:17 Paul specifically states that "faith comes by hearing and hearing by the word of Christ." The gospel, or God's word of truth, when accompanied by the power of God's Spirit not only regenerates deadened sinners but then continues to strengthen them, grow them, mature them, or make them to be like Jesus.

We perhaps see this point even more clearly when we pay attention to what Paul wrote in Rom 8:29. Paul wrote, "For those whom he foreknew he also predestined to be conformed to the image of his Son, in order that he [Jesus] might be the first-born among many brothers." The term that is translated *conform* in Rom 8:29 is a form of the same term that is used in Rom 12:2 and is translated *transformed*. What Jesus describes as being set free because we abide in his word, Paul describes as being transformed by the renewal of our mind. What every Christian needs consistently is to be fed by God's word; they need to abide or remain in God's word. This

6. Some translators believe that "spiritual" should be translated as "reasonable."

takes place first and foremost through the preaching and teaching of God's word within and by the church and those men gifted by the Holy Spirit to do this work (Eph 4:7–16; 1 Tim 2:8—3:7; Titus 1:5–9; 2:1–15; 2 Tim 2:15; 3:16—4:5; Heb 4:12–16; 1 Pet 1:22–25).

Paul summarized these same truths in Titus 3:3–7 (italics mine):

> For we ourselves were once foolish, disobedient, led astray, slaves to various passions and pleasures, passing our days in malice and envy, hated by others and hating one another. But when the goodness and loving kindness of God our Savior appeared, he saved us, not because of works done by us in righteousness, but according to his own mercy, by the washing of *regeneration* and *renewal* of the Holy Spirit, whom he poured out on us richly through Jesus Christ our Savior, so that being justified by his grace we might become heirs according to the hope of eternal life.

Notice that Paul also describes sinners as slaves, slaves to various passions and pleasures. Once again, the work that Jesus performed occurs by the work of the Holy Spirit, and is characterized as actually saving, not simply making salvation a possibility. While it is not altogether inaccurate to say "Jesus makes salvation possible," it is misleading. Jesus does not merely make salvation a possibility; in keeping with his name *Jesus* or Joshua ("deliverer"), Jesus actually saves. Jesus was given this name "because he shall save his people from their sins" (Matt 1:21).

## REGENERATION AND RENEWAL OF SINNERS—GOD'S WORK

Regeneration is God's work. Even our renewal is first and foremost the work of God the Holy Spirit, not our work, but we do participate in it. That is, the one who has received salvation, who has been acted upon by God, and continues to be acted upon by God is actively doing things that effect their salvation, but they are only able to do these things because, like Lazarus who was raised from the dead, they too were raised from the dead, giving them the ability to obey Jesus. The work of *regeneration* by the Holy Spirit has this corresponding companion work—the *renewal* by the Holy Spirit (Titus 3:5). God not only gives life, but also grows that life. It is God who nurtures his people, feeds them, and grows them in the grace and knowledge of himself. "He who began a good work in you will perfect it until the day of Christ Jesus," Paul wrote in Phil 1:6. Just as God set his people free from Egypt and then fed them with manna from the wilderness and gave them water from the rock, so too does Jesus set his covenant people free from sin, giving them a spiritual birth and then renews them by feeding them with his word (Exod 16, 17; 1 Cor 10:1–4; John 15:1–5; Rom 10:14–17; 2 Tim 3:16—4:5). All this is why Paul also wrote to the Philippian Christians, "Work out your salvation with fear and trembling, for it is God who is at work in you both to will and work for his good pleasure" (Phil 2:12–13). So, yes, to be Jesus's disciple means we are busy doing particular things, but we are only able to do these things because Jesus continues to be actively working in us through his Holy Spirit. This ongoing work by the Holy Spirit is what the Christian's renewal is all about.

## GOD'S REGENERATION AND RENEWAL OF ONLY SOME AND NOT ALL IS NOT UNJUST

The Bible does not speak of faith in God that saves from sin as a potential possessed by all people as a result of God distributing it to all humans. The Bible specifically teaches the very opposite. God shows mercy to some (Rom 9:1–29) and not to others for salvation, and in this he is perfectly just and glorified, because what we all deserve is death. It would be perfectly just for God to damn all humans to hell. God acted mercifully and graciously in establishing his covenant with his people. So, while God has obligated himself to save some, this obligation is an act of his mercy. In Rom 12:1, Eph 2, and Titus 3, Paul clearly attributes the salvation of a sinner to the mercy of God, and attributes to God a grace that actually saves a sinner. By definition, "mercy" is not getting what you deserve, which in turn leads you to get what you don't deserve—God's grace. This is why the terms and concepts of "mercy" and "grace" are virtually interchangeable in the Christian doctrine of salvation. God's mercy and grace are accomplished by the Holy Spirit in the *regeneration* (beginning point in salvation, being raised from the spiritual dead) and *renewal* (continuing the work of salvation) of the sinner. The sinner's *regeneration* produces *repentance* that leads to *renewal*.

## THE CULTURAL IDEOLOGY THAT HELPS OBSCURE THE GOSPEL

In the early-to-mid-seventeenth century, after over a hundred years of brutal and deathly conflicts over the right interpretation of the Bible, Europe made a decisive turn toward a humanistic ideology that rooted rationality and knowledge of the truth in the individual. Historians like to refer to the period that ensued upon this decisive turn, that was signaled by the pronouncement of the philosopher Rene Descartes, "I think, therefore I am," as "the Enlightenment." Oh, the irony. An enlightenment it was not. As some have said, it was more akin to an "endarkenment." It would take a few centuries for it to mature and blossom into a full-blown subjectivism and relativism. We will explore this point and some of its implications later. For now, we need to recognize that not only has this individualistic relativism swamped Western culture, but also seriously corrupted the church and Christian theology, and therefore many people's understanding of the gospel. It has led to those of us in the West—and wherever Western cultural influence has taken root—to easily default towards thinking and living as if humans can measure all reality, manipulate it, manufacture it, and then manage it—what I like to call the "Four M's" view of Western culture. If you notice, three of those terms begin with "man," and the other one begins with "me." This pretty well sums up the primary orientation of the West. Of course, this did not originate in the West or with Descartes, but in the human soul. More specifically, one of its consequences has been the corruption of the gospel that results in people assigning more power to the individual person for starting the Christian life. We discover its expression wherever someone thinks the individual needs to exercise faith in Jesus in order to be "born again." As we have seen, however, deadened sinners can't exercise faith in Jesus. First, they have to be born from above, then they are able to exercise faith in Jesus.

## CONCLUSION

The gospel of the Lord Jesus Christ is "good news" precisely because it is first and foremost about who Jesus is and what he does to save sinners from sin. This work by Jesus of saving sinners can be described as their regeneration, repentance, and renewal. It highlights that Jesus's disciples will be in his word and that his word will be in them, and this will result in them changing to be like Jesus. This work takes place as God's Spirit takes God's word and changes or transforms the Christian to be like Jesus as the Spirit convicts him or her of sin and enables them to repent of it. This gives us the basics of what the Christian gospel is and what it means in general for the life of every disciple of the Lord Jesus. When we recognize that our sin is unbelief, and that the Christian's renewal is seen in repentance from their unbelief, we can perhaps see more clearly that there is a sense in which the true disciple of Jesus is always being evangelized. When we recognize that repentance from sin is a mind being renewed in the truth of God's word so that the irrationality of sin is rejected, then we can perhaps better understand that offering a reason for the Christian faith, or apologetics, is what our renewal in the Christian faith is about. And so, once again, we see that discipleship, evangelism, and apologetics are united.

But there is another critical question that we need to answer as we seek to disciple others: What is the best way to explain the gospel? This question is necessary to ask at least for this reason—the gospel of the Lord Jesus is what the entire Bible is about. Among other things it means that before anyone becomes convinced that the gospel message in Scripture is true, they could have any number of questions regarding the Bible's content. In our next chapter we will attempt to answer this question regarding the best way to explain the gospel.

# 4

# Exploring the Explaining of the Gospel Through Jesus's Conversations

"Christ did come to found a kingdom. . . . He has saved us from ignorance; He has saved us from pain; but these are not the evils on which the hinge of His saving work turns. Above all and before all He has saved us from sin."[1]

B. B. Warfield

"It is, of course, as evident that men cannot turn from darkness to light, from the tyranny of Satan to God, in their own strength, as it is that men cannot open other people's eyes by their own power. As in the one case, so in the other, the immanent work of the Holy Spirit is not excluded because it is not mentioned."[2]

B. B. Warfield

"The great facts that constitute Christianity are just as 'naked' as any other facts, and are just as meaningless to us as any other facts, until they are not only perceived but understood, that is, until not only they themselves but their doctrinal significance is made known to us. . . . These great facts

1. Warfield, *Power of God Unto Salvation*, 45–46.

2. Warfield, "Summation of the Gospel," in *Faith and Life*, 176. To clarify: Warfield's point is that *just* because the Holy Spirit is not mentioned in some scriptural presentations or explanations of the gospel does not mean that those who provide those presentations or explanations are saying that the Holy Spirit is not needed.

of Christianity—is there anyone who has knowledge of their meaning and who has a right to our belief when he explains them to us?—who, in a word, has authority to declare to the world what this series of great facts means, or in other words, what Christianity is? . . . We find that doctrinal authority ultimately, of course, in Christ."[3]

B. B. Warfield

## INTRODUCTION

The Christian hope or gospel that we explain can be expressed in many ways, because of who Jesus is and what he does. Jesus is Lord of all creation. He is the Second Person of the Trinity. There are many ways to accurately explain the gospel of the Lord Jesus, and many ways to inaccurately explain it. The entire Bible reveals these points. Since the whole Bible is about the gospel, then we merely need to look at the variety that marks the Bible to understand that the gospel can be explained in many ways. We do not access this vast variety, however, apart from our sin. Among the many ways our sin is demonstrated is our attempt to interpret our lives and the lives of others in the way we want. As sinners we deny and reject the gospel. We need God to regenerate us from the spiritual dead, so that we have an accurate understanding of the gospel—an accurate interpretation of our life and the life of others—and trust in God for salvation. Still, even after deciding not to deny the gospel we can still distort it. Our need for renewal highlights that we need to grow or mature in understanding the gospel accurately. As we seek to get better at explaining the gospel, we learn more regarding who God is and what he has done, is doing, and will do. In other words, we conduct ourselves as Jesus's disciples. We cannot come close to giving an example of all the possible ways to explain the gospel. We can, however, discern some of the necessary features of an accurate presentation of it. We will seek to do this by looking at five presentations of it in the New Testament. Along the way we will see some of the points we have already touched upon. Faithfully explaining the gospel, then, will mean (1) an accurate presentation of what God has done in Jesus in order to save from sin, (2) a call to repentance from sin, and (3) a call to trust who God has revealed

3. Warfield, "Right of Systematic Theology," in *Selected Shorter Writings* 2:238.

himself to be and in what he does. Along the way, we will see that in God accomplishing the gospel, he also establishes the explanation of it. After all, since the explanation of the gospel is necessary for saving sinners, and God alone saves sinners, then God must be the cause of the gospel being explained.

## FIVE EXAMPLES

In this chapter we look at three instances in which Jesus confronted people with the truth regarding himself, two of which resulted in salvation, and one which did not. In our next chapter we will look at two presentations of the gospel from two of Jesus's apostles. In these we will see that the different audiences required different presentations. Yet each presentation confronted people with (1) the truth regarding Jesus, (2) a call to repentance from sin, and (3) a call to trust Jesus for salvation. We will look at Jesus's encounters with the Samaritan woman in John 4, the wealthy young man in Matt 19, and the thief on the cross in Luke 23. Then we learn from Peter's sermon on the day of Pentecost in Acts 3, and Paul's sermon at the Areopagus in Acts 17.

## A WORD OF CAUTION: WE ARE NOT JESUS

As obvious as it may seem we must remember that we are not Jesus. There are things that Jesus did that we cannot. One thing this means is that when explaining the gospel to others we cannot expect that we will be able to do all that Jesus did when he presented the gospel. Jesus is one person with two natures—a divine one and a human one, and he had no sin. While the Bible does not explain much regarding the union and interactions between these two natures, it reveals that Jesus has them and was therefore capable of doing things during his earthly life that we who are only human and sinful cannot do. Even though there is a sense in which Jesus set an example for us to follow, Jesus is not first and foremost our example to follow. Above all, Jesus enables those he saves from sin to come to God the Father and have fellowship, or a saving relationship with the Father. In doing this, Jesus serves as our Great High Priest (Heb 8–10). It is because no mere human is capable of doing what Jesus did that we needed Jesus to do the things he did in order for us to be saved from sin. Because Jesus is both God and man, he had powers during his earthly life that enabled him to know things about people that we cannot know. Among other things, these truths mean that Jesus's conversations reveal principles or guidelines that should direct our thinking about the general character of our conversations with others regarding Jesus. We are not to try and do everything that Jesus did in his conversations. Furthermore, some of the things Jesus did in speaking with others about himself can sometimes take many days, weeks, months, and even years to develop in our conversations. Finally, we must keep in mind that it is the whole church that is regarded as "the body of Christ" (Rom 12; 1 Cor 12; Eph 1:22–23; 4:4, 23; Col 1:18). Jesus's examples from which we should learn have application to, and implications for, the lives of every individual Christian. But such application and implications exist because such individual Christians are united to Christ, and therefore one another as the church. It is the church corporately that is the body of Christ, and it is to the church corporately expressed on earth within local congregations that has the duty and privilege to proclaim the gospel. This latter point we will explore in the chapters ahead, but for now we should be clear that it is not given to every individual Christian to fulfill the same function within the church's work of evangelism, discipleship, and apologetics.

## CROSSING CULTURAL BOUNDARIES

The account of Jesus speaking to a woman from Samaria is in John 4:1–26. Let's look at the first fifteen verses.

> Now when Jesus learned that the Pharisees had heard that Jesus was making and baptizing more disciples than John, although Jesus did not baptize, but only his disciples, he left Judea and departed again for Galilee. And he had to pass through Samaria. So he came to a town of Samaria called Sychar, near the field that Jacob had given to his son Joseph. Jacob's well was there; so Jesus, wearied as he was from his journey, was sitting beside the well. It was about the sixth hour. A woman from Samaria came to draw water. Jesus said to her, "Give me a drink." For his disciples had gone away into the city to buy food. The Samaritan woman said to him, "How is that you, a Jew, ask for a drink from me, a woman of Samaria?" For Jews have no dealings with Samaritans. Jesus answered her, "If you knew the gift of God, and who it is that is saying to you, 'Give me drink,' you would have asked him, and he would have given you living water." The woman said to him, "Sir, you have nothing to draw water with,

> and the well is deep. Where do you get that living water? Are you greater than our father Jacob? He gave us the well and drank from it himself, as did his sons and his livestock." Jesus said to her, "Everyone who drinks of this water will be thirsty again, but whoever drinks of the water that I will give him will never be thirsty again. The water I will give him will become in him a spring of water welling up to eternal life." The woman said to him, "Sir, give me this water, so that I will not be thirsty or have to come to draw water."

First, notice that Jesus has this encounter because he was busy doing what he was sent to do, and then, in turn, some had responded wrongly toward his actions. Jesus left Judea in order to avoid a conflict between his disciples and John's in light of his own rising popularity. There would come a time when his popularity would nurture the conflict between him and the Pharisees to the point that it would lead to his crucifixion. Yet, Jesus remained in control of that conflict, even as he remained in control of this situation between his disciples and John's. Jesus and his disciples leave Judea to avoid any apparent conflict with John's disciples, and as they do the opportunity arises to challenge this woman with his lordship and her need for salvation.

Principle 1: Our opportunities for proclaiming the gospel happen in the midst of all the circumstances of our lives, even those that seem unpleasant and unplanned. Knowing that God is in control of all creation teaches us to be at peace and perceive how we are able to present the gospel in the circumstances that arise through our obedience to God's will; we do not need to try and manufacture opportunities to speak to people regarding Jesus. It is not the job of pastors to create opportunities for church members to "engage in ministry." Such a notion would be simply silly if it were not actually believed by some and causing them to think and operate in a grossly unbiblical way. Among other things, it not only casts the pastor in the role of God, but also leads the members under such thinking to miss how biblical evangelism, discipleship, and apologetics actually take place. In the normal circumstances of our lives, as we seek to obey God's word, we *will* have opportunity to speak to others about the gospel. Whether we are at home with family, at work with colleagues, or out shopping, or doing any number of other things, we will encounter people who need to hear gospel truth. God determines what this looks like with every individual in the body of Christ, not the pastor or any other church leaders.

Principle 2: The demand to submit to Jesus's lordship, which is integral to the gospel, is not controlled or determined by anyone's cultural situation. Perhaps the second thing we should note is that people's questions often reveal assumptions about their interpretation of life, and all reality. Their interpretation of life is united to and in some sense influenced by the time and place in which they live. The Samaritan woman's question in v. 9 ("How is that you, a Jew, ask for a drink from me, a woman of Samaria?") is an example of this. Jews and Samaritans did not get along well. Samaritans were the result of some Jews marrying some Assyrians during the eighth century BC during a time when God's covenant people were judged and enslaved for their sin. To most Jews, Samaritans represented compromise with a wicked empire, and unfaithfulness to God. During Jesus's life, if God's old covenant people wanted to remain eligible to worship, they thought they had to obey laws that did not allow them to associate with Samaritans. So, when Jesus commanded the Samaritan woman to give him a drink, it was a bit shocking. Predictably, she interpreted her encounter with Jesus according to her cultural experience; she was surprised that Jesus spoke to her. Notice this: Jesus's lordship defines how we ought to think of our circumstances.

This does not mean that we should ignore or disregard our cultural situation, or be unconcerned about whether we offend people. Jesus was not giving needless offense. To say that Jesus's lordship is not controlled or determined by our cultural experience means that Jesus's lordship determines how we must interpret both our culture and our circumstances. Who we are willing to speak to, how we speak to them, and where we are willing to go are all matters that must ultimately be determined by our obedience to Jesus, and not our obedience or allegiance to a particular society's customs, or any human community's history, including our own biological family's. Notice that Jesus called into question a *custom*. Jesus did not break a law by a civil authority in his speaking to the Samaritan woman. Instead, he was going against an *illegitimate religious custom* within the Jewish religious culture.

Thirdly, a further extension of the second point above is Jesus's statements in vv. 10 and 13. Jesus counters the woman's questions with these points: If she knew who he really was, she would not have asked the question she did, but would have asked him to give her what she needed from him, and would have received it.

Principle 3: The way in which people wrongly interpret their circumstances gives us opportunity to both correct and instruct them by and with the gospel. To proclaim the gospel means we eventually reveal to people how they ought to interpret their circumstances in light of the truth regarding Jesus.

People who do not know Jesus as Lord and Savior wrongly interpret their lives; they do not think of their life circumstances as giving them reason to look to Jesus for salvation. Instead, they allow the culture in which they live to determine for them how they ought to think. They end up missing the true significance of both their circumstances and the people that are part of their lives, even as the Samaritan woman did not understand who Jesus was.

Principle 4: We can use the topics of our conversations, even as common as they might be, to steer the conversation to people's need for Jesus. Notice that Jesus uses the topic of conversation—water—to be his way of speaking about himself. Yet, we also want to observe how Jesus responded to the direction that the woman wanted to take the conversation.

The above points are further emphasized in the woman's question in v. 11. Her analysis and question ("Sir, you have nothing to draw water with, and the well is deep. Where do you get that living water?") reveals that she had a misunderstanding of what Jesus was talking about. But notice that it was Jesus's correction of her in v. 10 that precedes her analysis and question. As we provide correction and instruction that is consistent with gospel truth it will likely give us further opportunities to speak to people about the gospel. What we might call "gospel conversations" take place as we know the gospel, listen well to others, and are willing to bring correction and instruction.

Principle 5: Our goal in correcting and instructing is to nurture or continue the conversation, not shut it down. Notice that Jesus worked through the process of the conversation. Perhaps it is important to state one of the things that this does not mean. After all, when we look at the conversation Jesus had with the rich young man of Matt 19, we are going to see that the conversation ended a bit more quickly than the one with the Samaritan woman. We will look at this point in more detail later, but for now we should be reminded that God is in control of these conversations, not us. Yet, if we are to correct and instruct others regarding the gospel, we must experience it ourselves; only then will we know it well enough to explain it to others. In other words, knowledge of the Bible and the fruit of God's Spirit—love, joy, peace, patience, kindness, goodness, faithfulness, gentleness, and self-control, all of which demonstrate humility, wisdom, and courage—are all necessary features of engaging in gospel conversations.

The nurturing of a gospel conversation will sometimes lead people to ask for the very thing that they need, even though they will not understand very well the thing for which they are asking. This is what took place with the woman as revealed in John 4:15—she specifically asked Jesus to give her the water that he was talking about! *How great was that?* This is exactly what we would want, isn't it? But wait, how well did she understand Jesus when he spoke of this water, "welling up to eternal life"? Did Jesus immediately give her the water he was talking about? What is expressed in this conversation that reveals the union of evangelism, discipleship, and apologetics is that it took time for Jesus to reveal her sin to her; she had to mature in her understanding of who Jesus is and what he actually does for sinners. So, while Jesus eventually gave her the living water, it is the form in which this water or eternal life comes that we need to look at to understand this conversation, and see in it the features of the things we have already mentioned.

Observe how Jesus responded to the woman's request to be given the water of eternal life. We see in it in John 4:16–26.

> Jesus said to her, "Go, call your husband and come here." The woman answered him, "I have no husband." Jesus said to her, "You are right in saying, 'I have no husband'; for you have had five husbands and the one you now have is not your husband. What you have said is true." The woman said to him, "Sir, I perceive that you are a prophet. Our fathers worshiped on this mountain, but you say that in Jerusalem is the place where people ought to worship." Jesus said to her, "Woman, believe me, the hour is coming when neither on this mountain nor in Jerusalem will you worship the Father. You worship what you do not know; we worship what we know, for salvation is from the Jews. But the hour is coming, and is now here, when the true worshipers will worship the Father in spirit and in truth, for the Father is seeking such people to worship him. God is spirit and those who worship him must worship in spirit and in truth." The woman said to him, "I know that Messiah is coming, the one called Christ. When he comes, he will tell us all things." Jesus said to her, "I who speak to you am he."

Principle 6: Faithful proclamation of the gospel will eventually expose people to their rebellion against God and ignorance of his will. This is what we see in John 4:16–26. Nowhere are we told how Jesus knew that this woman had five husbands previous to the man with whom she was evidently living. Obviously, it got the woman's attention, because she thought Jesus was a prophet since he knew these things about her. Jesus's goal in stating these things was to show her how much she needed him. Exposing people to their rebellion against the Lord and ignorance of his will is likely the most difficult aspect of a faithful proclamation of the gospel. Unlike Jesus, we have sin of our own and so we can easily adopt the tendency to think that we have no business exposing people to their own rebellion against God. We perhaps find it easy to incorrectly apply Jesus's words in Matt 7:1, "Do not judge, lest you be judged." Isn't it a bit hypocritical for us to challenge people to take a look at their sin and call them to confess it, and repent of it? Isn't this judging other people? Who are we to tell other people that they should repent? This is where it is crucial that we understand that such a challenge and call is not based on who we are and what we do or don't do; it is based on who Jesus is and what he did, does, and will do. This is fundamentally why the gospel message is not about how a person's life can be better or how people can flourish, or have their best life now. Instead, it is about what God the Father has accomplished through Jesus the Son by way of the Holy Spirit so that sin is conquered. All this is why sin must be addressed in any gospel proclamation. The gospel is called just that because the good news is that Jesus has conquered sin and death. This means repentance from sin is possible and does become a reality in and through the work of God's Son and Spirit. A necessary part of this work is that the living and active word of God exposes sin and calls sinners to repentance (Heb 4:12–13). This is another way of saying that we don't have to do anything other than speak the truth of Scripture and people will be convicted of their sin. What we must prepare ourselves for is the wide array of responses such conviction stirs up. One of these responses was displayed by the Samaritan woman.

Principle 7: Prepare to be distracted by those to whom you speak the gospel; people will avoid looking at their rebellion against and ignorance of God's will. Notice how Jesus responds to the woman saying that she thinks Jesus is a prophet and to her question regarding where to worship—he does not get distracted by it. Her statement reveals how much correction and instruction she needs. We are not told what was running through her mind other than what her statements reveal, but based on Jesus's response to her in v. 10 we can know that her responses revealed various ways in which she did not know Jesus. She, therefore, did not ask him to give her what she needed. Instead, she asked questions and made statements that were a distraction from what needed addressing in her life; she avoided her actual need for Jesus. We do not know the degree to which she was aware that she was doing this. The point here is not that people only do this self-consciously. People's conscious awareness of avoiding their sin is not the issue. The issue is *that* people avoid their sin; we avoid looking at our need for Jesus. What this woman said to Jesus was ultimately a distraction from what needed to be addressed, even though her questions were not completely illegitimate or her statements false. Of course, this also raises the question regarding whether we are looking at our own need for Jesus. Only by recognizing our own need for the forgiveness of sins and the renewal that Jesus brings to us through the Holy Spirit are we enabled to faithfully proclaim the gospel to others. This is the fundamental difference between our proclamation of the gospel and Jesus's—his was on the basis of himself. In turn, this helps us understand one of the ways Christians can become weak in their own presentation of the gospel—their own avoidance of looking at their sin. We must be willing to address this issue every day or we will become ineffective in evangelism.

Principle 8: We must work with the truth that people are willing to admit and show how it connects to other truth that reveals their need for Jesus. Jesus did not allow her sin to control the conversation. Jesus did not answer her questions in vv. 11 and 12. Instead, Jesus kept speaking about himself and what he could give the woman, and when she directly asked Jesus for the water of which Jesus was speaking, Jesus pressed the subject regarding what it meant to have "a spring of water welling up to eternal life." It unavoidably meant dealing with sin. Notice that Jesus addressed her at the level of *meaning*. Jesus addressed her intellect and therefore her understanding. Jesus kept the focus where he knew it needed to be—helping the woman understand that her sin revealed her need for him.

When the woman was confronted by Jesus regarding her sin, as seen in her five husbands, notice that she admits some of the truth regarding it but stops short of saying the full truth. Still, Jesus acknowledged that she had spoken some truth. He then took the truth that she had stated and revealed how it was joined to more truth that specifically related to the woman's need for Jesus.

All this highlights the systematic nature of human knowledge and why systematic theology is not something human beings either choose or choose not to possess. The choice for people is not whether they will or will not think systematically or engage in systematic theology. Instead, the choice is whether a person will consciously work at bringing their thinking in submission to what God reveals as true through his general revelation in creation and in his special revelation in Scripture. Because such revelation is so vast and reveals the glory of the Triune God, we, and others, find it easy to become distracted from looking at our sin. This will be one of the greatest challenges, if perhaps not the greatest one, that we will encounter in defending and commending the gospel of the Lord Jesus to others.

Principle 9: Because an individual's salvation is united to their participation in corporate worship, we must emphasize connection to the church and participation in corporate worship when presenting the gospel. In vv. 19–20 the woman sought to avoid her sin by confessing that she believed that Jesus was a prophet. She then asked him a question about a debate between the Jews and Samaritans regarding worship. On one hand, it seemed like a legitimate question, but Jesus draws our attention in vv. 21–24 to how it did not address what was most important in the woman's life. Here we have an example of the correction that God's word continues to bring. Notice how Jesus pressed the matter with this woman even to the point of telling her that she and the Samaritans (the "you" of v. 22 is plural) were ignorant of what they were doing in their worship. Jesus was not saying that the woman and the other Samaritans knew absolutely nothing about God, or even that they had no sincerity in what they were doing. Rather, his point was that their worship was not marked by the full truth and right knowledge about the one true and living God; it was worship that was not according to God's revealed word, the Old Testament (remember the New Testament had not been written yet), that had been given to the Israelites or the Jewish people. Jesus was not saying that all Jews would be saved, but that the message of salvation that is true for all people came through the Jewish people.

Jesus's statement in v. 23 points to him and helps us see that calling people to salvation in and through Jesus leads to addressing the matter of worship. In John 2:13–22, when Jesus removed some men from the temple—the place of worship—because what they were doing hindered the true worship of God, he identified himself as the true temple. Through his death and resurrection, he would raise up a new temple—himself—through which true worship would take place. This is what Jesus meant when he said, "Destroy this temple, and in three days I will raise it up" (John 2:19–22). To be called to salvation in Jesus is to be called to the right corporate worship of God. We will address this further in our next chapter when we look at Peter and Paul's preaching, but for now we should at least state that an individual's salvation unites them to the entire body of Christ, the church, and its one fundamental duty and privilege—the worship of the Triune God. Biblical evangelism, discipleship, and apologetics is not about calling people to have a private, personal encounter with Jesus so that they can have a spiritual experience that helps them in life. While biblical salvation can be described as "help," this term, by itself, is too vague; it simply does not clarify what kind of help Jesus is for us. What biblical evangelism, discipleship, and apologetics press upon those who do not have salvation is that they must become faithful worshipers of the living and true God. This means that participation with the whole body of Christ in its weekly worship is indispensable to biblical salvation.

Many in American society in particular are prone toward an individualistic perspective on life and tend to interpret the Bible according to it. Part of the result of this is that the corporate or communal dimensions of life that God created are missed by many sincere professing Christians in America. But God makes clear that he has always been at work saving a community of people from sin, and that he has done so in order that they might worship him. This is better understood when we pay attention to why God set his Old Testament people, Israel, free from Egypt (Exod 4:23; 7:16; 8:1, 20; 9:1, 13; 10:3, 7, 8, 11, 24, 26), that the first two commandments in the Ten Commandments address worship of God (Exod 20:1–5), and how the apostle Paul summarizes all sin as engaging in idolatry, or false worship (Rom 1:18–32).

The truth that Jesus said to the Samaritan woman, that the hour had already come when true worshipers would worship the Father in spirit and truth, reveals that Jesus was already enabling this to take place. In particular, Jesus revealed to the Samaritan woman that the debate as to *where* worship was to take place was not what actually mattered regarding the true worship of God. Instead, the issue revolved around whether the worship was centered on Jesus. Other parts of God's word help us understand what the true or faithful worship of God looks like, but in this conversation with the Samaritan woman Jesus clarified that salvation through and by him was unavoidably united to a person's participation in God's people's corporate worship. In part, it helps us see that the individual's salvation is unavoidably united to their becoming part of God's covenant community, the church, and to the one basic purpose for which

God created them—to worship or serve him (in addition to the texts listed above, see also Heb 10:19–25; 12:18–29).[4]

Principle 10: Eventually, we must be direct, clear, and explicit in telling people that Jesus, and Jesus alone, is the only way to salvation. The woman makes one more comment, though: "I know that Messiah is coming—he who is called Christ. When he comes, he will tell us all things." It was a true statement that Jesus, once again, used to reveal himself. Jesus directly, clearly, and explicitly told her, "I who speak to you am he." There comes a point at which we must challenge people to recognize that Jesus is the only one *through* whom, *by* whom, and *in* whom anyone can have salvation. Jesus alone is the Son of God, the Second Person of the Trinity, the only one who paid the God-appointed penalty for sin, because he alone lived always obeying God's law, and therefore became the perfect sacrifice for sin. Jesus alone died and rose from the dead, defeating death and sin. If we are to have forgiveness of sin, a right relationship to God the Father, and be able to live in ever-increasing obedience to God's law, then we must believe in Jesus or trust him to deliver us from our sin. This is what we must commend to those who are not trusting in Jesus for their rescue from sin.

## A FAITHFUL PROCLAMATION MAY GET REJECTED

Not all, or even likely most, of our proclamations of the gospel will result in the salvation of those who hear them, but this cannot determine whether we will proclaim the gospel. Furthermore, one of the important

4. It is likely important to mention that worship can be understood in both a narrow and broad sense. Both senses are a part of each other, and therefore help to define one another. In the narrow sense, worship addresses what God's redeemed covenant people do in their corporate gathering each Lord's Day when they assemble together to give to God the praise that is rightfully his. This corporate worship is to be planned and conducted by the elders of the church, centered on the person and work of the Lord Jesus Christ, empowered by the Holy Spirit, and thereby glorify God the Father. This corporate worship was seen most vividly in the creation of Israel and carried on through the establishment of the Levitical priesthood and the sacrificial system that the writer of Hebrews tells us was fulfilled by Jesus (Heb 8–10). Jesus's fulfillment was always God's plan as can be seen in numerous ways from the New Testament, but in particular through the writer of Hebrews quoting from Exod 24:8; 25:40; Ps 40:6–8; Deut 32:35, 36; Jer 31:31–34; and Hab 2:3, 4 and attributing what God was doing through Old Testament Israel and applying it to what Jesus accomplishes for, in, and with the church. Worship in a broad sense refers to what every human does in their whole life. Thus, idolatry or false worship is not merely something that can and does take place with some who are self-consciously religious, but with everyone who fails in various ways and to varying degrees to obey God in all aspects of life.

aspects of defending and commending the gospel is knowing how to respond to those who reject it. One such encounter that Jesus had that guides us in these matters is seen in Matt 19:16–26 which Jesus had with a young man. The text reads as follows:

> And behold a man came up to him saying, "Teacher, what good deed must I do to have eternal life?" And he said to him, "Why do you ask me about what is good? There is only one who is good. If you would enter life, keep the commandments." He said to him, "Which ones?" And Jesus said, "You shall not murder, you shall not commit adultery, you shall not steal, you shall not bear false witness, honor your father and your mother, and, you shall love your neighbor as yourself." The young man said to him, "All these things I have kept. What do I still lack?" Jesus said to him, "If you would be perfect, go, sell what you possess and give to the poor, and you will have treasure in heaven; and come, follow me." When the young man heard this he went away sorrowful, for he had great possessions.
>
> And Jesus said to his disciples, "Truly I say to you, only with difficulty will a rich person enter the kingdom of heaven. Again I tell you, it is easier for a camel to go through the eye of a needle than for a rich person to enter the kingdom of God." When the disciples heard this, they were greatly astonished, saying, "Who then can be saved?" But Jesus looked at them and said, "With man this is impossible, but with God all things are possible."

## WHAT ABOUT THE DIFFERENCES AMONG THE GOSPELS?

Mark 10:17 and Luke 18:18 begin their accounts of this same exchange. We should note that Mark and Luke differ slightly in their accounts from Matthew's, and in relation to each other. While this is not the place for a full treatment regarding how to think about all the differences that mark the four canonical Gospels, it is likely important to make a few observations. First, differences in accounts do not necessarily mean contradictions. When Matthew omits that the young man said "Good teacher" and tells us that he said "Teacher," we ought not to conclude that these differences automatically mean that Matthew or Mark or Luke have given false accounts. Matthew's omitting the adjective "good" before "Teacher" does not automatically mean that he was stating that the young man did not call Jesus "Good teacher." At most, it simply means Matthew decided not to include that detail in his account. It leads us to our second observation.

Every account of an historical event is, by the very nature of the case, selective. When writing any history, no one can include every possible detail that marks the events about which they write. This leads to our third observation. Since all historians—and this is a proper way to think about Matthew, Mark, Luke, and John—must be selective about what they include in their accounts, then their selections are a helpful way of understanding their intentions in their written account. While we cannot know everything that was in the author's mind as he wrote, we must allow what he wrote to guide our thinking, and therefore our interpretation of it. This is why it is perhaps better to highlight the important role of the *text's content and direction* for interpreting it rather than the author's intentions. It is not that the latter is necessarily bad, but it can be misleading. Does an author's text, by itself, tell us everything that the author was thinking when he wrote? Not hardly. As we read the Bible our duty is not to try and imagine all of what was running through the human author's mind when he wrote Scripture. Our duty is to pay attention to what was written.

Matthew's account of Jesus's conversation with this young man stresses how Jesus exposes our pride or self-righteousness that is revealed when we think that we know and have the ability to keep the standard of goodness that must be met to enter God's kingdom. In this conversation we see some of the same principles on display in Jesus's conversation with the Samaritan woman but applied in a little different way.

## JESUS EXPOSES OUR BELIEFS AND COMMITMENTS WITH HIS QUESTIONS

Principle 11: Learn to ask questions that expose people's assumptions (or presuppositions) that control their thinking. Jesus responded to the young man's question with his own question. Jesus's question exposed the young man's beliefs and commitments regarding eternal life or entrance into God's kingdom. The young man's beliefs and commitments were not only shared with many others of that day, but also down through the centuries. It is the belief that we have the ability to both discern what is good and do it. Jesus's question, "Why do you ask me about what is good?" and his next statement, "There is only one who is good," confronted the young man with his pride, powerlessness, and presumptions. Think about what Jesus's question exposed.

To ask Jesus the question "What good thing must I do to have eternal life?" was for the young man to presume that he could do what was necessary to have eternal life. It also revealed that the young man evidently thought that Jesus knew the answer to the question. When Jesus asked the young man, "Why do you ask me about what is good?" Jesus was, at the very least, highlighting that the young man believed Jesus had the answer that he needed. Jesus was not acknowledging his ignorance to answer the question, as some have taught. Rather it was a way to stir the young man to think about his motive for the question and what he hoped to gain from talking to Jesus. Did he really believe that Jesus had the answer? If so, he should do what Jesus said. If he did not believe Jesus had the answer, then why was he asking Jesus the question? Was he playing a game? Did he arrogantly think he had something to teach Jesus? The question also may have been driving at the point that the young man actually knew the standard of goodness that he ought to obey and that he had not met that standard. This is seen in that Jesus commented: "There is only one who is good." If the young man was good, he would not have needed to ask Jesus the question. It also implied that the young man was asking the wrong question. Jesus's statement highlighted that God is the standard of goodness. And very likely the young man knew exactly what this meant—he had not kept the standard that was required of him.

Perhaps the young man was playing a game, and not really being sincere. But above all, notice that Jesus was stirring the young man's thinking. This is perhaps an often overlooked point in evangelistic encounters. By Jesus asking the young man the question and making the comment that he did, he was, without directly stating it, challenging him to rethink what he was saying.

The term *presupposition* is often used to refer to the controlling beliefs that determine how we think. It is perhaps safe to say that people are often unaware of how their words and behavior are connected to what they think and believe. Having our presuppositions exposed to us can often help us repent.

In the conversation Jesus had with this rich young man, we once again see rebellion against and ignorance of God's will exposed. Such exposure calls the person to repent. One of the interesting things about the Greek term *metanoia(n)* that means *repentance* is that it means "a change of mind or thinking." Of course, because the Bible teaches that our thinking is united to all that we are as creatures who are created in God's image, we only think rightly about our thinking when we affirm that it is joined to what we feel and do. In other words, to repent means a change in our whole being, our whole self, and not simply with one aspect of us or our lives.

Perhaps one of the most helpful things we can do in our conversations about the Christian faith is to learn to ask questions that help expose people's presuppositions. This is a skill that can be developed, but it requires us to not only learn the doctrinal content of God's word that shapes true Christian thinking, but also to be willing to be good listeners. But a caution is in order here.

## BE CAREFUL ABOUT GETTING CARRIED AWAY WITH QUESTIONS

We need to be careful to balance questions with direct statements of truth. What this balance looks like in any one conversation depends largely on the people with whom we are conversing. Jesus did not always throw questions at people. He often proclaimed truth directly, clearly, and concisely. Even in this encounter with the young man of Matt 19, Jesus gave direct statements of truth that pushed the conversation along to where it needed to go with *that* young man. Knowing with whom we should and should not ask questions is rooted in knowing the people with whom we are conversing and paying attention to what they have said. Not every person needs questions. Sometimes people need a direct and clear statement of gospel truth.

I am reminded of a former colleague who seemed to get carried away with this approach of asking questions. He greatly frustrated many of his students. Some of them came to me expressing their frustrations over his near-constant refusal to give any direct answer to a question, or make a statement of truth to give clarity on a matter. Frankly, he did not understand his audience very well. This approach of asking questions is best used with people who have enough life experience and knowledge in order to benefit from the questions. The younger the person is to whom we are talking or the less knowledgeable someone is about the Christian faith, then, generally speaking, the less effective this approach of asking questions becomes. It is not that it can never be used with young children or even some teenagers, but its effectiveness is diminished when the one receiving the questions lacks the necessary life experience and knowledge from which to draw upon when attempting to reflect upon and answer the questions. Sometimes whether we ask questions is simply governed by how much time we have to converse with the person. Do we have a long-term relationship with the person, or not? If not, then perhaps a more direct and clear statement is needed. We will see that this is precisely the approach that Jesus adopted with the man on the cross in Luke 23.

Keep in mind, however, that there are different reasons why people are assured of their assumptions. Sometimes people have developed an assurance of their thinking because they have self-consciously and willingly adopted over many years a particular approach to life. Young people can often have an assurance of their thinking, because they have not lived long enough to even be aware that there are such things as assumptions, or have just begun to learn that there are such things that operate in our thinking and actions. There is an "assuredness" that reflects pride and arrogance, and an "assuredness" that reflects lack of experience and ignorance. They are related but not identical. If we confuse the two, we are liable to frustrate some people and be woefully unhelpful to those who are genuinely looking for answers, because they lack experience and they actually recognize they have ignorance that needs to be overcome!

## JESUS BALANCED QUESTIONS WITH DIRECT STATEMENTS OF THE TRUTH

While stirring the man's thinking with questions, Jesus directly confronted him with God's law and therefore his sin. This is what God's law always does with us. Since Jesus was willing to receive the young man's question as an honest one, he answered it. "If you would enter eternal life, keep the commandments." *How simple is that?* Be careful not to "overthink" presentations of the gospel. The gospel really is quite simple. At the same time, do not mistake simplicity for something that is shallow. While there is a simplicity to the gospel, it is nonetheless profound. That young man had violated God's law because he was a sinner, and as a result he was under the power of sin and completely incapable of doing the good that God required for him to enter into eternal life. Part of his being under the power of sin was seen in the questions he asked Jesus. It was perhaps seen most clearly in how he responded to Jesus's statement that he must keep the commandments. The young man asked, "Which ones?" This question clearly exposed the young man's sin.

## JESUS FOCUSED ON THE CENTRAL ISSUE—HUMAN PRIDE AND INDEPENDENCE

Notice that Jesus's question and subsequent statement led the young man to ask the question, "Which ones?" Jesus continued going down the path the young man apparently wanted to go down. Jesus responded to this question by listing some of the commandments, but not all of them. Jesus was simply giving a representative sample. It was also a way of continuing to allow the young man to expose his sin. After all, his question, "Which ones?" seemed to imply that he thought he only lacked obedience to some of the commandments, an implication that was confirmed when Jesus only mentioned some of the commandments and the man stated, "All these I have kept. What do I still lack?"

Was the young man really that ignorant of God's law? Did he really fail to recognize that God's law requires complete perfection all the time not only in behavior, but in thoughts and desires? Or was he simply arrogant? Did he really think that he had met God's perfectly righteous standard his whole life? Did he really not recognize that it is impossible to only keep part of God's law? Well, the truth is that he was both ignorant and arrogant—the two, it seems, often go together, although as mentioned previously they are not identical. A right understanding of God and his law humbles us. To the degree that we are ignorant of God's law, then to that degree we are likely proud or arrogant. To have salvation, to be evangelized or made disciples of the Lord Jesus, we must see the folly of our arrogance; we must rightly understand our failure to meet God's holy and righteous standard. The apostle Paul stated it clearly: "All have sinned and fall short of the glory of God" (Rom 3:23). Only as people understand their need for God's mercy and grace do they seek it, and understanding that need is about rightly recognizing the depth and breadth of your sin.

Jesus's next statement did not mean that Jesus believed that the man had actually obeyed God's law; it meant that the young man still lacked full and complete obedience to God's law. After all, Jesus began his statement to him with "If you would be perfect . . ." The way Jesus completed the statement and how the young man responded was an example of how

God's law reveals our sin. Jesus told him, "Go, sell what you possess and give to the poor, and you will have treasure in heaven; and come, follow me," but the young man went away sorrowful, "for he had great possessions." The young man had an allegiance to his wealth that he was not willing to give up. We need to be clear about two very important points regarding Jesus's directive to the young man.

First, Jesus was not saying that every person needs to sell all their possessions in order to follow him. Some have taken Jesus's words in this way, but to do so ignores the specific nature of this young man's sin, the rest of the conversation with the disciples, and other places in God's word that teach us how to be faithful stewards of all the possessions and wealth God gives. The young man's problem was his sinful preoccupation with his wealth, and his dependence on it.

Jesus's exchange with his disciples in vv. 23–26 revealed that material wealth is a serious obstacle to faithful discipleship to Jesus. Notice that while the young man to whom Jesus spoke went away sad, there was still a teaching opportunity in the event. Sometimes our conversations with others about the gospel will not result in their salvation, but that is not to say that no one can benefit from those conversations.

Jesus used his conversation with this young man to teach his disciples two very important truths about salvation or discipleship to him: *(1) Material wealth can be and often is a great obstacle to placing faith in Jesus for salvation*, and *(2) Salvation is not possible for us to accomplish; God alone saves from sin.*[5] Jesus's statement in v. 24 about a camel emphasized the impossibility for humans to save themselves from their sin. The disciples got the point. It was why v. 25 says that "they were greatly astonished" and asked, "Who then can be saved?" These two truths together reveal a common truth—that when we think that our lives depend on us and what we can accomplish (as often seen with those who have much wealth) we possess the very opposite way of thinking and living that is embraced by those who have faith in Jesus for salvation. *When we depend on ourselves for life, we leave no place for dependence on Jesus.* This was demonstrated by the young man. What we should keep in mind is that

5. We ought to keep in mind that this conversation was part of Matthew's presenting how Jesus challenged the Pharisees' interpretation and application of God's law. The Pharisees loved money and they operated with thinking and actions that revealed that they were absorbed with their own sincerity and failing to understand the depths of their sinfulness and thereby dependence on God. While we are never told that the young man was a Pharisee or a budding one, he nonetheless showed all the distinguishing marks of their sin.

what ultimately amounts to "much wealth" is not so much our possession of a particular amount of money or particular material goods, but rather how much our possessions and wealth possess us. The whole exchange between Jesus and the rich young man alerts us to ask ourselves: Of what do we think our life consists?

Principle 12: Evangelism and discipleship take place even among those committed to Jesus, so we must explain the gospel even to those who claim commitment to it. Of course, this conversation was also difficult for Jesus's disciples to accept because they possessed the common belief of their religious culture that the rich person had been blessed by God. See, they too, like the Samaritan woman, needed culturally controlled beliefs exposed and removed. Rather than seeing material wealth as an obstacle to salvation they, with some warrant from the Scriptures, had believed that wealth was *always* a sign of God's covenant blessing. What they and some others had failed to understand was that such wealth could only be a true blessing from God if it resulted in humility before and dependence on God.

Notice that once again, Jesus confronted a presupposition that was part of the disciples' and the young man's religious culture. Notice that it was, in part, based only on a superficial understanding of God's word, and so it resulted in a wrong interpretation of it. Even those claiming to be committed to faith in Jesus for salvation need to be regularly corrected regarding their understanding of what it means to have faith in Jesus. This is what every faithful pastor will do in every sermon he preaches, even to those who are truly saved by their belief in the gospel. Again, it is why the New Testament letters are to the church.

## THE DESPERATE DEPEND ON JESUS

Luke 23:39–43 tells of Jesus having an evangelistic conversation with one of the men who was crucified along with him. It ought not to surprise us that as he died Jesus had a conversation that expressed what his death accomplished.

> One of the criminals who were hanged railed at him, saying, "Are you not the Christ? Save yourself and us!" But the other rebuked him, saying, "Do you not fear God, since you are under the same sentence of condemnation? And we indeed justly, for we are receiving the due reward of our deeds; but this man has done nothing wrong." And he said, "Jesus, remember me when

> you come into your kingdom." And he said to him, "Truly, I say to you, today you will be with me in Paradise."

On first glance this does not seem like a very beneficial conversation through which to learn much about evangelism, discipleship, or apologetics. On closer examination, however, we discover much.

Principle 13: Biblical salvation requires death to sin, and does not promise the full experience of God's covenant blessings during this life. We must be on guard against promising false hopes that the gospel does not give. Notice that the first criminal who spoke appears to have a very accurate sense of what it means that Jesus is the Christ, or Messiah—he is the one who can save both himself and others from death. If there was ever an ironic statement in Scripture, this is it! The criminal who declared to Jesus "Save yourself and us!" really had no idea what he was saying. One cannot help but wonder if Jesus was not tempted to say, "*What do you think I am doing up here?*" The only means for salvation and the kingdom of God to come was happening because Jesus was on that cross! Yet, based on what the second criminal said, it is clear that the first one did not mean his declaration to be taken as anything other than an expression of his belief that Jesus might be able to save them from physical death. It is important to note that according to Luke 23:35–37, the portion of Scripture just prior to the one we are studying, the "people stood by watching, but the rulers [Israel's religious rulers] scoffed at him, saying, 'He saved others; let him save himself, if he is the Christ of God, his Chosen One.'" So, very likely the criminal who asked Jesus the question about whether he was in fact the Christ and implored him to save them picked up on this accurate admission by the Jewish religious leaders that Jesus had in fact rescued others from death. Still, those religious leaders, while saying something truthful about Jesus, did not understand how that truth was related to other truths that should have led them to repent. Notice, again, the systematic nature of truth and our knowledge. Observe also that what was true of the two men was precisely true of the Samaritan woman. Faced with death, it appears that this criminal was desperate for help and so he seized upon this truth spoken by others about Jesus in hopes that he might be able to get out of his situation.

This is another good example of how the words that people use in conversation about Jesus must not simply be taken at "face value." Was this criminal really interested in being saved from sin or simply saved from one of the consequences of his sins? We often need to penetrate past the words that people use regarding Jesus and get at their actual meaning. We have already seen how Jesus did this with the Samaritan woman and the rich young man. Jesus had to do it even with these men, and in what Jesus said and did not do we are shown that all sin and its consequences are not removed in this lifetime from those who truly trust Jesus for salvation.

Some people are merely interested in having better circumstances in this life and try to use Jesus and the Bible to get those better circumstances. Sadly, throughout the history of the church, and in various parts of the world today, many people believe that to be a Christian means that all our earthly difficulties are overcome, and all of sin's consequences will be removed. Some people wrongly preach what is called "the health and wealth gospel." They teach that if you truly believe in Jesus, you will be healed of all sickness and be rich; they wrongly teach that Jesus solves all our problems and removes all our difficulties now. This is a lie; the Bible does not teach this. But the gospel can be distorted to teach this.

But perhaps we are not so foolish to think that Jesus will make us very rich so that we can have the car, boat, house, or even jet that we want, as some actually teach and preach. There is a "softer" version of the health and wealth gospel. After all such a belief is nothing less than thinking that salvation from sin is about us experiencing what we want to experience. Perhaps we do not want a lot of material wealth. Perhaps we simply want academic, athletic, or artistic success. Perhaps we simply want a happy marriage and obedient children—a peaceful family life. Doesn't obedience to God bring blessing that heals relationships? Perhaps we think that faithful biblical ministry means people always being added to church membership, more ministry activities taking place within our church congregation, and a better reputation in the community. There is a very subtle and seductive danger that lurks in what we do with the gospel promise of blessing. You see, eventually all our earthly difficulties will be overcome and all of sin and its consequences removed from the lives of those who truly believe the gospel. But not in this lifetime. Instead, Jesus's great victory over sin and *all* its consequences will only be experienced in the new heavens and new earth when Jesus fully renews the creation (Rev 21:1–8). "In this world," Jesus said, "you have tribulation" (John 16:33). Notice that Jesus did not remove the man from the cross whom he took with him to paradise, and above all Jesus did not rescue himself from physical death. Instead, Jesus died and he allowed these men to die with him. But praise be to God, he also rescued the one man from spiritual and eternal death, because in his own death Jesus secured eternal redemption from sin (Heb 9:12).

Principle 14: Recognize when all that has been said is all that needs saying. Even while dying, Jesus and one of the thieves gave faithful testimony regarding the gospel. But they did it quickly. We can learn from this. Notice that the first criminal's inaccurate understanding of Jesus is confronted and corrected by his fellow criminal! Jesus's response to the second criminal's words stands as confirmation that this rebuke by the other criminal and his call for Jesus to receive him was correct and good. Sometimes we can allow others to say what needs to be said and simply confirm the correctness and goodness of it. Perhaps Jesus was so tired at this point that all he had the energy to say was what is stated in v. 43. However, it also might be that he simply did not need to say anything else and so he did not. I can certainly recall many instances when I was teaching in Christian schools when my students' answers to questions were not only correct and good, but also carried so much weight among their classmates that I did not need to add to their answer. There is a sense in which the sufficiency of God's word and the entire sweep of church history requires us to recognize something about this principle. In our conversations with others about the Christian faith we perhaps do not need to arrive at something creative and original as much as we need to echo the words of many who have come before us. The first way we can do this is by quoting Scripture itself! A second way is to point people to others who have shown how the gospel is sufficient to address their concerns and questions. This is one reason why I spend time reading some books that address issues I know how to address, and questions that I know how to answer. What I want to discover is: Has this person done a better job than I do, or can in answering this question or addressing this issue? If so, then in some instances it is quite appropriate for me to say: "You know, you should read ____________________ on that. They have done a very nice job of addressing that matter." Or, I can provide a quick summary of an author's treatment and then recommend their book. It would be foolish and arrogant for me to think that I need to try and be the sole source of the gospel for everyone with whom I come in contact. Even Jesus did not add to words to which nothing needed to be added.

But let's look at those words that the "second" criminal spoke. In Luke 23:40–41 we read, "Do you not fear God, since you are under the same sentence of condemnation? And we indeed justly, for we are receiving the due reward of our deeds; but this man has done nothing wrong."

Wow! I suppose being nailed to a cross has a way of giving one an acute sense of the truth and one's need! Here is another example of clear, direct, and concise proclamation of the truth. Here is an abrupt exposure of rebellion against and ignorance of God's will. The second criminal addresses the heart of the matter—his fellow criminal did not fear or reverence God, but he should have, and he should have because he was being justly condemned for his behavior in the midst of one who had done nothing wrong. Notice that he challenged the man to recognize in Jesus his only hope for salvation, his only hope from being rescued from the just penalty of their condemnation. The "second" criminal recognized that even in his physical death he could still be saved. He knew salvation in Jesus transcended mere physical life, even as it included physical life.

The text tells us nothing about how this man knew that Jesus had done nothing wrong, or why he spoke as if the other man should have known this. Perhaps both men were Jews, and were quite familiar with Jesus's ministry; it would seem so. Certainly, crucifixion was a sentence that Roman citizens suffered only under rare circumstances, so it is not likely that both of them were Roman citizens. Notice, however, what his words most certainly meant—he believed (1) that Jesus had done nothing wrong, (2) that he and his fellow criminal deserved to die, and (3) that to fear God meant to believe these things and to look to Jesus to grant him access to Jesus's kingdom. The latter was affirmed when he said, "Jesus, remember me when you come into your kingdom." It meant that this criminal believed that Jesus's death was not going to prevent Jesus from establishing his kingdom. At the very least it was an implicit belief in the resurrection from the dead.

For anyone to have salvation they must confess that because of their sin they justly deserve death, that Jesus alone is the means to eternal life, has come into his kingdom, and he alone grants entrance into it. Jesus's statement to the man on the cross near him tells us that there is nothing that we can accomplish to bring ourselves into Jesus's kingdom. We have to admit the truth about ourselves and Jesus and look to Jesus to rescue us from the death we deserve. If we are to be helpful in evangelizing others to the Christian faith, we must communicate these truths to them.

These are the truths that Jesus's disciples explained after Jesus rose from the dead and ascended into heaven. We have numerous examples of their proclamation in the New Testament. We will now turn to explore two of them—one from Peter and one from Paul—and see what we can learn from them.

# 5

# Exploring the Explaining of the Gospel Through the Apostles' Preaching

"The church did not grow up by natural law: it was founded. And the authoritative teachers sent forth by Christ to found His church, carried with them, as their most precious possession, a body of divine Scriptures, which they imposed on the church that they founded as its code of law. . . . The Christian church thus was never without a 'Bible' or a 'canon.'"[1]

B. B. Warfield

"In him [Christ] we discern one in whose knowledge of the meaning of the great series of Christian facts in which he was chief actor, we can have supreme confidence; and to whom, with the apostles whom he appointed to teach all nations, we may safely go for the interpretation of the Christian facts. In the teachings of Christ and his apostles therefore we find authoritative Christian doctrine—'dogma' in the strictest sense of the word: and this 'dogma' enters into the very essence of Christianity."[2]

B. B. Warfield

1. Warfield, "Formation of the Canon," in *Works* 1:451. Warfield's explanation regarding the presence and authority of the Bible is based on the important distinction between being and knowing. That is, the historical process by which humans arrive at knowing something is distinct from, although inseparably joined to, the presence of the reality that they come to know.

2. Warfield, "Right of Systematic Theology," in *Selected Shorter Writings* 2:238–39.

"The apostles did not transmit the tradition only after it had been given a fixed form by the faith of the church but because of the authority that they had received from Christ to be the bearers and custodians of this tradition."[3]

Herman N. Ridderbos

## INTRODUCTION

As we stated at the beginning, the whole Bible is about the gospel of the Lord Jesus Christ. Even with all its various events, people, and places, the Bible tells one main story and it is about the gospel of Jesus. The biblical gospel has an historical character to it; all the doctrine that is expressed in and by the gospel is marked by history. There are many things this means, and we cannot explore much of what it does mean. That would take many books, and many books have been written about these things! Still, we need to recognize that as we present the gospel to others, we are not simply presenting some ideas or beliefs. Instead, we present a particular interpretation of life that is joined to a person—the Lord Jesus! The gospel is not only the true story *about* Jesus, but also the story given *by* Jesus regarding himself. The gospel is the true or right interpretation of Jesus by Jesus. Jesus established the authoritative interpretation of his life, death, resurrection, and ascension. The New Testament is this authoritative interpretation. The New Testament completes the Old Testament and is organically rooted in and dependent on the Old Testament; the Old Testament by itself is not a completed book; it expected or anticipated further revelation from God. Jesus continues, then, through the power of his Holy Spirit, to proclaim himself through his church proclaiming the Scriptures of the Old and New Testament. In this chapter and the next we look at the two models for this proclamation from the apostles Peter and Paul in the book of Acts.

## JESUS'S AUTHORITY THROUGH THE APOSTLES

From the very beginning of his ministry Jesus shared his authority with a group of men whom he chose—his disciples, or men who would later come to be called his apostles (Matt 10:1–42). The union between Jesus

3. Ridderbos, *Redemptive History*, 18.

and his twelve disciples was so close that to receive them was to receive Jesus (Matt 10:40). This union or relationship that Jesus established between him and his apostles was based on the union that Jesus has with his heavenly Father. Jesus also stated in Matt 10:40 that "whoever receives me receives him who sent me." The Greek verb *apostellō* means "I send" and is the term from which we get the English word *apostle*. Quite literally the apostles were the men whom Jesus sent to proclaim his gospel. In order for anyone to receive the gospel, or be evangelized, or receive the doctrines of the Christian faith, they need to receive the interpretation of Jesus proclaimed by Jesus's apostles. As Lord of all creation, Jesus is Lord of the interpretation of himself and all creation. Only by first receiving this authoritative message are we equipped to proclaim it to others. There is power in the gospel for life, because this authoritative gospel message is not merely the presentation of information to the mind (although it contains information), but the presentation of Jesus, a true encounter with the divine man, the Son of God, the Lord of Glory, who is the Creator and Redeemer.

While all of Jesus's apostles who remained with him (excluding Judas, who betrayed Jesus) possessed the same apostolic authority, Peter and Paul had unique roles to fulfill within this authority. Peter led the way in proclaiming the gospel to the Jews, and Paul led the way in proclaiming the gospel to the gentiles. These two audiences serve as the two broad categories that people will be in to whom we proclaim the gospel. These two groups—Jews and gentiles—are not merely identified by their ethnic character. Instead, these two categories are primarily referring to people's knowledge of God's written word based on how God chose to reveal himself to them through their history. According to the Bible, Jew and gentile are more precisely ethical (moral) and epistemological (knowledge) categories.

## APOSTOLIC AUTHORITY EXERCISED: JESUS'S UNIQUE ONGOING WORK THROUGH THE HOLY SPIRIT

At the beginning of Acts, Luke wrote that it was a continuation of what he had previously written (in the Gospel that bears his name) about "all that Jesus began to do and teach, until the day when he was taken up, after he had given commands through the Holy Spirit to the apostles whom he had chosen. He presented himself to them after his suffering by many proofs, appearing to them during forty days and speaking about the kingdom of God" (Acts 1:1–3). In other words, Jesus, through the Holy Spirit, gave the apostles the ability to speak and write the authoritative interpretation of himself, or the gospel message. Jesus gave "commands through the Holy Spirit to the apostles whom he had chosen." As the apostle Paul wrote in Eph 2:20, the church is "built on the foundation of the apostles and prophets, Christ Jesus himself being the cornerstone." The apostles, whom Jesus chose, possessed a unique authority and function in the history of salvation.

In order to possess this authority and function such a man had to have been a physical eyewitness of Jesus's life, death, resurrection, and ascension and chosen by the Holy Spirit to have this authority and function. In Acts 1:15–25 we read that two men had the possibility of replacing Judas, but only one was chosen. The man who was not chosen to replace Judas was in fact "one of the men" who had been with the apostles while "Jesus went in and out among" them "from the baptism of John until the day when he was taken up." This man, Joseph or Barsabbas (Acts 1:23), had been an eyewitness of Jesus's ministry, and had been with the apostles listening to Jesus and seeing him perform miracles. The issue of whether he would become an apostle was not simply a matter of whether he had salvation, nor simply particular historical circumstances, but a particular ministry function, or a particular authority that Jesus alone had the authority to give or not give through the Holy Spirit. It is why the apostles prayed, "*You, Lord,* who know the hearts of all, show which one of these two *you have chosen* to take the place in this ministry and apostleship from which Judas turned aside to go to his own place" (Acts 1:24–25, italics mine). Notice, then, that Luke affirms that the establishment of the apostles as Jesus's authoritative witnesses to his gospel after his resurrection is united to all that Jesus did before his death and resurrection. It is another way of stating that the proclamation of the gospel is part of the gospel.

## THE PROCLAMATION AND WRITTEN PRESERVATION OF THE GOSPEL IS PART OF THE GOSPEL

According to the book of Acts, the apostles Peter and Paul belong to that unique group of men who were given authority by Jesus to speak and write the interpretation of his life, death, resurrection, and ascension that is binding upon all God's people (and ultimately even those who are not). In other words, what the gospel of Jesus is and how it is communicated is not determined by us.

Jesus's apostles and the Old Testament prophets fulfilled a unique role in God's plan of redemption. It was through these men that God revealed himself to his people regarding the authoritative interpretation of Jesus that was and still is binding on God's covenant people. God made his word known through these men. First through their preaching and teaching and then their writing, they brought God's word or written revelation. The covenant people of God, the church of the Lord Jesus, rests upon these men. God's people are created and sustained, or built by and upon, this revelation about God and from God (Matt 16:13–20; Acts 9; Eph 2:19–22; 4:1–16; 1 Pet 1:22–25; 2 Pet 1:16–21) that possesses God's power for salvation through the Holy Spirit. It is this revelation that is God's word, and it produces, preserves, and perfects God's people. This revelation is the very life of God's people because it reveals God, who is life, and is used by God's Spirit to give life (1 John 1:1–7; 2 John 9). This is seen most supremely in that Jesus, who is God, is called the Word (John 1:1–14). No one has the authority or power to interpret Jesus however they want. Nor does Jesus leave us in confusion or ignorance wondering how to interpret him. No, Jesus preached and taught the gospel! He evangelized, discipled, and gave the authoritative defense of himself. By his explanations Jesus established his gospel because he is the unique King of kings, and Lord of lords. In part, this means that Christian evangelism, discipleship, and apologetics are what Jesus says they are as revealed in his written word, and are only able to be done as God's people are transformed by his word through his Spirit. The church is not primarily in need of creativity on these matters, but humility to follow the example of the apostles Jesus chose to first explain the gospel. We need to pay attention to what the Lord Jesus gave his apostles to give to us and we need to receive it.

In Eph 2:13–22, the apostle Paul gives us a clear and concise statement regarding the redemptive or saving work of Jesus and the role that the prophets and apostles possess in our benefiting from Jesus's work. Part of God's redemptive work is Jesus ensuring that the authoritative interpretation of him would be clearly explained. These clear explanations of the gospel are so that the gospel would be firmly established in people through the work of God's Spirit. These are God-given explanations that are authoritative for God's people. Part of what this means is that the explanations given by the apostles are to direct us in how we explain the gospel.

## GOD WORKS THROUGH HUMAN MEANS

The only Triune God uses humans in the conversion of sinners to the gospel. While the Holy Spirit can certainly work apart from humans, God has chosen to work through humans, and he uses the proclamation of the Scriptures to accomplish this (Rom 10:14–17). As we have already seen, the apostle Peter commands the Christian to give a reason for the hope he or she possesses. Jesus commanded his disciples, and us through them, to make disciples of all nations. God gives us his eternal life through the Scriptures, or his word. As the Westminster Confession of Faith so accurately expresses it, the Holy Spirit works "by and with the word" (WCF 1.5). Saving faith comes by hearing the word of Christ, that word that is not only about Christ but is Christ's because it is him. We could put it this way: The gospel *message* is the gospel's *means* to its power. Paul expressed this point when he wrote, first in Rom 1:16, that he was not "ashamed of the gospel, because it is the power of God for salvation to everyone who believes, first for the Jew, and then for the Gentile," and then in Rom 10:17 that "faith comes by hearing and hearing by the word of Christ." God's supernatural power for saving sinners is present in the preaching of God's word by those authorized to preach it through the work of the Holy Spirit. Later we will look at the important distinction between (1) the preaching and teaching of the gospel by those who have been rightfully given the authority to do this in the church, and (2) the proclamation of the gospel by any Christian. For now, we need to recognize that every accurate proclamation of God's written word is the means that God's Holy Spirit uses to regenerate spiritually dead sinners and then renew them so that the fruit of God's Spirit marks their life. As we seek to understand what it means to give a reason for the Christian hope and accurately explain the gospel, it is necessary that we pay attention to how Jesus's authoritative representatives fulfilled this duty and privilege.

## JEWS AND GENTILES: MISSIONAL AND ETHNIC CATEGORIES

In history, God chose to first reveal his written word primarily to ethnic Jews, and he chose the apostle Peter to be the foremost preacher to them (Matt 16:13–20; Acts 2:14–41; 3:1–26; 4:8; 5:3, 29; 8:14, 20; 9:32—11:30). It was Peter who took the lead in preaching the gospel in the earliest days of the church to the Jews after the Holy Spirit was sent by God the Father and God the Son, and it was Peter through whom the message was first declared that Jews should not regard gentiles as separated from them regarding the reception of God's saving revelation. As we have already seen, Jesus stated clearly that "salvation is from the Jews" (John 4:22). Paul would later write in Rom 1:16 that he was not ashamed of the gospel because it is the power of God for salvation to everyone who believes, "first for the Jew, then for the Gentile." God chose to first reveal his word in a saving way to a primarily ethnic Jewish community. I say *primarily* because there was always a provision during the Old Testament era for a person who was not an ethnic Jew to become part of Old Testament Israel. Still, merely being a member of physical Israel did not automatically mean one had salvation. Through this history, then, we need to recognize that the categories of Jew and gentile are not merely ethnic categories, but missional ones as well.

Many Old Testament Israelites were not saved from their sin (1 Cor 10). Many of them failed to trust in God and his word; they failed to obey God, even though they had a significant amount of knowledge of God's word. Paul later stated of them that "they have a zeal for God, but not according to knowledge" (Rom 10:2). It was people who are described in this way to whom Peter was primarily sent to preach the gospel. Peter's primary mission was to take the gospel to Jews, but what identified them as Jews was not merely their ethnic character but what marked them in terms of their exposure to, knowledge of, and response to God's word.

This distinction between a physical ethnic character trait identified with the term *Jew* and a spiritual trait identified by the same term can be seen from Rom 2. One of the most important points mentioned by Paul in his Letter to the Romans is that ultimately what it means to be "a true Jew" is that one possesses a particular inward spiritual characteristic that is "a matter of the heart" (Rom 2:29). Paul specifically wrote, "For no one is a Jew who is merely one outwardly, nor is circumcision outward and physical. But a Jew is one inwardly, and circumcision is a matter of the heart, by the Spirit, not by the letter. His praise is not from man but from God" (Rom 2:28–29). Among other things, this speaks to the truth that while a person can be born into a situation where they are surrounded by God's word and the activities of God's people, and have an important kind of knowledge of God's word, this experience alone does not give salvation. The Spirit of God must still take God's Word and apply it to our souls, so that we are changed by it so that we trust that Word in both its forms—written and made flesh (Jesus)—for salvation. The latter experience is what makes a *true Jew*, as we see from Rom 2.

The apostle Peter was primarily sent to those people in his lifetime who fit the description of being well acquainted with God's word and God's people, and yet still had not trusted God for salvation. Thus, Peter was to regard the Jews to whom he was sent from a *missional* perspective, even as Paul's mission was to gentiles, or those who were not well acquainted with the Scriptures. It is from this missional perspective that I believe we are warranted in appropriating the categories of "Jew" and "gentile." Those people who have grown up within or around God's covenant people, the church, and demonstrate a general knowledge of the Bible and yet have not trusted in God for salvation are those who fall under the missional category labeled *Jew*. Again, notice that the issue in all this is a person's knowledge of and response to God's word, not merely their ethnic character. Those who have very little knowledge of the Bible and a limited experience within the church fall into the missional category of "gentile." All of this is to say that today one very well may encounter many ethnic Jews who actually are in the missional category of "gentile."

The apostle Paul in Eph 2:12 describes the spiritual heritage of *gentiles* as those who were "separated from Christ, alienated from the commonwealth of Israel [God's old covenant people], and strangers to the covenants of promise." From a theological and spiritual perspective, a *gentile* has reference to a person who has very little, if any knowledge, of God's written word and the ways of God's covenant people. The apostle Paul was primarily sent to people who fit this latter description. Keep in mind that both Peter and Paul preached and wrote to people who fit in both categories. Still, they primarily worked among people that fit one of the categories: Peter to Jews, Paul to gentiles. Again, this is not to say that these groups had nothing to do with a particular ethnic character, but rather, that their ethnic character was neither the sole nor primary feature about them. By paying attention to what Peter and Paul preached and wrote to the people in each of these categories, we are better able to understand how we ought to proceed in our presentation of the gospel to people who today fit within these two broad categories.

## PETER AND PAUL: THE CHIEF DEFENDERS AND EXPLAINERS OF THE GOSPEL

Two examples given in Scripture of the apostles Peter and Paul evangelizing, making disciples, and defending the gospel help us understand what it will mean for us to do the same. Peter's sermon in Acts 2:14–40 and Paul's in Acts 17:16–32 are two clear examples of the preaching of the gospel.

On first glance it may appear that Peter's sermon does not fall into the category of what he refers to in 1 Pet 3:15, when he tells us to always be ready to give a reason or defense to anyone who asks us for the hope we have. We should recognize, however, that there are many ways in which people can actually "ask" concerning the reason for the Christian's hope. Any attempt by someone to secure an explanation for what the Christian is to believe and do gives us opportunity to fulfill the command Peter gives. This is because the Christian's hope is organically related to all aspects of the Christian life. Of course, it is perhaps important for us to note that Peter wrote his first letter to the first-century church in the midst of sporadic persecution of Christians in various places in the Roman Empire. It also may be that the audience already believes that they know the correct explanation for the Christian's hope, and they are simply mistaken. Or, it may be that there is a confession of ignorance and desire to know the gospel, or a direct challenge of the truthfulness or relevancy of the biblical gospel. Regardless, all such situations give the Christian the opportunity to explain the reason for his or her hope in the Lord Jesus.

## KNOW THE AUDIENCE TO WHOM YOU ADDRESS THE GOSPEL

Peter and Paul knew their audiences quite well. They were aware of the basic knowledge of God that their audiences possessed. They stressed different aspects of the gospel message in the two sermons that we will look at, but these different emphases did not mean proclaiming two essentially different gospel messages. So, we can also say that while they spoke to two different audiences, those two audiences had the most important need in common—they needed to repent and believe the gospel. They knew their audiences' need for regeneration by the Holy Spirit. Peter and Paul knew that the Holy Spirit used the gospel to convince people of their sin and of the remedy for it in Jesus's life, death, resurrection, and ascension. In other words, they knew people needed to hear the truth about Jesus, to believe it and entrust themselves to it.

## PETER'S AUDIENCE

Peter spoke to an audience *primarily* of ethnic Jews, although some were not. Their most important feature, though, was not their ethnicity, but their significant knowledge of the Old Testament. They were also familiar with the events surrounding Jesus. Peter did not need to explain the basics of such things to them. Peter's address, as recorded in Acts 2:14–40, explains how they should have thought about the coming of the Holy Spirit and Jesus's life, death, resurrection, and ascension. We should note that what is recorded in Acts 2 may not be the complete sermon given by Peter, but an accurate sample of what he said. Whichever it is does not change that it is God's holy inerrant word, nor does it change what we should learn from its contents. Peter proclaimed the gospel as recorded in Acts 2:14–40 to an audience that had a fairly good understanding of the Old Testament, even while diverse in terms of the languages they spoke and the locations where they resided. Acts 2:9–11 indicates that the audience was comprised of both Jews and "proselytes." The latter term refers to non-Jews who had aligned themselves with the Jewish people, and therefore had come to learn the Old Testament and believe it to be true. While speaking to an audience of both ethnic Jews and non-Jews, most of whom would have confessed to believe the Old Testament, Peter preached the gospel by explaining the right interpretation of Jesus in relation to the Old Testament.

## THE SUPERNATURAL SOURCE AND POWER OF PETER'S SERMON IN ACTS 2

Peter's sermon begins in Acts 2:14, but just prior to it the Holy Spirit came upon the twelve apostles and gave them the supernatural ability to speak the gospel in a language that they had not previously known

(Acts 2:1–13). These languages were not unknown to some in the audience, but rather were the native languages of some of them. It is why they said, "We hear them telling in our own tongues the mighty works of God." It is another way of saying that the Holy Spirit gave the apostles the ability to speak the gospel in a language foreign, or unknown previously to them. Notice, then, that the first way in which the Holy Spirit revealed himself through the apostles was in giving them the ability to speak the gospel in a language that they had previously not been able to speak. The Holy Spirit gave the apostles the ability to communicate the gospel effectively so that people with whom the apostles had not previously been able to communicate with were now able to understand them. Please notice that this was a supernatural power given by the Holy Spirit to the apostles. From beginning to end a right understanding and passing on of the gospel of the Lord Jesus is a supernatural power given by the Holy Spirit; it is not something under human control that humans can manufacture, manipulate, and manage. We cannot control this so that *we* can evangelize, disciple, and defend the gospel by our own strategies; we do not plant and grow churches in accord with our own strategies. With regards to this truth, we are no different from the apostles. Like them, we need to receive God's power both to understand and pass on the gospel. Among other things, this means that prayer is foundational to our work at understanding and passing on the gospel. Again, what is called for in these matters is not our creativity, but faithfulness to act in accordance with how God has determined that his gospel should be explained.

## THE NEW TESTAMENT GOSPEL IS THE FULFILLMENT OF THE OLD TESTAMENT

Peter's main point can be summarized as follows: Jesus fulfilled the Old Testament through his life, death, resurrection, and ascension and is the Lord and Messiah, or deliverer of people from sin. At the time that Peter preached his sermon, the New Testament or new covenant ("testament" is the Latin translation of the word "covenant") Scriptures had not been completed. Peter explained how Jesus's life, death, resurrection, and ascension resulted in the sending of the Holy Spirit, and how these events had already been written about in the Old Testament. Peter quoted from Joel 2:28–32, Ps 16:8–11, and Ps 110:1. Of course, Jesus had stated that he had *not* come to abolish the Old Testament but to fulfill it (Matt 5:17).

But Peter did not simply proclaim these truths. In response to this message, they asked Peter and the other apostles, "Brothers, what shall we do?" Peter answered, "Repent and be baptized every one of you in the name of the Jesus Christ for the forgiveness of your sins, and you will receive the gift of the Holy Spirit. For the promise is for you and for your children and for all who are far off, everyone whom the Lord our God calls to himself" (Acts 2:37–39).

## THE GOSPEL AND THE RELATIONSHIP BETWEEN THE OLD AND NEW TESTAMENT

To engage in biblically Christian evangelism, discipleship, and apologetics we need to understand the fundamental way in which the New Testament message of Jesus relates to the Old Testament. The relationship between the Old and New Testament is sometimes a significant point of confusion for people who have yet to believe in Jesus. And it often continues to be a point of confusion, even for those of us who know Jesus as Lord and Savior! While there are certainly some aspects of the relationship between the Old and New Testament that are difficult to understand, the main character of their relationship to each other is not complicated. After all, since Jesus fulfilled the Old Testament and he established and empowered the writing of the New Testament that is all about him, then the New Testament is what explains the Old Testament, and the Old Testament is the root from which the New Testament originates. The New Testament is the organic fulfillment of the Old Testament. The Old Testament is the root of the New Testament, and the New Testament is the fruit of the Old Testament. Neither Testament can be understood on its own.

Peter did not shy away from the Old Testament when proclaiming the gospel. If we are to become equipped to explain the gospel to others, or to engage in Christian evangelism, discipleship, and apologetics, we must learn what it means that Jesus fulfills the Old Testament and be able to explain this accurately to others. In brief, it means that Jesus fulfilled God's covenant promise, first made to Adam, continued with Noah, and expanded with Abraham, Moses, and David. Jesus as Savior is the Son of David (Matt 1:20; 9:27; 21:9, 15; 22:42). It was Jesus who said that Moses wrote of him (John 5:39–47). It was Moses who wrote the first five books of the Bible. It was the gospel of Jesus that was preached and applied to Abraham (Gal 3:1–9) and Abraham who rejoiced over the revelation of

Jesus given to him (John 8:56). And it is Jesus who is the Second Adam, who succeeded where the first Adam failed (Rom 5:12–21; 1 Cor 15:45–46). The Old Testament pointed to, and prepared all new covenant believers for, Jesus.

## WHO REPRESENTS "PETER'S AUDIENCE" TODAY?

The audience to whom Peter addressed his sermon in Acts 2 is analogous to what some of us will encounter as we seek to engage in evangelism, discipleship, and apologetics within the church. Giving a reason for the Christian hope will sometimes be done with people who know a good bit about the Bible, and who may believe that they are Christians but are not. In fact, the early history of the church as revealed in the New Testament shows us that the church had many false teachers who had to be exposed for preaching a false or distorted version of the true gospel (Gal 1:6–10; 1 Tim 4:1–11; 2 Tim 3:1–13; Titus 1:5–16; 2 Pet 2; Jude; Rev 2). It is *in* the church, not merely outside it, where the gospel must be proclaimed, and where the attack against the gospel can come. In fact, I believe that both Scripture and church history reveal that the most dangerous attacks against the gospel have come from within God's covenant community, and yet they are not wholly unrelated to the attacks that come from outside it. Both are expressions of failing to believe the gospel and to willingly submit to Jesus as Lord. The attacks from outside the church are simply clearer forms of these expressions of unbelief and rebellion. The attacks inside the church, however, are disguised as belief in the gospel and willing submission to Jesus. Jesus's own warning in Matt 7:21–23 and his constant disagreements with the Jewish religious leaders reveal the danger that lurks among those professing faith in God.

The majority of texts cited above regarding false teachers in the church were written by the apostle Paul, who was the apostle to the gentiles. Among other things, this helps us see that Peter and Paul's tasks to different groups did not mean they were involved in radically different ministries. Even as Paul preached primarily to gentiles, he was deeply involved in bringing the gospel to those already in the church. Yet, as the second half of the book of Acts reveals, Paul was sent primarily to the gentiles. We do well to learn from Paul's engagement with those outside the church, and there is likely no better example of Paul's preaching to the gentiles than his engagement with the men of Athens as recorded in Acts 17:16–32.

## PAUL: PREACHER TO THE GENTILES

At the beginning of the account of Paul's encounter with the men of Athens in Acts 17:16–34, we learn two basic truths about those whom God uses to engage in apologetics, evangelism, and discipleship—they are those who have a soul greatly burdened about true and false worship of God and they have an intellect equipped to reason with non-Christians. Both characterized Paul, as we see from the text. "Now while Paul was waiting for them at Athens, his spirit was provoked within him as he saw that the city was full of idols. So he reasoned in the synagogue with the Jews and the devout persons, and in the marketplace every day with those who happened to be there" (Acts 17:16–17). Here again, we see an example of Paul not merely among the gentiles, but also the Jews. Yet, in a real spiritual or theological sense these Jews had much in common with the Greeks of Athens, because both groups were confused about God and what true worship of him looked like. This is what compelled Paul to reason with them. Contrary to what some have thought in the history of the church, the unregenerate or unrepentant sinner who has yet to believe in Jesus for salvation *is* able to understand, objectively speaking, some of the truth of the gospel. There is an overlap or commonality between the Christian and non-Christian on knowledge of the truth as it pertains to Jesus, and, by implication, this extends to many other realities.[4]

In v. 16, Luke used a term for *provoked* that is used in the Greek translation of the Hebrew Old Testament (the Septuagint) to refer to how God responds to idolatry (Deut 9:7, 18, 22; Ps 106:28–29; Isa 65:2–3; Hos 8:5). The verb tense also indicates a sustained inspection or observation by Paul. Of course, Paul, as a first-century Jew, who was well educated and well traveled, already knew a good bit about the idols of the Greco-Roman culture. More than likely, what is referred to here is his gaining

4. The question of what the Christian and non-Christian hold in common regarding knowledge of truth is a rather lengthy and complicated discussion in the history of Christian theology in general and apologetics in particular. As it pertained to Warfield's view, we should note that he affirmed this commonality and criticized Abraham Kuyper and Herman Bavinck for failing to recognize sufficiently enough to place a proper value on apologetics. See Warfield, "Introduction to Francis R. Beattie's *Apologetics*," in *Selected Shorter Writings* 2:93–105; "Review of *De Zekerheid Gesloofs*," in *Selected Shorter Writings* 2:106–23.

precision in how the Athenians were demonstrating their commitment to their idols. Above all, it means that it took time and effort for Paul to learn about their idolatry and in learning about it his soul was greatly disturbed or provoked. His response was not temporary rage, but as the verb tense communicates, a *continuous settled concern or disturbance in his soul*. It is consistent with God's jealousy for his own name (Exod 20:4; 34:14; Isa 42:8).

So, perhaps we ought to ask ourselves two things: (1) Are we knowledgeable about the idols of the culture in which we seek to engage in evangelism, apologetics, and discipleship, and (2) does the false worship we observe disturb us? Does it compel us to want to reason with people about the claims of the Lord Jesus upon their life? Are we equipped to do that? Obviously, a genuine love for the Lord Jesus is necessary, and yet, this only possesses us when we have learned about him and from him. You see, the Bible doesn't set our intellect off against our affections and our will; rather, it teaches us how they function in harmony with each other. We will not be compelled to reason with others about Jesus unless we are fully convinced in our own minds that the Bible is true and Jesus is the Son of God, the Second Person of the Trinity, and the only Savior from sin. The apostles were certainly men who possessed this conviction.

In reasoning with people about the claims of Christ we will eventually have to address their presumptions and presuppositions (controlling beliefs that determine how you think) about God and the gospel, which will also mean that we will have to learn to deal with the ignorance and arrogance of the non-Christian. This is what Paul did with the men of Athens, as we see from Acts 17:18–21. There we read:

> Some of the Epicurean and Stoic philosophers also conversed with him. And some said, "What does this babbler wish to say?" Others said, "He seems to be a preacher of foreign divinities"—because he was preaching Jesus and the resurrection. And they took hold of him and brought him to the Areopagus, saying, "May we know what this new teaching is that you are presenting? For you bring some strange things to our ears. We wish to know therefore what these things mean." Now all the Athenians and the foreigners who lived there would spend their time in nothing except telling or hearing something new.

From these verses we see that as we address the non-Christians' presumptions and presuppositions, we can expect to receive verbal attacks. Correcting misunderstandings of the gospel and answering baseless judgments against the gospel means telling people that they are wrong—this is not something most people receive well! The apostle Paul's experience from the men of Athens testifies to this.

These men belonged to two groups—the Epicureans and the Stoics. These were two groups that embraced some beliefs that were common in their time and place, but are out of accord with what Scripture teaches. The Epicureans were known for the pursuit of pleasure as their supreme commitment, but this did not mean that they merely pursued physical or sensual pleasures. Instead, it meant that they believed humans sought what was most pleasurable in the ultimate sense. Indeed, they believed if one pursued merely physical pleasure one would not be living according to ultimate pleasure, and thus it would be a denial of the Epicureans' true commitments. They regarded the absence of bodily pain and the gentle relaxation of the mind as the most desirable state, and they called it repose. While arriving at this commitment, they also denied that there was a God who created. All that existed was physical matter and life was best lived not by speculating about things unknowable but to deal with the material realm and one's life in it.[5]

The Stoics believed that the human race began from a single point of origin and that one should live based on logic and discipline and in harmony with the natural order that was permeated by a divine principle or logos. They were committed to a strict and morally disciplined life that was about living in harmony with the divine principle found in life and that permeated all things. They endorsed something very similar to what Christian theologians would later call natural law. But natural law in Christian theology, when defined as the expression of God's divine nature seen in the created order and by which the created order operates, is not precisely what the Stoics meant by natural law, but it was close. They were essentially pantheistic, that is, believing that life and the natural order was itself God. But they also believed that there was an order or rationale to events and wisdom, and the "good life" was experienced by not trying to fight against it but in submitting to it. So, they believed that if one reasoned rightly about life and conformed one's life to such reason, then one would experience the good life. Since they regarded all people as part of the one material world orderly system, they contributed both a natural law theory and a notion of universal brotherhood to the Western

5. Stumpf, *Socrates to Sartre*, 113.

intellectual tradition.[6] In the end, the Epicureans and Stoics were not so far apart—both thought that human fulfillment could be experienced apart from Jesus. They certainly weren't far apart in their criticisms of the apostle Paul.

They referred to Paul as a "babbler." The Greek term for "babbler" refers to a seed-eating bird or scavenger. Metaphorically, it referred to people who grabbed ahold of other people's ideas and passed them off as their own. Thus, they were accusing Paul of "being an ignorant plagiarist and a religious charlatan."[7] There is some question as to whether the Greeks were genuinely interested in learning from Paul or whether they were sitting in judgment of him, or basically affirming that they would decide whether what Paul was saying was true and legitimate. The language here matches Acts 16:19–20 when Paul's opponents in Philippi seized him and Silas and brought them before the magistrates. That scene was one in which Paul and Silas stood as defendants before a civil "jury" as it were. There was no formal civil court or jury aligned against Paul in Athens and there was also terminology here that is similar to Acts 9:27 where we are told that Barnabas took Paul and brought him to the apostles in order to alleviate the apostles' fear of Paul. Furthermore, the language regarding where they took Paul could refer not merely to a geographical place but to the administrative body that took its name from the place. The fact that they called Paul a "babbler," or ignorant plagiarist and religious charlatan, indicates, at the very least, that they were pressing Paul for more information so that they could render a final verdict on what they perceived to be nonsense. One thing is for sure, they had already rendered a judgment about Paul and his message up to that point.

Still, Paul had a great opportunity to proclaim the gospel and he took it. These men, like so many other people, had little to no knowledge of God's written word. Indeed, this is becoming increasingly the case in many parts of the world, including the United States. So, we would do well to learn from the apostle Paul what a faithful gospel presentation includes. We can organize Paul's thoughts under three main points. A faithful gospel presentation includes (1) identifying people's spiritual predicament as confused idolaters (17:22–23); (2) correcting false ideas about God and people (17:24–31); and (3) stressing repentance from sin and resurrection from the dead (vv. 30–31).

6. Stumpf, *Socrates to Sartre*, 113–20.

7. Peterson, *Acts*, 490.

## PEOPLE ARE CONFUSED IDOLATERS

Paul's opening statement to these men was not exactly a compliment, but he wasn't trying to be harsh either. Paul was simply being honest, as every Christian ought to be. Yet, in the process he was affirming that there was some common ground between him and them. Still, in the midst of doing this he presented himself as having something worth saying. We might say that Paul identified them as "all over the religious map" (v. 22) and ignorant of the one true and living God (v. 23). But notice how Paul uses the knowledge he gained from doing research into their way of life. It was the equivalent of him saying, "You have even admitted that there may be a god that you don't know about. So, let me tell you about him."

So, what are the truths that Paul emphasizes? First, God is the creator who is utterly independent and in complete control of his creation (vv. 24–25). Second, God created all people from one man and providentially governs their lives (v. 26). Notice, then, that Paul affirms that Adam was a particular, historical man. Third, God's providence reveals his presence that defines people's lives, but is misunderstood, leading to wrong worship (vv. 27–29). Notice how Paul did not start by talking about Jesus. Paul's approach here is consistent with the entire history of revelation. The Bible starts with the doctrine of God as creator. We do not present God's gospel accurately unless we understand its organic union to the doctrine of creation, with its emphasis on God as creator. Who Jesus is and what he does cannot be rightly understood apart from the doctrine of creation. For professing Christians to misunderstand this point raises serious questions about the accuracy of their understanding of the gospel. The biblical doctrine of redemption or salvation can only be rightly understood in relation to the biblical doctrine of creation.

But let us pay attention to the fact that Paul proceeds on the basis of what he has in common with his audience. He speaks respectfully to them precisely because he knows that they too are created in the image of God and have some knowledge of the one true and living God. From what they know—whether they are willing to admit it or not—Paul proceeds to move toward the most important truths of the gospel.

Paul's stress is on people being subject to God, defined by God, controlled by God, and accountable to God. Paul does not start by telling them about Jesus, and still less, how Jesus can fulfill their lives. No, all that Paul says to them leads up to him telling them about their need to repent, about the coming judgment by God, and finally, the resurrection of Jesus from the dead. For Paul, the gospel, and thus all biblically faithful apologetics, evangelism, and discipleship revolve around the biblical doctrine of God as creator and redeemer, or humans as creatures created in God's image, corrupted and condemned by sin, and in need of a savior. Jesus can only be rightly presented when God as creator-king and judge is presented first. The wider context of the biblical doctrine of creation then gives clarity to apologetics, evangelism, and discipleship. The latter three are just as wide and deep as the creation, and, perhaps most importantly, the Creator's plans for creation.

Finally, what the apostle Paul stresses at the end is the need for sinners to repent of their sin, because Jesus rose from the dead. Jesus's resurrection is not only why people *must* repent, but also why they *can* repent. Jesus continues to give new life, resurrecting deadened sinners from the dead.

## CONCLUSION

Whether it was Peter to primarily a Jewish audience or Paul to primarily a gentile audience, the gospel message about the life, death, resurrection, and ascension of Jesus that they proclaimed was the same. Peter, Paul, and all the apostles spoke the gospel not only to those who had never believed it before, but also those who believed it or at least claimed to. This is because even those who have been regenerated, and have believed in Jesus for their salvation for many years, still need further renewal or sanctification. They still need to grow as disciples by receiving God's Word through God's Spirit. Only as we receive God's Word by God's Spirit are we then equipped to explain to others about the Lord Jesus. Some with whom we reason will have much knowledge of the Bible and the Christian faith and life. Some will not. Thankfully, we have in Peter and Paul's sermons clear ways in which we can address people who fall into the two general categories of ignorance and knowledge of God's Word. What both need is a right knowledge of God's Word that highlights what God has accomplished in and through his Word made flesh, the Lord Jesus Christ. In other words, they need to understand the power, authority, and sufficiency of God's written Word. Let's explore this next.

# 6

# Establishing the Gospel: Exploring the Authority and Power of Apostolic Preaching

"We accept Christianity in all its distinctive doctrines on no other ground than the credibility and trustworthiness of the Bible as a guide to truth; and on this same ground we must equally accept its doctrine of inspiration."[1]

B. B. Warfield

"Christianity is in its very nature an aggressive religion; it is in the world just in order to convince men; when it ceases to reason, it ceases to exist. It is no doubt the truth; but the truth no longer proclaimed and defended rots quickly down."[2]

B. B. Warfield

"The dense darkness in which men live, the terrible bondage into which they have been brought; this is part of the revelation of the Ascended Saviour, connected with which is the necessary implication of their hopelessness apart from the preaching of the Gospel. The appointed means of breaking this darkness is the proclamation of the Gospel by which alone can men's eyes be opened."[3]

B. B. Warfield

1. Warfield, "The Real Problem of Inspiration," 214.
2. Warfield, "Christianity the Truth," in *Selected Shorter Writings* 2:216.
3. Warfield, "Summation of the Gospel," in *Faith and Life*, 176.

## INTRODUCTION

The biblical gospel is not merely information about Jesus, but the life-giving power of God for everyone who believes it. This life-giving power is not *from* those who believe it, because they are spiritually dead. As the apostle James wrote regarding God the Father, "Of his own will he brought us forth by the word of truth that we should be a kind of first-fruits from his creatures" (Jas 1:18). It is this word of truth that is the gospel. It is the gospel itself through the presence and power of the Holy Spirit that is the power of God for salvation. The gospel, then, is not merely the message about what the Lord Jesus has done "to save his people from their sins" (Matt 1:21), but is the means to receiving all the benefits of Jesus's life, death, resurrection, and ascension. As a result, God has chosen the preaching of the gospel to be the primary means by which the gospel advances on earth (Rom 10:14–17; 1 Cor 1:18–25; 2 Tim 3:16—4:5; 1 Pet 1:22–25; 2 John 9–10). This reveals the powerful organic union between God's Word and Spirit, and how God's Spirit works by and with God's Word to accomplish all that God has promised to accomplish in rescuing his creation and his covenant people from sin. Yet we cannot understand this union between God's Word and Spirit that is necessary in order for us to receive the power of the gospel unless we are willing to receive God's explanations regarding his Word and Spirit. Such explanations are God giving himself to us because in order to have the power of the gospel for eternal life we must believe the rightful explanation of it. There is content to be believed, and by believing it one is receiving it. The "it" one is receiving is not mere information but God himself. By receiving God, we are receiving new life or spiritual life by which we are changed or transformed to be like God in our character (2 Cor 3:18; Rom 8:29; 12:1–2; Gal 5:22–24; 2 John 9–11).[4] Thus, the explanation of the gospel is part of the gospel.

The Scriptures reveal an intimate and organic union between God's word and his covenant-redeemed people—Israel (OT) and the church (NT). This intimate and organic union reveals that God's covenant-redeemed people have always been created, sustained, nourished, and perfected by God's Word through the power of God's Spirit for the glory

4. Old, *Reading and Preaching*, 8: "If we are truly to understand Christian preaching, we must see Jesus Christ as its center. First, we must see Jesus as the fulfillment of generations of preaching and teaching that went before him, and second, we must see Jesus as the type, or perhaps prototype, of generations of preaching that have followed him. He is both the pattern of preaching and the gospel to be preached."

of God the Father. Integral to this work is God's ordained means through which he mediates his Word and Spirit to the people who are the objects of his mercy and grace. Throughout history, God has chosen particular men in his covenant community to whom he brought his word and by which he distributes his covenant blessing and curse. This is not to say that God could not or did not bring his word to particular men and women in extraordinary circumstances that were outside his ordinary chosen means of delivering it through his prophets and apostles. Instead, it draws our attention to the truth that God has chosen to work through his ordained authority structure by which he mediates himself to his people. In other words, in order to be evangelized and discipled in the Christian faith and be equipped to defend it, we must understand that both becoming a Christian and growing as a Christian means receiving from God what God alone is able to cause us to receive, not just once, but continuously throughout our lives. God does this first and foremost through the preaching of his word by those who have been established by his Spirit to preach it in the church. This means that it is profitable for equipping God's people for every good work (2 Tim 3:17).[5]

Even when God brought his word in extraordinary circumstances, such as during the times of the judges, it was designed to bring his people back to the ordinary means of grace by which God had commanded them to operate. We see God's ordained authority structure in seed form in Noah and Abraham (Gen 18:17–19), and coming to its fullest fruition in the old covenant era through Moses culminating in King David. We see this same authority structure fulfilled in the new covenant era through Jesus creating and establishing the apostles. The apostles, then, were the foundation upon which Christ established and nourished his church through their preaching, teaching, and writing of God's word by the ministry of the Holy Spirit. God not only created his redeemed covenant community, but also nourished and multiplied them. Just as God commanded Adam and Eve to be fruitful, multiply, fill the earth, and subdue

5. Old, *Reading and Preaching*, 42: "When the prophets claimed to pronounce the word of God, they had something quite dynamic in mind. They understood that word to be a powerful force, an authoritative word by which God rules his kingdom, a creative word by which the heavens and the earth came into existence, a word of judgment that made the crooked straight and the rough places smooth, a redemptive word by which God's ultimate purposes were brought to fulfillment. For the prophets, God's word was not so much a phonetic reality as an ultimate reality, not so much a communication of ideas as turning on a light in a dark room, a light that fills the void of human existence with purpose, or turning on the headlights of a car making clear the road ahead."

it, God, through the Last Adam, who is the Word made flesh—Jesus, the Son of God, the Second Person of the Trinity—is fruitful, multiplies, fills the earth, and subdues it, as he creates, sustains, nourishes, and perfects his covenant people.

The creation, sustenance, nourishment, and perfection of God's redeemed covenant people means that God shepherds them through the administration of his word in their corporate life (Exodus, Leviticus, and Deuteronomy). In the Old Testament era God's word was administered through the offices of the prophet, priest, and king. These offices find their root and fulfillment in the Lord Jesus Christ. Through the offices of prophet, priest, and king, God gave himself to his people, because these three offices administered God's Word to God's covenant community redeemed from sin. As an organic part of his work of redemption, Jesus established the apostles—the men to whom he gave the authoritative interpretation of his life, death, resurrection, and ascension. Integral to this is the Spirit of Truth, sent by Jesus and proceeding from the Father, bearing witness about and glorifying Jesus to the disciples that Jesus had chosen (John 14:15–27; 15:26–27; 16:13–15; Acts 1:1–2). It is the apostolic testimony preserved and given through the New Testament Scriptures by which people have both God the Father and Son mediated to them (2 John 9–10), and they are shepherded and built up in the knowledge and love of God (Eph 4:11–16). In other words, Jesus fulfilled all that was begun in the old covenant era that was integral to God rescuing creation and his people from sin. Essential to this new covenant administration of God's covenant is the preaching of the apostolic testimony regarding Jesus.

The power for creating, sustaining, and perfecting the church, or the making of disciples, evangelizing of sinners, and defending the gospel, is rooted in and received by the apostolic proclamation regarding Jesus as given in and through the New Testament. Through the Holy Spirit, the power and authority of Jesus is administered through the proclamation of the Old and New Testament by those gifted by the Holy Spirit, and who have been confirmed by and to the church through that same Spirit. In all this we see, fundamentally, what the Protestant Reformation was about—the recovery of these truths in all their glorious implications. In what follows I hope to more specifically trace out what I have just affirmed and help us see the indispensable authority and power of apostolic preaching for the creation, sustenance, growth, and perfection of the church. Thus, it is through faithful biblical preaching in the church that evangelism, discipleship, and apologetics first and foremost take place.

## THE WORD OF THE CREATOR: SPOKEN, WRITTEN, MADE FLESH

The Bible, of course, begins with God creating by his Word and Spirit. God spoke his word and it was accompanied by his Spirit and life came. God is life. He alone has life within himself, and there is no life apart from his sovereign decision to create and sustain it. God is Lord over life and death, and to know God is eternal life (John 11:25; 17:3; Rev 1:17–18). God's response to sin is to bring his *Word* for judgment and rescue, or in covenant terms, curse and blessing (Gen 3). God spoke to Adam and Eve, as well as the serpent. Repeatedly, throughout the Old Testament, we read of God speaking, and of course, we only know this because God empowered particular men, beginning with Moses, to write his word. Thus, there is an intimate, intricate, and organic union between the spoken and written word of God and judgment against, and rescue from, sin. God's final and fullest manifestation of his word was that he became flesh.[6]

God is called the Word at the beginning of John's Gospel, and John begins his account of the gospel in a way that is unmistakably meant to alert us to Genesis: "In the beginning was the word, and the word was with God, and the word was God." From beginning to end the Bible teaches us to identify God with his word. Among other texts, Matt 19:5 and Gen 2:24, Rom 9:17 and Exod 9:13–16, along with Gal 3:8 and Gen 12:3 demonstrate that the terms *Scripture* and *God* are used interchangeably.[7] God *is* his word, and his word spoken, written, and made flesh is God

6. While the point of this chapter is to highlight the power and authority of the apostolic testimony that is God's word to his people for their life, it is God's word that was always confirmed to and through the senses of God's servants and the whole covenant community. Thus, in Genesis 15 where we have the first explicit mentioning that "the word of the Lord came" we also have God confirming his word to Abram's senses through his looking at the stars, and then through the covenant ratification ceremony. Among other things it highlights the unbreakable union between God's word and the sacraments of baptism and the Lord's Supper. It is no mere coincidence that it is in Genesis 17:10 where we read of the covenant sign of circumcision for the first time shortly after reading that God told Abram that he was changing his name because God had already made him the father of many nations. In Romans 4:17 Paul states that Gen 17:5 was proof of the resurrection, and that the Christian faith and life is the revealing of the resurrection.

7. See especially Warfield, "'It Says,'" in *Works* 1:283–332.

to us and for his people; God accomplishes all that he accomplishes by his word, and because there is never disunity between God's Word and Spirit, we must always think of God's Spirit as working by and with God's Word; God's Word always brings us his Spirit for blessing or curse. To emphasize God's Word is to emphasize his Spirit, whether we know it or not, because God's Word and Spirit always remain united. While we may erroneously isolate God the Father, Son, and Holy Spirit from each other in our thinking, or misunderstand their relationship to each other, nonetheless, God the Father, Son, and Holy Spirit are never disconnected from each other or dissolved into each other; we can distinguish between them, yet they are forever united as one.

The reception of God's word, then, was and still is necessary for the reception of salvation, and in the Old Testament era this took place through the three primary offices that governed the life of God's old covenant people—the offices of a prophet, priest, and king.

## OFFICES AND FUNCTIONS OF PROPHET, PRIEST, AND KING

The offices of prophet, priest, and king were central to the life of God's old covenant people and were revealed through Moses, the great prophet and priest of God in the old covenant era. Each office was fulfilled or brought to its perfection by Jesus.

Perhaps the most concise and accurate descriptions of the functions of each office are given in the Westminster Confession of Faith in its Shorter Catechism. Question #24 reads: "How does Christ execute the office of a prophet?" The answer is: "Christ executes the office of a prophet, in revealing to us by his Word and Spirit, the will of God for our salvation." Question #25 states: "How does Christ execute the office of a priest?" Answer: "Christ executes the office of a priest, in his once offering up of himself a sacrifice to satisfy divine justice, and reconcile us to God, and in making continual intercession for us." Question #26 asks: "How does Christ execute the office of a king?" Answer: "Christ executes the office of a king, in subduing us to himself, in ruling and defending us, and in restraining and conquering all his and our enemies." The Larger Catechism expands on these answers.

While Moses did not hold the office of a king, he demonstrated its function by leading God's old covenant people, Israel, out of Egypt and to victory over the Egyptians. The offices of prophet, priest, and king were designed to govern the worship and life of God's old covenant people. These offices and their functions existed in an organic relationship to each other, as can be seen, among other places, in Deut 17 and 18. By affirming that Moses wrote of him, Jesus identified himself as the fulfillment of the prophetic, priestly, and kingly offices.

What the Old Testament prophets accomplished was not primarily the foretelling or prediction of the future, but rather the forth-telling or proclamation of God's word. This is confirmed by the test for a prophet in Deut 18:22. Our English translations have difficulty doing justice to the Hebrew in Deut 18:22. The text is not merely saying that if a prediction does not come true, then the one making the prediction is not a prophet. Instead, it affirms that if what the prophet spoke *is not* (the literal rendering), that is, *is not true*, or *not in accordance with what God had already spoken*, then that person was not a prophet.[8] There *was* a predictive element within what the Old Testament prophets did, but this was not their primary function. Instead, their primary role was to first set forth God's covenant, and then second, to prosecute against God's people the covenant law case God had against them by virtue of their disobedience within the covenant relationship and law he had established with them through Moses. This culminates in Moses's lifetime in the speeches of Deut 28 and 29 in which the blessing and curse of God's covenant are set before God's covenant people through Moses.

8. Craigie, *Book of Deuteronomy*, 263. If we think that the predictive element alone was the test of a prophet it sets up a rather difficult scenario. What if the prophet predicts something to take place many years into the future? The people would obviously have to wait until that date to discover whether the alleged prophet was indeed a prophet. The test of speaking what was consistent with what God had already spoken is highlighted not only in that the proper translation of the present tense verb results in "*is not*" in 18:22 (italics mine), but also in the words of 18:20: "But the prophet who presumes to speak a word in my name that I have not commanded him to speak, or who speaks in the name of other gods, that same prophet shall die." The emphasis, in other words, was whether the alleged prophet was calling God's covenant people to think and live to honor Yahweh. What honored God was all he had previously spoken through Moses. This is why this portion of Scripture begins with Moses stating what he does in 18:15: "The LORD your God will raise up for you a prophet *like me* from among you" (italics mine). See, too, 18:18. So, Deut 18:22 must be understood in the context of 18:20 and the emphasis on what God had already revealed through Moses.

## JESUS AND THE APOSTLES FULFILLING PROPHET, PRIEST, AND KING

Thus, when Jesus said that Moses wrote of him (John 5:39–47), he identified himself as the fulfillment of the offices of prophet, priest, and king. Among other New Testament books, the book of Hebrews makes these points especially clear. Its opening statement emphasizes and illumines the union and fulfillment of the prophetic, kingly, and priestly offices and functions of the Old Testament. In Jesus accomplishing and applying these works he affirmed that he is not only the one in whom God's people would experience all the blessings of God's covenant, but also the one who would deliver God's covenant curse. Jesus reinforced this point when he explained why he spoke in parables and quoted Isa 6:9–10. To Jesus's disciples the mysteries of the kingdom had been granted but not to at least some of the crowds to whom he spoke (Matt 13:10–16). In these emphases we need to see, among other things, that God not only blesses and curses through his Word, written, spoken, and made flesh, but also that God is sovereign regarding who receives the curse and blessing. Still further, Peter in Acts 3:22–26 proclaims that Jesus is the fulfillment of Deut 18:15–22. Now, what we might too easily miss is this: Because Jesus is the fulfillment of Deut 18:15–22, Peter and the other apostles are also the fulfillment of Deut 18:15–22 because it was Jesus who empowered and ordained Peter and the apostles to proclaim the authoritative interpretation of Jesus's life, death, resurrection, and ascension (John 14–16; Acts 1:1–8).

## GOD: SOVEREIGN OVER THE PROPHETS AND APOSTLES

Just as God was sovereignly in control as creator and redeemer of the prophets, so too was he sovereign over the apostles. Neither the prophets nor apostles were ever in ultimate control over the power and authority administrated through them. The *keys* of the kingdom that Jesus gave to the apostles are identified with God's revelation of himself that leads to a true confession of him (Matt 16:13–28). Because the keys of the kingdom are identified with God's revelation of himself, these keys were never fully controlled by the apostles; this revelation was and always will be sovereignly controlled by Jesus through the Holy Spirit (contrary to Roman Catholicism). The apostles did not replace Jesus, and the church built upon the prophets and apostles (Eph 2:20–21) does not replace Jesus; God is not dependent on the church, or anyone or anything in any way at any time. It is in God that all live and move and have their being, not the reverse (Acts 17:28). In their act of first speaking and then writing the authoritative interpretation of Jesus's life, death, resurrection, and ascension, the apostles, like the prophets, were men who were vessels, instruments, or administrators of God's power and authority. To be sure, the Lord, having created and redeemed each of the men who proclaimed and wrote his word, also developed each man through that man's whole life so that under the control of the Holy Spirit each one wrote in a way consistent with his personality and history. Yet, the power to speak and write God's word was not, strictly speaking, theirs. It was neither theirs to ultimately give to or withhold from others. God did not need them to get his revelation out. Among other things, we learn this through God speaking through Balaam's donkey (Num 22:30)! In and of themselves, the prophets and apostles could hardly regard themselves as anything special, and this also applies to those of us who are given the privilege and duty to preach God's word.

Furthermore, God determined by his Spirit who would understand and bow to the testimony concerning him. There was nothing that the apostles had at their immediate control that determined the success or failure of their declaration; the Spirit of God moves as he wills, as Jesus told Nicodemus (John 3:8). Even when the apostles spoke and a miracle was performed, they did not speak in their name, or give what was not first *given* to them (Acts 3:6). The life and death of Judas serves as an example that even a particular, exclusive earthly experience that on all accounts appears to human senses to ensure God's covenant blessing does not in fact give that blessing. Still, the apostles whom Jesus established carried out a unique office and function in the history of God's redemption. The apostles and their testimony are the fulfillment of Isa 6:9–10 and Matt 13:10–16. Philip preaching to the Ethiopian eunuch in Acts 8:26–40 is an example of the need for and the provision of this authoritative interpretation of the gospel that is about Jesus's fulfillment of the Old Testament. In other words, it is God's explanation of himself—who he is and what he has done, is doing, and will do—that establishes his kingdom.

Before we go further, though, perhaps we need to remind ourselves that every human deserves God's covenant curse. It is only through God's sovereign mercy and grace that a sinner receives God's blessing. Such blessing only comes through God's Word and Spirit.

## JESUS, THE HOLY SPIRIT, THE APOSTLES, AND THE CHURCH

All that Jesus, the Word made flesh, did in his earthly ministry, he did in the power of God's Spirit (Matt 3:13–17; Luke 4:14). The union between Jesus, the Holy Spirit, the Old Testament, the gospel, and the proclamation of the Scriptures is succinctly expressed in Luke 4:16–21, when Jesus read from Isa 61:1–2 and announced that in the hearing of those present that text had been fulfilled. Included in Jesus's works done by the power of the Spirit was his establishing his apostles as the authoritative interpreters of his life, death, resurrection, and ascension (Luke 6:12–16; Acts 1:1–3). God gave his people himself as they were given the truths of the Old and New Testament. Further, we have seen that part of the Old and New Testament is the truth regarding the authority structure ordained by God through which he gives himself to his people. This ordained authority structure is integral to, and an organic part of, all God's covenant community (Israel in the Old Testament and the church in the New Testament) is and does. B. B. Warfield illumined the point well:

> There lies at the basis of Christianity not only a series of great redemptive facts, but also an *authoritative interpretation of those facts*. Amid the perhaps many interpretations possible to this series of facts, who will help us to that one through which alone they can constitute Christianity? In the ordinary affairs of life we are enabled to arrive at the true interpretation of the facts that meet us, by the explanations of those who have knowledge of their meaning and who have a claim upon our belief when they explain them to us. . . . These great facts of Christianity—is there anyone who has knowledge of their meaning and who has a right to our belief when he explains them to us?—who, in a word, has authority to declare to the world what this series of great facts means, or in other words, what Christianity is? It is evident that we are face to face here with an anxious question. And it means nothing less than this, that the existence of a doctrinal authority is fundamental to the very existence of Christianity. We find that doctrinal authority, ultimately, of course, in Christ.[9]

In other words, to understand the nature and function of God's word written, spoken, and made flesh is to understand the church, what it is and does. However much we fail to understand the one we fail to understand

9. Warfield, "Right of Systematic Theology," in *Selected Shorter Writings* 2:238. Italics mine. Observe that this has to do with the entirety of *what Christianity is*.

the other, because the church is the body of Christ. We could just as accurately say the church is the "body" of God's Word. I would also add then that to the degree that we fail to understand these matters we fail to understand the church's worship. This is because the church's worship is empowered by Christ (God's Word), is about Christ (God's Word), nourishes God's people on Christ (God's Word), causes us to rejoice about Christ (God's Word), and makes God's people to be like Christ (God's Word). Again, God's Spirit is integral to all this. The Word was made flesh, and he, by the power of his Spirit, creates, sustains, matures, and perfects his bride, the covenant community, the church (Eph 4:7–16).

The fulfillment of Jesus's mission is mediated or administered through his apostles (Matt 10:1–40; Mark 6:7–13; Luke 6:12–16). Thus, the apostles are established and empowered by Jesus to declare the authoritative interpretation of Jesus. This authoritative interpretation of Jesus is the gospel to which people are continuously evangelized in and through the church, in and by which sinners are made to be Jesus's disciples, and is defended against all arguments set up against it. This authoritative interpretation of and by Jesus was first expressed verbally and then in written form. The apostles knew they had this authority and that it was about Jesus's Spirit equipping them for this task. First Corinthians 7, 2 Pet 3:16, and the truth that the writings of the apostles were to be read in the church reveals that these apostolic writings had the same authority as the Old Testament Scriptures. Moreover, it meant that the apostles knew of what their authority consisted. An integral part of it was the recognition that God's Spirit would continue to bless his church with men who the Spirit had given the ability to rightly interpret the word of God and declare it to others (Eph 4:7–16; Rom 12:3–8; 1 Cor 12, esp. vv. 28–31).

Upon the dispensing of God's word by such men, the church would continue to multiply, mature, and be perfected. So united is God's word with God's people that repeatedly in Acts we read of God's word increasing or multiplying when it refers to people being brought into the church. The following texts highlight these matters: Acts 1:1–3; 2:41–47; 3:12; 4:33; 6:7; 8:25, 40; 9:20–21, 28–29, 31; 10:33–48 (note especially 10:40–42); see also 12:24; 13:5–7, 47–49; 15:22–27 (note the apostolic authority to declare the truth); 15:36; 16:17 (note the name she uses for God); 17:13, 22–34 (here we have an example, along with previous sermons in Acts, that there was in this preaching theological exposition of the meaning of Jesus's life, death, resurrection, and ascension [only those with apostolic authority, or who had the approval of the apostles, did this]; they did not merely read the Bible); 18:5, 8, 23–26; 19:20; 20:18–32; 28:23, 25–31. We should note that the last words quoted from Paul's preaching is his quoting Isa 6:9–10 and that "salvation has been sent to the Gentiles; they will listen." Of course, none of this is to diminish in any way the importance of and benefits from reading God's word. Instead, it highlights how crucially important the preaching of God's word by God's Spirit-empowered servant is to the creation, multiplying, and maturing of God's people.

## SENT TO SPEAK THEN WRITE

The authority structure that Jesus established by creating his apostles gave them the power and authority to first speak and then write the authoritative interpretation of Jesus. This reflects the Hebrew conception of the apostolate in which a representative sent by another could represent the one who sent him, even to the point that the representative in delivering the message was considered the very person whom he represented.[10] Thus, Jesus told his chosen apostles, "He who receives you receives me, and he who receives me receives the one who sent me" (Matt 10:40). Jesus said, "Truly, truly, I say to you, the one who receives whomever I send, receives me, and the one who receives me receives the one who sent me" (John 13:20). To his chosen apostles, after his resurrection, Jesus said, "Peace be with you; just as the Father has sent me, even so I am sending you" (John 20:21). To receive this revelation regarding Jesus one had to have been an eyewitness to the life, death, and resurrection of Jesus, and have received from him the authoritative teaching regarding those events as they pertained to the kingdom of God (Acts 1:1–26 [see esp. v. 3 and vv. 21–26 regarding the choosing of Matthias]; Acts 9:1–31; 2 Cor 12:1–10; Gal 1:11—2:21). These men fulfilled a unique role in the history of redemption.

The authority that the apostles possessed was first administered through their preaching the gospel and then secondly through their writing its interpretation. First Thessalonians 2:13, 2 Thess 2:13–15, and 1 Cor 15:1–11 are helpful in clarifying for us that the apostles' authority to declare the gospel was first done verbally. These texts also clarify that

10. See Ridderbos, *Redemptive History* for the most concise treatment of these matters.

this declaration of the gospel was synonymous with the term *tradition* and this term operated as a synonym for the Scriptures, or the word of God.

This word of God received through hearing is said by Paul to have been "at work" in the believers. "And we also thank God constantly for this, that when you received the word of God, which you heard from us, you accepted it not as the word of men but as what it really is, the word of God, which is at work in you believers" (1 Thess 2:13). This is, of course, consistent with what Paul wrote in Rom 1:16 regarding the gospel—that it is the power of God for salvation to everyone who believes. Still further, "But we ought always to give thanks to God for you, brothers beloved by the Lord, because God chose you as the first-fruits to be saved, through sanctification by the Spirit and belief in the truth. To this he called you through our gospel, so that you may obtain the glory of our Lord Jesus Christ. So then, brothers, stand firm and hold to the traditions that you were taught by us, either by our spoken word or by our letter" (2 Thess 2:13–15). Note that when Paul says that God called them through the gospel so that they may obtain the glory of our Lord Jesus Christ, he is not communicating that God was merely giving them permission to reach that goal. We know this is not the case because of what I have underlined above: "God chose you as the first-fruits to be saved." Paul is emphasizing the means through which God *does* accomplish their salvation. God chose them as the firstfruits to be saved and he was doing it through the gospel. The term *called* is equal to the term *chose* in 2 Thess 2:13–15. This is just one example of why faithful pastors and Bible teachers have affirmed for centuries that there is a difference between the free offer of the gospel to all people and the effectual call of God that raises sinners from the spiritual dead. Even as Jesus raised Lazarus from the physical dead by Jesus calling out to him, so too a similar thing takes place by God's Spirit as men faithfully preach God's word. It is also why we are correct in defining the gospel as both the *message about* the life, death, resurrection, and ascension of Jesus and the *means by which* these events reach their fulfillment.

We should also note what Paul wrote in 1 Cor 15:1: "Now I would remind you, brothers, of the gospel I preached to you, which you received, in which you stand, and by which you are being saved, if you hold fast to the word I preached to you—unless you believed in vain." The term *stand* is a perfect active indicative verb that communicates that a past action is affecting their current situation. But Paul goes further. Paul wrote that they were being saved, or that their salvation was ongoing, but only as they held fast to the word Paul had preached. This is the same kind of language and action that God had told his covenant people to do in relation to him (Deut 10:20; 11:22; 13:4; Josh 23:8). The Corinthians were, at that time, standing and would continue standing by virtue of the gospel. In other words, the preached gospel was the means by which they were being saved. Paul then helped them, and us, see what this looks like from their side of the matter. It means their holding fast to the word Paul preached. We should emphasize that there really is no reason for Paul to refer to *his preaching* unless *his preaching* was somehow united to everything else he affirmed. Why not just write "the gospel you received" or "hold fast to the word"? But Paul, twice in a very short span, alerts them to *his preaching* of the gospel. Why? Because he had the authority to preach the authoritative interpretation of Jesus's life, death, resurrection, and ascension by which they were being saved, and it was through *his preaching* of the *gospel* that they had been called out of darkness and brought into God's marvelous light, as Peter wrote (1 Pet 2:9).

We agree then with Herman N. Ridderbos:

> The apostles were not simply witnesses or preachers in a general, ecclesiastical sense. Their word is the revelatory word; it is the unique, once-for-all witness to Christ to which the church and the world are accountable and by which they will be judged. . . . The New Testament itself inseparably unites the central events of redemption on the one hand and their announcement and transmission on the other. *The announcement of redemption cannot be separated from the history of redemption itself.* That proclamation was left neither to chance nor to human tradition or reporting nor to preaching, whether of religiously gifted individuals or of the church. Indeed, as apostolic proclamation, the announcement of redemption first of all belongs to the reality of revelation itself, and as such it has its own unique, once-for-all character. In that exclusive sense, apostolic proclamation is also the foundation of the church, to which the latter has known itself to be bound from the very beginning.[11]

11. Ridderbos, *Redemptive History*, 15. Emphasis Ribberdos's.

## THE POWER OF GOD TO SAVE THROUGH PREACHING

Of course, it was Paul who wrote in Rom 10:14–17 of the centrality of preaching for believing the gospel. But it is important that we understand precisely what Paul was affirming by his words in Rom 10:16–17. Paul wrote, "But they have not all obeyed the gospel. For Isaiah says, 'Lord, who has believed our report?'" This is a quote from Isa 53:1. Paul had previously used a quote from Isa 52:7 to refer to the need for gospel preachers to be sent: "How beautiful are the feet of those who preach good news." In the Greek of Paul's quote from Isa 52:7, he used the term that refers to the preaching of the gospel. Here is the full quote from Isaiah: "How beautiful upon the mountains are the feet of him who brings good news, who publishes peace, who brings good news of happiness, who publishes salvation, who says to Zion, 'Your God reigns.'" The Hebrew verb form that is expressed in the English phrase "who publishes" is communicating that the announcement of the peace, the good news, and salvation is *made* to be heard. In other words, it is not a mere verbal declaration, but rather an *effectual* declaration, just as Paul affirmed an effectual call to the Thessalonians. This same idea is communicated in the two questions of Isa 53:1: "Who has believed what he has heard from us? And to whom has the arm of the LORD been revealed?" To have the arm of the Lord revealed to us is to have God cause us to know and experience his saving power. This is why Paul draws the following conclusion in Rom 10:17: "So faith comes from hearing and hearing by the word of Christ." Saving faith comes from hearing the preaching of the gospel, the gospel that is both the word about Christ (he is the content) and belongs to Christ (he is the owner). In other words, in Rom 10:17 Paul is saying that Christ, through his word preached, creates the ability to spiritually hear and respond in faith to Christ's message that comes through his ordained servant. Perhaps this can be seen even more easily when we note how the Lord's "arm" and "hand" are referred to in the Old Testament.

## GOD'S SAVING POWER: THE PREACHED WORD THAT IS REVEALED AS TRUE

Frequently in the Old Testament God's right hand and/or arm are used as symbols of his power to conquer the enemy of his people, to save his people from sin, or judge them for their sin (Exod 6:6; 15:12, 16; Deut 4:34; 5:15; 7:19; 9:29; 11:2; 26:8; 1 Kgs 8:42; 2 Kgs 17:36; 2 Chr 6:32;

Ps 44:3; 89:10, 13, 20–21; 98:1; 136:12; Isa 30:30; 40:10–11; 44:12; 51:5, 9; 53:1; 59:16; 62:8; 63:5, 12; Jer 21:5 [an instance of God judging and fighting against his people]; 27:5 along with 32:17 and 21 [helps us see the connection between God's act of creating with his actions to redeem]; Ezek 4:7 is a clear connection between the use of *arm* and the verbal proclamation of God's word through his chosen prophet; 20:33–34). God's people understood this connection between God's arm and God accomplishing salvation, as can be seen not only from the abundant Old Testament citations above, but from Mary's declaration in Luke 1:46–55 (see esp. v. 51), when she responded to Elizabeth's words regarding Mary, the Christ child, and Elizabeth's own child. These things are further illumined for us in John 12:36–50.

When Jesus arrived in Jerusalem six days before the Passover, he encountered some Greeks who had come for the feast. Jesus recognized this as a sign that his time of glorification through his death and resurrection was at hand (12:20–32). In the midst of Jesus speaking about this, John tells us a "voice came from heaven" (v. 28). The crowd heard thunder. Keep this in mind. Jesus went on to speak about the judgment of the world, the ruler of the world being cast out, and Jesus being lifted up to draw all people (in light of this being prompted by the Greeks it was a veiled reference to all *types* of people, i.e., Jew and gentile, in God's kingdom) to himself. Then Jesus gets a bit more ambiguous and spoke about people walking in the light while the light is with them and that they needed to *believe* in the light. Then John tells us that Jesus departed and hid himself and that the people did not believe in him despite all the signs Jesus had done. Pay attention to what John wrote concerning this. John wrote that this was so "the word spoken by the prophet Isaiah might be fulfilled: 'Lord, who has believed what he heard from us, and to whom has the arm of the Lord been revealed [Isa 53:1]?' Therefore they could not believe. For again Isaiah said, 'He has blinded their eyes and hardened their heart, lest they see with their eyes, and understand with their heart, and turn, and I would heal them.' Isaiah said these things because he saw his glory and spoke of him" (John 12:38–41). The very text that the apostle Paul uses to stress that faith comes from hearing the word of Christ the apostle John uses to confirm why people could not hear rightly and believe in Jesus. Perhaps someone might ask, "Well which is it?" It is both. It could not be otherwise. God is Lord of the revelation of himself; God determines who hears or rightly understands his word and who does not; his sheep hear his voice because they are his sheep (John 10:26–27); to them the arm or power of the Lord has been revealed.

Knowing who God is, understanding him as the worthy object of your faith for the saving of your soul, is a gift from God. God creates, saves, and destroys by his mouth or word (Ps 18:8; 33:6; Job 4:9; Isa 34:16; 40:5; 45:22–23; 48:3, 13 [note the union of God's "hand" and "right hand" creating along with God's word going out]). Perhaps the effectual nature of God's word is expressed nowhere more concisely and clearly than Isa 55:10–11: "For as the rain and the snow come down from heaven and do not return there but water the earth, making it bring forth and sprout, giving seed to the sower and bread to the eater, so shall my word be that goes out from my mouth; it shall not return to me empty, but it shall accomplish that which I purpose, and shall succeed in the thing for which I sent it." And then that is followed in the last two verses of Isa 55 with a declaration of the joy that is experienced by God's people because they have been saved by God. God has mercy upon whom he has mercy and hardens whom he hardens (Exod 9:16; Rom 9:17–18). Perhaps again we should remind ourselves that no one, not a single person, deserves to be able to hear, understand, and believe for salvation; what we all deserve is death. So then, what Isaiah is asking in 53:1 and that Paul uses in Rom 10:16 amounts to asking this: "Who, in the preaching of the gospel, has been given the power to believe the gospel and be saved?" That Paul did not think this was simply for converting people to the Christian faith, but in building them up continually in the Christian faith their whole earthly life, i.e., the making of disciples, is seen, among other ways, in that Romans was written to Christians, and that the most accurate way to translate Rom 1:16 is that "the gospel is the power of God for salvation to everyone who *keeps on believing*" (italics mine).[12]

That the power to continuously save us as sinners comes through the preached gospel is expressed by Paul in Rom 1:15 that preceded his statement regarding why he was not ashamed of the gospel. "So I am eager to preach the gospel to you also who are in Rome. For I am not ashamed of the gospel, for it is the power of God for salvation to everyone who believes, to the Jew first and also the Greek. For in it the righteousness of God is revealed from faith to faith, as it is written, 'The righteous will live

12. The term is *pisteuonti*, a present active dative participle. The act of believing is ongoing and reflects the nature of the gospel, the Christian faith, and life. To the degree, then, that we recognize belief in Jesus to be central to evangelism, discipleship, and apologetics, to that degree we will recognize their union to one another.

by faith.'" The power of God to bring salvation by his "arm" and the connection of this to apostolic preaching was expressed by Paul in Acts 13.

As Paul began preaching in the Antioch synagogue, he referred to God's history of bringing Israel out of Egypt "with uplifted arm" (v. 17). Paul highlighted Jesus as the fulfillment of Israel's hope of salvation. It sparked the interest of many and so Luke tells us that the next Sabbath day "almost the whole city gathered to hear the word of the Lord" (v. 46). But some of the Jews began to contradict Paul and Barnabas. This is what Luke reports next: "And Paul and Barnabas spoke out boldly saying, 'It was necessary that the word of God be spoken first to you. Since you thrust it aside and judge yourselves unworthy of eternal life, behold, we are turning to the Gentiles'" (italics mine). Notice that in thrusting the word of God aside they were regarding themselves unworthy of eternal life. In other words, the word of God is equated with eternal life. Now, what Paul and Barnabas said next is, I believe, one of the most stunning statements in the Bible regarding the character of apostolic preaching. They stated: "For so the Lord has commanded us, saying, 'I have made you a light for the Gentiles, that you may bring salvation to the ends of the earth.'" This is a quote from Isa 49:6 referring to the one commonly called the "suffering servant," who was God's way to save his people, both Jew and gentile, from their sins, and, who, of course, is Jesus. Paul and Barnabas said that it applied to them in their preaching the gospel. It is the equivalent of saying, "Our apostolic preaching is Jesus."[13] It was, of course, the continued expansion of what Jesus had said in Acts 1:8. The response of the gentiles was appropriate: "And when the Gentiles heard this, they began rejoicing and glorifying the word of the Lord, and as many as were appointed to eternal life believed." The union between the saving work of Jesus in his life, death, resurrection, and ascension and the apostolic preaching of these things could not be tighter or clearer. The apostle Peter proclaimed the same truths.

Consider what Peter wrote in 1 Pet 2:2: "Like newborn infants, long for the pure spiritual milk, that by it you may grow up into salvation—if indeed you have tasted that the Lord is good." What is this pure spiritual milk? It is the gospel preached. Consider how Peter began his letter. He greets his hearers (the letter would have been read out loud in the congregation of God's people) and states that those who have salvation have been born again to a living hope by God the Father through the resurrection

13. Here is an example of why in the first chapter of the Second Helvetic Confession we read that "the preaching of the word of God is the word of God."

of Jesus Christ from the dead and that this is what they rejoice in despite their various trials (1 Pet 1:3–9). Then he wrote that the prophets (of the Old Testament) were serving this salvation to God's church. Note what Peter wrote in 1:12: "It was revealed to them that they were serving not themselves but you, *in the things that have now been announced to you through those who preached the good news* to you by the Holy Spirit sent from heaven, things into which angels long to look." The words in italics illumine us to a vital point. The power of God for salvation that not only brings one into the kingdom for the first time (conversion) also purifies the Christian throughout their life (sanctification or discipleship); this purification from sin was accomplished through the Holy Spirit in what was preached. This is why Paul wanted to preach the gospel to those in Rome who were already Christians. It is why Peter went on in 1 Pet 1:22–25 to write the following: "Having purified your souls by your obedience to the truth for a sincere brotherly love, love one another earnestly from a pure heart, since you have been born again not of perishable seed but of imperishable, through the living and abiding word of God; for 'All flesh is like grass and its glory like the flower of grass. The grass withers, and the flower falls, but the word of the Lord remains forever.'" Now, if he had stopped right there, we would truly have in his statement a most exalted view of the Scriptures, the word of God written, and we would have an exalted view of the Word of God made flesh, Jesus. But Peter did not stop there. He said one more thing: "And this word is the good news that was preached to you." Again, we have emphasized not merely the written word of God, but the preached word of God.

Paul emphasized these same points by telling Timothy what Scripture is—God-breathed (2 Tim 3:16). And what does God accomplish through his breath or mouth or word? He creates, interprets, or judges, destroys, and redeems. Paul next explained what God's word was good for—teaching, reproof, rebuke, and the training in righteousness, so that the man of God would be thoroughly equipped for every good work. This is why Paul lays upon Timothy a most solemn charge: "I charge you in the presence of God and of Christ Jesus, who is to judge the living and the dead, and by his appearing and his kingdom: preach the word" (2 Tim 4:1–2). Here we see not only the emphasis on preaching the word of God, but also that the apostles recognized that the authority that they possessed to preach God's word would be passed on to others through the Holy Spirit and thereby the preached word, just as all the other gifts of God Spirit were given to God's people through the preached word of God.

## THE CHURCH, PREACHING, GOD'S SPIRIT, AND HIS GIFTS

Acts 6:1–7; 1 Cor 12:1–31; Rom 12:3–8, Eph 4:7–16; 1 Tim 3:1–13; 5:17–18; Titus 1:5–9; and 1 Pet 5:1–5 all address the topic of spiritual gifts in various ways. What is affirmed through these texts, and emphasized by each in various ways is the unitary and organic character of the church. After all, the church is the body of Christ or the bride of Christ. While it is true that inanimate objects are used as metaphors for the church, such as stones and a house (1 Pet 2:4–5), it is noteworthy that in this same text those stones are referred to as living stones, and the house is a spiritual one in which God's people are being built up as a holy priesthood. In stating that God's people are being built up, Peter affirmed that something or someone was acting upon them. What is this thing acting upon them? It is God's word preached as we already saw from 1 Pet 1:22–25.

In 1 Cor 12:28 Paul lists some spiritual gifts. Without getting sidetracked on the question of whether they are all operative today in the exact same way they were during the apostolic age, let me alert your attention to the order that Paul presents. We find a similar order in Eph 4:11. First apostles, then prophets. (Here there is some debate over whether this refers to "preachers" in general, or those with the supernatural ability to predict the future. My point does not mandate an answer to the question.) First Corinthians 12 lists teachers third, while in Ephesians he mentions evangelists, then shepherds, or pastors, and then teachers. What we need to recognize is what Paul says about the relationship of these works to the growth and health of the church.

Paul affirms in 1 Cor 12:4–11 that all the gifts of God's Spirit are given for the common good of the church according to how God wills. Thus, the individual Christian is never to be the focus of the gifts he or she possesses. The focus is service to others for building them up or strengthening them in the church to the glory of God. In Ephesians, Paul makes much the same point, but with the gifts he highlights he places an emphasis on the gifts that emphasize verbal proclamation of God's word and that "equip the saints for the work of ministry, for building up the body of Christ" (Eph 4:12). What Eph 4:13–16 emphasizes is that the

Holy Spirit causes the church to mature, to be strengthened through its knowledge of doctrine that then leads the body of Christ to speak truth to one another and spur one another on to growth. This is the same as making disciples and continually believing the gospel. While the emphasis in Eph 4 does not exclude quantitative growth, the emphasis is on qualitative growth that takes place through God's word applied by those gifted by God's Spirit to take that word and proclaim it faithfully.

This emphasis on the preaching and teaching gift in the church is revealed by Paul's words in 1 Tim 5:17: "Let the elders who rule well be considered worthy of double honor, especially those who labor in preaching and teaching."[14] The terms Paul uses for preaching and teaching could also be translated "word" and "doctrine." Why would Paul distinguish "those who labor in preaching and teaching"? It would seem that it is because such a ministry is the root from which the entire church is created, fed, and grows.

The church is shepherded or ruled through preaching and teaching, because it is God's living and active word that is able to renew our minds that we might be transformed to be like Jesus. In Rom 8:29 Paul says that God is saving his people in order to conform them to the image of his Son, and then in Rom 12:2 Paul uses a modification of this same term for *conform* to say that the entire Christian life is summarized as each one being *transformed* by the renewal of their mind. God does this work. Even in Rom 12, Paul's command to be transformed is a passive imperative. In other words, he is commanding those who already have the power of God's Spirit to submit themselves to a process that God controls and applies. The building up of Christ's body is done by those with the authority or Spirit-enabled power to faithfully preach and teach God's word. This authority is not highlighting the individual who holds it but rather the Spirit that holds that individual. To honor the office that such a man holds and the function he performs because of that office is to truly honor the Holy Spirit's entire work of multiplying and maturing the church. The truth that the Spirit apprehends certain men to do this

14. The terms Paul uses for "preaching" and "teaching" are the Greek terms *logo* and *didaskalia*. The latter term is normally translated "teaching" or "doctrine" and is used to refer to the authoritative teaching that governs the church. *Logo* is the dative of *logos*, and the contextual use of the term greatly shapes how it should be translated. Knight, *Pastoral Epistles*, 233, summarizes Paul's point: "He is speaking of a subgroup of the 'overseers' that consists of those who are especially gifted by God to teach, as opposed to other overseers, who must all 'be *able* to teach' (1 Tim 3:2)." Emphasis Knight's.

means the church has the responsibility to see that its life centers on or revolves around what the Spirit has gifted those men to do.

This union between the regenerating and renewing work of God in and through his Son and Spirit by the written and preached word of God is also seen in Titus 2:11–14. There we read that the "grace of God has appeared bringing salvation for all people, training us to renounce ungodliness and worldly passions, and to live self-controlled, upright, and godly lives in the present age, waiting for our blessed hope, the appearing of the glory of our great God and Savior Jesus Christ, who gave himself for us to redeem us from all lawlessness and to purify for himself a people for his own possession who are zealous for good works." Notice the two things that Paul joins to the term for *appear*. The grace of God that saves has *appeared* and it does this by *training* God's people to live holy lives, and this is joined to "waiting for our blessed hope, the *appearing* of the glory of our great God and Savior Jesus Christ." You see, the word of God made flesh who accomplished the redemption, or rescue of sinners from sin, continues to be applied through the written word of God being proclaimed, so that Christ's bride is prepared for him when he appears a second time. Jesus's church is being prepared by God's word for God's Word. In turn, this is summarized just a few verses later as the Holy Spirit's work of regeneration and renewal (Titus 3:5).

There is a use of the term *evangelism* that refers to the verbal proclamation of the gospel that the Holy Spirit uses for the conversion of a sinner into God's kingdom or that corresponds to the Spirit's work of regeneration. There is, at some point, in one who is truly a Christian a transfer of them out of darkness and into God's marvelous light (1 Pet 2:9–10). No, they do not have to be aware of when this actually occurs or occurred in them in order for it to occur. More important is our awareness that such a use of the term *evangelism* must be understood as organically united to discipleship and apologetics. Regeneration is the creating of a disciple; it is one of the fruits (not the only) of a successful defense of the Christian gospel. Because, according to Titus 3:5, there is no regeneration without its corresponding renewal, which together comprise salvation, we are to not only think of evangelism as ongoing in the one regenerated, but also to recognize that the act of regeneration by the Holy Spirit is God giving birth to a disciple of Jesus and successfully commending or defending the gospel.

Perhaps the most vivid picture of this is seen in the Old Testament through the prophet Ezekiel. In the thirty-seventh chapter we read of the

"Valley of Dry Bones" over which God called Ezekiel to prophesy. Ezekiel was to say to them, "O, dry bones, hear the word of the LORD." What will God say to them? "Behold, I will cause breath to enter you and you shall live." Ezekiel does this, and through a gradual process of his continuing to speak God's word the bones come to life (37:7–10). It illustrates what God not only did for his people in the Old Testament era, but also what he continued to do for them in the New Testament era culminating in God's Word becoming flesh, speaking his word to the chosen objects of his mercy and thereby cleansing them, raising them from the spiritual dead, and continuing to nourish them, and thus causing them to abide in his word (John 15:1–17). It is no coincidence that Rev 20:4 alludes to or echoes the language and results of this.

Finally, we should note that the apostle John made clear in 2 John 9–10 that intimate fellowship with God the Father and Son, and by implication the Holy Spirit, takes place as we abide in the teaching or doctrine of Christ. John's statement clearly reveals that we cannot set the ongoing verbal proclamation regarding Christ off against vibrant, passionate, and intimate communion with God. John wrote, "The one who does not abide in the teaching [*didache* = authoritative doctrine] of Christ does not have God; the one who abides in the teaching of Christ has the Father and the Son." But John went a step further. He gave a sober warning in vv. 10–11. "If anyone comes to you and does not bring this teaching [the teaching of Christ, including the truth of v. 9 that he had just written, because it is part of the *didache*, or teaching] do not receive him into your house [that is, the church] or give him any greeting. For the one who greets him shares in his wicked works." These are very stern and sobering words. Why would John issue this warning? Because anyone who denies this truth that he had written is denying the very root by which God's people grow and multiply. To deny this truth and to encourage others to deny it is to teach a disconnect between them and the only God-ordained means by which they *have God*. Notice that he did not say that in having the teaching about Christ that they did not have the Son and Father's teaching or doctrine; he said that in not having their teaching we do not have *them*. To deny this truth among confessing Christians is to attempt to displace God at the center of the worship and life of the church and to encourage and facilitate idolatry within the church. It is to seek salvation and growth in Christ through human-engineered schemes and methods. It is to establish the very sinister situation that will lead some who were involved in the church to be rejected by God on judgment day, because what they were really doing was nothing more than using the language of Scripture and Christian theology and their own conceptions of good works to express their own self-centered and self-absorbed agendas (Matt 7:21–23). But those who understand that from God and through God and to God are all things (Rom 11:36) and that he alone from beginning to end gets the glory for what takes place in the saving of his people, they will exalt not only the gospel message of Jesus through verbal proclamation, but also recognize and exalt the truth that the gospel message establishes a gospel means or method by which God's people are created, nourished, and perfected to do all the good works God has ordained for them to do. This is simply another way of saying that God's word or the gospel is its own apologetic, or defense.

## CONCLUSION

God's word spoken, written, and made flesh is the source and sustenance of God's people. God first births his people by his word through his Spirit, and then he grows or matures them by it. In other words, God has established his redeemed covenant people by explaining enough of the truth to them that he has mediated his very life to them. Through history God has been bringing his word so that he would accomplish his purposes in his creation. These purposes can be summarized as his covenant blessing and curse. God either rescues us from sin, or condemns us for it. He accomplishes both by his word through His Spirit. From the very beginning, God was selective regarding to whom he revealed his saving truth. God told Noah to build the ark, because God was going to bring a flood of judgment. God determined to bless the nations through Abram, who became Abraham. God's power and not human power was revealed in the birth of Isaac (Rom 9:6–9). God made his promises and he has fulfilled them, and continues to do so.

God has always given particular men the authority to declare his truth to others, and God has uniquely blessed through this preaching of his word. God thus established his people by his word by his Spirit, and God's people only knew his word as God revealed it first, historically, to his prophets and then his apostles. By doing this, God gave such men an authority that he did not give to everyone. This did not make these men inherently better than others in the kingdom of God; they were still sinners who needed to be saved. Those who are given the inestimable privilege of proclaiming God's word will always need to be saved by the very word they proclaim; they need God's mercy and grace like all other sinners. But the authority that God gave these men was the authority to declare to God's people God's word. They were given the authoritative explanations of Jesus's life, death, resurrection, and ascension. In the old covenant era these men were called the prophets. At the beginning of the new covenant era, they were called the apostles. The Old Testament prophets and New Testament apostles first had the authority to verbally declare God's word and then they wrote it. This was an authority unique to them. This function, and the authority entailed in fulfilling it by writing God's word, has ceased among God's people. But the authority to declare God's word still holds in the church, because the Spirit of God declared through the apostle's writings that he would gift some to be able to preach and teach God's word by declaring the meaning of what the apostles wrote. This word of truth is what continues to be explained, and by it Jesus has established and continues to establish his church and kingdom.

None of this is to say that the proclamation of God's word by those gifted by God's Spirit is all that the church does in its corporate life. God's Spirit gifts individual Christians to do a variety of necessary works in the church, but he does so through the preached word of God. In all this we have said nothing of those other means of grace—the sacraments (baptism and the Lord's Supper), prayer, and the right exercise of church discipline.[15] Yet, strictly speaking, even with these acts that God has established we see the supremacy of God's word or the verbal explanation of God's truth. Apart from God's word and Spirit we do not know the role these other means and acts have in the life of God's church corporately and his individual disciples; we do not know how we are to engage in them, nor delight in receiving and administering them. Furthermore, none of this should be taken to mean that there is no benefit from every individual believer reading and studying the Bible. Every individual believer ought to read and study the Bible, in part, in order to hold the men accountable who are given the duty to preach and teach it. Still, we need to see that there is a vitally special place for the preaching and teaching

15. Whether we want to name the Lord's Supper or baptism as *sacraments*, *ordinances*, or *means of grace* is not a vital matter. The issue with them is not primarily what we call them but how we view and use them. The critical matter is how they function within our lives individually as Christians and how a congregation uses them in its corporate life. The same goes for using *means of grace* to describe or name prayer and the exercising of church discipline. This highlights, among other things, the enduring importance of the debate between nominalism and realism in the history of Christian theology.

of God's word among God's people by the men uniquely gifted to do this, because it is first and foremost by that function that God has revealed that he creates, sustains, nourishes, and perfects his redeemed covenant people, as well as judges all people.

All this is integral to what it means to be made disciples of the Lord Jesus, to be evangelized to his gospel, and to be able to defend it. In all this a particular interpretation of God's word has been presented as organically united to Christian apologetics, discipleship, and evangelism. In our next chapter we explore and explain more fully that humans as creatures created in God's image cannot help but interpret their life circumstances. We will see how this is an integral part of what many have called a *worldview.* Although the worldview concept and its use has come under recent criticism, it has played an important role in the history of apologetics in particular, and the history of Western culture in general. So, we need to explore its strengths and weaknesses so that we can more effectively explain the gospel to people who interpret life in ways that are to varying degrees contrary to God's word.

# 7

# Exploring and Explaining People as Interpreters

"For what are the great facts that constitute Christianity? Strip them free from 'dogma,' from that interpretation which has transformed them into doctrine, and what have we left at the most but this: that once upon a time a man was born, who lived in poverty and charity, died on the cross and rose again. An interesting series of facts, no doubt, with elements of mystery in them, of the marvelous, of the touching: but hardly in their naked form constituting Christianity. For that they require to receive their interpretation. . . . Give the facts no interpretation, and we cannot find in them what we can call Christianity; give them a different interpretation and we shall have something other than Christianity."[1]

B. B. Warfield

"All science without God is mutilated science, and no account of a single branch of knowledge can ever be complete until it is pushed back to find its completion and ground in Him. . . . It is thus true of sciences as it is of creatures, that in Him they all live and move and have their being. The science of Him and His relations is the necessary ground of all science. All speculation takes us back to Him; all inquiry presupposes Him; and every phase of science consciously or unconsciously rests at every step on the science that

1. Warfield, "Right of Systematic Theology," in *Selected Shorter Writings* 2:237–38.

makes Him known. Theology, thus, as the science which treats of God lies at the root of all the sciences."[2]

B. B. Warfield

## INTRODUCTION

Because we are created in God's image, we have rational abilities that enable and require us to interpret our experience. We are to do this in accordance with God's word, but because of our sin condition (fallen nature) and our finite condition as limited time-and-space-bound creatures, we are doubly handicapped in interpreting our experience according to God's word. Yet, because of God's saving grace through the Lord Jesus Christ by way of the Holy Spirit, Christians are enabled to not only have an accurate-enough interpretation of reality to place their trust in the Lord Jesus for salvation, but also mature in that interpretation, or have it become increasingly more accurate. This interpretation, by the very nature of the case, involves the Christian in every subject matter of reality, because God is the creator of all reality. Thus, the Christian faith is not merely about an interpretation of one part of reality that we might call spiritual or theological in a narrow sense but is an interpretation of all reality in the broadest and most comprehensive sense. Over approximately the past two hundred years, the term *worldview* has been used to describe and analyze people's comprehensive interpretation of reality. In this chapter, we explore and explain the matters related to the worldview concept and consider its validity for Christian apologetics, discipleship, and evangelism.

## FILTERING THE BIBLE THROUGH OUR THINKING

To interpret anything is to assign meaning or significance to that which we are interpreting. Interpreting the Bible is like making coffee. The coffee grounds and the filter are like our *presuppositions*, or the controlling beliefs that determine how we think. The water going over the coffee grounds and through the filter is like the Bible passing through our thinking. As the water goes over the coffee grounds and through the filter, we have the

2. Warfield, "Idea of Systematic Theology," in *Works* 9:70–71.

dark liquid known as coffee. This is an apt illustration, because just as the coffee I drink carries with it some, but not all, of the properties of the coffee grounds, so too is everyone's interpretation of anything, including the Bible, to some degree marked by properties of their own thinking, or presuppositions. This is not to say that everyone's interpretation of the Bible is completely misleading, inaccurate, or false, but rather to affirm that (a) there is no such thing as a presuppositionless interpretation of anything, including Scripture, and (b) that we always stand in need of an improved interpretation of anything we interpret, including Scripture. If we are to have an accurate or right interpretation of Scripture—and yes, we need to explore much regarding what this means—we will need truth to wash over our thoughts and purify them. Among other things, this will mean us allowing God's word to govern our thinking. This reminds me of another illustration regarding human thinking.

Another way of thinking about our presuppositions, or the controlling beliefs that determine how we think, is to regard them like railroad tracks that direct our thinking. Once certain beliefs are accepted as true, those beliefs unavoidably move our thinking in a particular direction.

If I think that all reality is simply physical so that it is only possible to know that which can be empirically verified through my five senses, then it will be literally *unbelievable* for me to think that in Palestine in the first century AD a young virgin had God place the Second Person of the Trinity within her womb and caused her to give birth to him. In such a case, my presupposition about the nature of reality prevents me from accepting a belief that directly contradicts or goes against my belief about reality. If I was to come to believe in the miracle of the virgin birth of Jesus, I would have to let go of my belief that only what I or anyone else could empirically verify through one of the five human senses could be regarded as real.

The conclusions that we embrace about what the Bible teaches unavoidably involve us in understanding and wrestling with the presuppositions through which we process or filter the Bible. This is why Richard Lints stated, "A genuine biblical theology will strongly affirm that humans (Christian and non-Christian) are inevitably influenced by their own culture, tradition and experience. Until and unless the evangelical community wrestles more seriously with this fact, they will not overcome the unreflective biases that characterize the evangelical appropriation of the Bible."[3] Those presuppositions or "biases" through which we filter the Bible, and all our experience of reality, comprise what some people call a *worldview*.

## CHRISTIANITY AS A WORLDVIEW

Ronald Nash, a Christian philosopher, defined "worldview" as "*a conceptual scheme by which we consciously or unconsciously place or fit everything we believe and by which we interpret and judge all reality*."[4] While controversy surrounds the degree to which we are able to think of Christianity as a worldview, I do believe there is some legitimacy to it. Two of the benefits of thinking of biblical Christianity as a worldview is that it (1) presents the Christian as actively participating in the interpretation of all reality, and (2) may allow us to compare biblical Christianity more effectively to those worldviews that conflict with it to varying degrees.[5] While the concept of a worldview can be helpful in apologetics, discipleship, and evangelism, we must recognize that the worldview concept has been used in the past in non-Christian ways. Understanding a little about the history of the worldview concept can be of further help in our apologetical encounters so that we clearly communicate what we mean and do not mean when we speak of Christianity in general and Christianity as a worldview in particular.[6]

3. Lints, *Fabric of Theology*, 27.

4. Nash, *Faith and Reason*, 24.

5. For the utilization of the worldview concept to do this see Sire, *Universe Next Door*.

6. Kennedy, *Against Worldview* is critical of how he perceives that worldview has been used in Christian education circles over the past several decades. While Kennedy affirms some valuable points regarding how Christian educators ought to reflect upon their use of the worldview concept, his treatment suffers from a number of weaknesses. Among them are: (1) direct contradictions, (2) a lack of clarity or specificity regarding the use of worldview that he criticizes, (3) functioning with a caricature of how worldview has been used in the past within Christian education circles, (4) a failure to cite examples of the misuses he mentions, (5) a muddled analysis of the relationship of deductive and inductive reasoning, (6) repeated false either/or reasoning (among the many: "We need not be interested in faithfulness to a particular intellectual framework that we might label a 'Christian worldview.' Rather, we should be seeking faithfulness to the message of the gospel of Christ," p. 117), and (7) a superficial analysis of the history of the worldview concept as it relates to the present ("We need to move on from the combat mindset that originally ignited Christian worldview thinking," p. 116). When is the Christian ever not involved in spiritual warfare that necessitates a "combat" mindset?

## A HISTORICAL UNDERSTANDING OF THE WORLDVIEW APPROACH

Considering human thinking and living from the perspective of a "worldview" is not new. In his book on the history of the worldview concept, David Naugle clarifies that the term "worldview" can be traced back, it appears, to the eighteenth-century Prussian philosopher Immanuel Kant (1724–1804).[7] It seems that Kant used the German term *weltanschauung*, or "worldview," first, and yet only once. It would be theologians and philosophers after Kant in the nineteenth century who would utilize this concept, and they would often do so in opposition to biblical Christianity. It is not exactly clear, however, that everyone who used this concept in opposition to biblical Christianity was fully aware that their work was opposing biblical Christianity. In particular, the nineteenth-century German theologian Friedrich Schleiermacher (1768–1834), at least based on his own profession, meant to defend Christianity against its opponents, and yet in using Kant's theory of knowledge he did significant damage within the church and Western culture in general, because he in fact deviated from Christianity.[8] Through an analysis of the worldview concept, we see how theology and philosophy are inseparably united. The nineteenth-century theologian Charles Hodge was correct when he

7. Naugle, *Worldview*. Naugle's treatment is substantial and helpful, except he actually seems to lose sight of his own title and project by committing a word-concept fallacy in the history he presents. The concept of a worldview, by definition, cannot be reduced to the word itself. Naugle begins by noting the importance of John Calvin as the "headwaters of the worldview tradition among evangelical Protestants" (5). And yet, as he rightly points out, Calvin never used the term "worldview." That being the case, one's presentation of the *concept* that is communicated by the *term* "worldview" within evangelical Protestant circles goes well beyond Naugle's narrower focus that lays predominant stress on the Dutch Reformed tradition. Naugle rightly identifies the nineteenth-century Scottish theologian James Orr as instrumental in communicating the worldview concept. But this is precisely because he was part of a broader Reformed and Presbyterian heritage that stressed the concept without using the term "worldview." A fuller and more accurate treatment of the worldview *concept* should have included the American Presbyterians to whom Orr was unavoidably related. Such a history is seen in the work of the Old Princeton theologians such as Archibald Alexander, Samuel Miller, Charles Hodge, B. B. Warfield, and J. Gresham Machen, as well as the Southern Presbyterians Robert Lewis Dabney, James Henly Thornwell, Benjamin Morgan Palmer, John Girardeau, and Thomas Peck, to name a few.

8. For an accurate assessment of Schleiermacher's theology and its relationship to American Liberal theology and that is sympathetic to it, see Dorrien, *Making of American Liberal Theology*. For a fuller treatment of Schleiermacher's relationship to Kant and their influence on American Liberal theology see Smith, *B. B. Warfield's*, 63–87.

acknowledged that every theology is in some sense a form of philosophy.[9] It has been the union of Kant's philosophy with Schleiermacher's theology that has seriously undermined Christian apologetics, discipleship, and evangelism throughout the last two hundred years, and is the headwaters of the non-Christian thinking and living that has corrupted Western academia and culture over the last two hundred years. The influence of Kant is captured well by John M. Frame:

> It was Kant who developed a comprehensive *rationale* for autonomous reasoning. It was Kant who argued that we must reason autonomously and *must* never reason in any other way. . . . So Kant is arguably the most influential philosopher from his time to our own.[10]

Perhaps the most important thing to understand about the unbiblical way in which the worldview concept was used in the past is how it was employed to communicate a deeply *humanistic*, or "human-centered," approach to thinking and living. Theologians, philosophers, poets, and novelists of the nineteenth century often taught that everybody had their own worldview and no one could sit in judgment of anyone else's worldview. All of this was consistent with Kant's theory of knowledge that affirmed that knowledge was not about people discerning what was objectively true about the external world, but instead determining how they wanted to interpret that external world. When it came to thinking about human knowledge claims, these nineteenth-century thinkers placed priority on the individual's cultural experience that led him or her to perceive reality in a particular way. It did not take long before the belief was embraced that truth claims were simply people's way of talking about their perceptions of reality. Such truth claims, however, were not to be thought of as achieving a correspondence to a reality to which everyone could or did have access. Put another way, such thinking was another

9. Hodge, "What Is Christianity?", 121.

10. Frame, *History of Western Philosophy and Theology*, 251–52. Emphasis Frame's. This is why it is a bit misleading for Trueman, *Strange New World*, to present Jean-Jacques Rousseau as the most significant source for "the authorization of feelings" (34) in the West since the eighteenth century. While the book has much to commend it, relegating Kant to a single marginal comment (61) is not helpful in presenting the larger picture of the source and justification for the subjectivism that Rousseau, Marx, Darwin, Nietzsche, Freud, et. al. embraced and exposited in their own ways. The latter men ought to be regarded first as symptoms before they are thought of in any sense as source for how the West, many Christians, and allegedly Christian institutions have been corrupted and gone astray. For Trueman's fuller treatment see his *Rise and Triumph*.

way of saying, "You have your worldview, and I have mine, but they are neither 'wrong' nor 'right'; they are simply our way of speaking about our experience." Because it was becoming acceptable to believe that human thinking was unavoidably captive to a particular time and place, it was also becoming acceptable to believe that no statement could ever correspond to a reality that was true for everyone in *all* times and places. All this contributed to what has come to be called "the Fact/Value Divide." The following table presents that divide and what subject matters have been thought to belong to which realm.

## "THE FACT/VALUE DIVIDE": TERMINOLOGY AND CONCEPTS[11]

| **Facts** | **Values** |
|---|---|
| Empirical Data | Personal Experience |
| Objects and Objectivity | Subjective and Subjectivity |
| Reason and Rational Discourse | Faith and Feelings |
| Science, Knowledge, and the Intellect | Spirituality |
| Education and Scholarship | Religion and Theology |
| Politics | Worship |
| Public Policy | Ethics |
| Government and Laws | Interpretation |
| Public | Private |

So, initially the worldview concept was actually used to reinforce this unbiblical disconnect of objectivity from subjectivity. All of this reflected some of the thinking during that revolutionary movement of the seventeenth through the eighteenth centuries commonly referred to as "the Enlightenment," and that continued to be nourished during the nineteenth and twentieth centuries. Despite this history, however, there are still legitimate reasons for using the worldview concept to explain biblical Christianity. In order for us to recognize this legitimacy, however, it is necessary that a brief exploration and explanation of this history be given.

11. Reproduced from Hoch and Smith, *Old School, New Clothes*, 24.

## A SKETCH OF "THE" ENLIGHTENMENT: FIRST A WARNING

One of the challenges historians face is trying to provide adequate and accurate summary explanations about people and events in history. These summary explanations are for helping people understand the nature and significance of the past. These summary explanations often are more difficult to achieve than it may appear. If one is truly attempting faithfulness to the historical record, then one begins to realize that brief summary statements often fall very short of doing justice to that record. People and life are much more complex than brief summary statements communicate. Unfortunately, to some degree, in order to even begin getting a handle on history, we are forced to possess categories in which we can begin to organize and understand the people and events of the past. So, on one hand, we need these brief summaries and categories, but on the other hand, we need to understand their limitations and dangers. Hopefully a detailed study of the past will inform our summaries so that despite their brevity they can retain accuracy. If we fail to understand the limitations and dangers of these summaries, we are likely to have a distorted and damaging understanding of the past. The understanding becomes damaging when it leads us to misunderstand other people and events of both the past and present. One subject of history where distortion and damage has taken place and continues to take place is with respects to the subject known as "the Enlightenment." Since it is "the Enlightenment" from which the term and concept of worldview actually originates, any use of the term and concept needs to substantively address that part of the Western intellectual heritage.

## THE(?) ENLIGHTENMENT? THE AGE OF REASON?

During the seventeenth and eighteenth centuries, Europe was an extremely volatile place. Religious wars were taking place, political intrigue and upheaval marked the governmental landscape, life-transforming advances and discoveries occurred in the physical sciences, and great controversies raged in biblical scholarship. One of the most interesting, if not ironic, titles for this time period is "the Age of Reason." When one considers what is often meant by this title and one explores the character of this time period, one almost has to keep from choking on that title. Now, please do not misunderstand my point. There is definitely some legitimacy to naming this time period "the Age of Reason." Such a title would not have been perpetuated for so long were there not some legitimacy to it. The seventeenth and eighteenth centuries did see a new emphasis on human reason as the judge of what was true and good. Further, it is also true that particular branches of the church were actively subordinating the Bible to human reason. Yet, we seriously distort the picture if we believe that this was true for everyone, or even a majority of the people. Further, we alter the picture if we think that this alleged avalanche of "reason" completely enveloped everyone's life so that all people were simply under an unavoidable influence from it. This commitment to human reason that marked some people's life during this period was not like perfume released into the air by which everyone was affected simply by breathing. Maybe one example can help complicate the picture just enough to help us to see how misleading pithy titles can be.

Most intellectual historians identify the French philosopher Rene Descartes's declaration, "I think, therefore I am," stated in the late 1630s, as the cornerstone concept upon which "the Age of Reason" was built.[12] Certainly, there is quibbling over the extent to which Descartes was simply echoing others, or affected by them. Still, Descartes's philosophy helped cultivate a *rationalistic* philosophy that came to be identified with the seventeenth and eighteenth centuries.[13] His philosophy is generally recognized as a sort of "tipping point" in history, and one that is thought to represent this "Age of Reason."

By *rationalistic* I mean a way of thinking that either believes that human reason, unaided by anything outside of itself, ought to have primary authority in how one interprets reality, or a philosophy that places too much weight or importance upon reason in order to acquire knowledge.[14] When we recognize that this is the general perspective of those who think "rationalistically," and when we learn the truth about what characterized most people's lives in the seventeenth and eighteenth centuries, we might question whether the title "the Age of Reason" is the best title for the seventeenth and eighteenth centuries.

12. Cf. Carson, "Dangers and Delights of Postmodernism," 11–17.

13. Strictly speaking it would be misleading to identify Descartes as advocating a full-blown rationalism since he was working these matters out within a self-confessed Christian framework as a devout Roman Catholic. One might certainly argue that he accommodated his beliefs to rationalism, but that was not Descartes's intention. See Stumpf, *Socrates to Sartre*, 235–48; Copleston, *History of Philosophy*, 63–152.

14. Cohen, "Rationality," 415–20.

## REASON WITHIN THE BOUNDS OF RELIGION[15]

Six years after Descartes's declaration, the English parliament petitioned a number of Puritan pastors and theologians to draft a document that would express what it was that all of the British Empire should believe about what the Bible taught. Since church and state were still considered to exist in a vital union to one another during this time, both in Europe and in the American colonies, it was an unavoidable aspect of one's life as a participant within civil society to have a correct theology! In other words, in both Europe and the British colonies, *religious faith* was the dominant perspective from which people viewed themselves and society as a whole. These Puritan pastors and theologians drafted what came to be called the Westminster Confession of Faith, and since its production, it is safe to conclude that millions of people in Europe, America, and around the world have confessed it to be true to what Scripture teaches, even if they did not either fully understand it or live according to it. Such a dominance of biblically directed religious faith during the seventeenth and eighteenth centuries did not disappear overnight only to be replaced by unaided human reason. In many ways, the seventeenth and eighteenth centuries could just as properly be labeled "the Age of Christian Faith." We come to further understand this when we realize that England was not alone in its preoccupation with Christianity. In the seventeenth century, all Europe was characterized by conflicts over the proper understanding of Christianity, as well as military engagements of one kind or another that were designed to establish the rule of various nation-states and their view of the Christian faith. Though the physical fighting began to diminished as the eighteenth century began, the conflicts and debates about Christianity did not.[16]

The eighteenth century was marked by debates and developments over biblical interpretation and what should characterize the relationship between various church communities and the civil governments. It was

15. This is also the title of a helpful philosophical and theological work by Nicholas Wolterstorff. In this work Wolterstorff is arguing for how we should think about the relationship of human reason to theological beliefs or religious commitments. Cf. Wolterstorff, *Reason Within the Bounds of Religion*. I believe the title also aptly characterizes much of the history of the seventeenth and eighteenth century, if not of all human existence. I base this on Rom 1:18–32 and Eph 4:17–19 in which all people's relationship to God (religious) is understood with respects to their reasoning or thinking, and how thinking in turn affects their living.

16. Cragg, *Church and the Age of Reason*; *Freedom and Authority*; Hazard, *European Mind*.

precisely these debates and developments over biblical interpretation that became one of the primary factors that affected how people began to think about how the church, both Protestant and Catholic, should relate to civil governments. To be sure, it was beliefs regarding the role of human reason, as represented by Descartes, and its ability to access and evaluate truth claims that affected the changes that were taking place in biblical interpretation. These changes were the blossoming of what is known as the historical-critical method or modern biblical criticism.[17] Still, such changes, though taking root in the European universities, were not widespread among the general population. So, even though it is true that, during the seventeenth and eighteenth centuries, people begin to trust more in human reason rather than divine special revelation (the Bible) for interpreting reality, we ought not think that such a shift was accepted by the majority of the population. Historians that try and present it as otherwise are simply not accurate.

Thus, it is extraordinarily misleading to label the seventeenth and eighteenth centuries in Europe as "the Enlightenment," or "the Age of Reason," as if that time period can be accurately summarized by such a title. Those two hundred years in Europe and the British colonies were not marked by one particular way of thinking, or worldview, that determined how people accessed knowledge, interpreted the Bible, and thought about their place in the world. Intellectual history is a great deal more complex than such storylines indicate. Humans and the things that affect their thinking are filled with too many variables that possess too many intricacies to allow for such simplistic analyses and conclusions. Simplistic analyses of historical time periods and overgeneralized labels, however, certainly make it easier to present a particular theology, philosophy, or worldview as having supremacy during a given time and place. They also make it easier for historians to communicate an ideological agenda that can help shape people's perceptions of the past, and the present. But faithfulness to the historical record disallows such procedures, and we do well to resist them.[18]

17. For histories of modern biblical criticism see Baird, *From Deism to Tubingen*; *From Jonathan Edwards to Rudolf Bultmann*; Harrisville and Sundberg, *Bible in Modern Culture*. For critical assessments of the historical-critical method see Linnemann, *Historical-Criticism*; *Is There a Synoptic Problem?*; Maier, *Biblical Hermeneutics*. For an overview of the German roots of the historical-critical method see McGrath, *Making of Modern German Christology*. See too Brown, *Jesus in European Protestant Thought*.

18. Trueman, "Renaissance," in *Revolutions in Worldview*, 178, gave expression to the same point regarding the period called "the Renaissance" when he wrote: "Is it at

As we study the history of ideas that helped shape people's thinking in the past and present, we need to exercise caution. Identifying the relationships that exist between people and the philosophies that characterize the time period in which they lived or live is not a simple matter. Yet, it is necessary to understand these relationships if we are to understand the biblically Christian worldview that Scripture directs us to possess. One of the difficulties of possessing a biblical worldview is that to differing degrees we are influenced by the ideas that fill the culture in which we live. In other words, we are prone to adopt ways of thinking that are embraced by our culture, or the way of life that surrounds us. We all possess a worldview and live within a culture that endorses and puts on display various nonbiblical worldviews. So, we need to be clear about what we are involved in doing as we seek to possess a biblically Christian worldview.

## A BIBLICAL USE OF THE TERM "WORLDVIEW"

In light of the way the term *worldview* has been used in the past, it is very important that Christians clarify what they mean when they use the term. Of course, clarity of expression is always necessary, regardless of the history of a term, but in the case of the term *worldview* and its history the matter is quite significant. In summary, we are faced with two significant challenges when using the term "Christian worldview"—both terms can be difficult to precisely define. Each term in itself is highly controversial, so we are not exactly going to avoid difficulties by putting the two together! Using the term *worldview* to express and explain Christian thinking and living can be legitimate, but we need to be careful that we clarify what we do not mean by our use of the term *worldview*.

We should not use the term to mean that the Christian worldview is only one among many permissible options. We ought not to communicate that the Christian worldview is simply the individual's perceptions and feelings about God, or merely about the individual's private, religious experience. In other words, what the individual expresses as his or her experience does not lie outside the sphere of evaluation and verification by others. Finally, we should also *not* affirm that everything that we are to

all meaningful to speak of '*the* worldview' of such a diverse and diffuse phenomenon? I suspect not. Therefore, in this chapter I will trace the various threads that form the warp and woof of the movement we call the Renaissance, rather than present a single set of dogmas, as if such were sufficient to define 'the Renaissance worldview.'" Emphasis Trueman's.

believe as Christians can be rationally comprehended and explained or that even the finite rational explanations that are consistent with Scripture will automatically satisfy the reasoning of non-Christians.

What we ought to affirm with the terms *Christian worldview* is that there are some thoughts, feelings, and actions that are Christian, and there are some that are not, and these can be known, and even to a certain degree are known even by all people (the works of God's law are written on every person's heart, according to Rom 2:15). In other words, part of a Christian worldview is the acknowledgment that there is a God who determines all reality. Reality is known to some degree by all people, and some, if not perhaps many, statements about that reality can be evaluated as to their degree of accuracy. Furthermore, a Christian worldview affirms that all reality is united and so human knowledge has a systematic character to it. One can even say that the whole notion of a worldview is synonymous with what many in previous generations would have called systematic theology. Sadly, however, these Christian beliefs, as well as others, continue to be largely rejected by the majority of people in Western cultural settings, and even by many people who profess to be Christians.

## ACQUIRING A BIBLICAL WORLDVIEW THROUGH YOUR WORLDVIEW

As we continue to explore the answer to the questions "What is biblical Christianity?" or "What is the biblical gospel?" we have to recognize that we do not pursue the answers to these questions as "clean slates" waiting to receive a "biblical worldview." It is precisely this truth that is part of a biblical worldview. It is another way of expressing the biblical truth that humans are sinners who are biased against the truth. Such a bias leads to our both distorting and denying truth. This is one of the main points of Rom 1, as well as a number of other passages in Scripture. Theologians often refer to this condition as the noetic effects of sin. The word "noetic" has reference to the mind. One of the Greek words translated "mind" is *noos*. To speak of sin having "noetic" effects is to say that sin affects our thinking. The Greek word for "repentance" is *metanoia*, which means "change of mind," or "change of thinking." Since the Christian life is one of repentance, we might also express the Christian life as the process of exchanging one set of thoughts for another, or one worldview for another. As we do this, we need to explore more precisely what comprises a person's worldview.

## MOTHER'S EXCELLENT TEA

I was born near Chicago, but have spent more of my life in the South than any other region of the country. Growing up I initially detested iced tea. I thought it tasted awful. As a young boy, when we ate dinner where iced tea was served, I would drink as little as I could. This, of course, took place while living in places other than the American South. I soon discovered, after moving to the South, that "Yankees" don't know how to fix iced tea. What was sadly missing in the iced tea that I had been drinking was *sugar*. All the tea I was familiar with, if it had any sugar at all, had the sugar added after the tea had cooled. That's *not* when you add sugar to tea! If you are going to have tea worth drinking, you have to add the sugar while the tea is hot. What I soon discovered after moving south was that *real* sweettea (Yes, down south it is *one* word. That's in keeping with the sugar and the tea being united!) is definitely worth drinking.

## THE FIVE SUBJECTS IN EVERYONE'S WORLDVIEW

So, what does all of this have to do with the worldview concept? Plenty. Who made the best tea you ever drank? Just remember, whether you want to admit it or not, it was your mother. Remember, *M*other's *E*xcellent *TEA*. Why? Because, if you will, then you might be more likely to remember the five subjects that are part of everyone's worldview. Those five subjects are: *M*etaphysics, *E*pistemology, *T*heology, *E*thics, and *A*nthropology. Well, maybe such a ridiculous memory device won't be that helpful, but if not, then work at creating one of your own, because it is very important to remember these five subjects. In fact, it is not only important to remember that they are part of everyone's worldview, but also to know what each of these subjects addresses, and how the content of one subject area relates to the others.

## EXPLORING WHAT'S IN OUR WORLDVIEW

There are a number of ways in which to analyze a person's worldview. In *The Universe Next Door*,[19] James Sire explains how to do it by asking eight basic questions. Another one that is helpful is given by Ronald Nash in his book *Faith and Reason* (cf. 4n). What follows is largely indebted to his work. We will keep our definitions brief, and then look at some examples of questions that are most immediately addressed in each subject area. Some people would argue that we could and should reduce these five to simply the first three. Ethics and anthropology are then considered as some aspect of the first three subject matters. This is legitimate, but for the sake of clarity, it may be helpful to work with all five so that we understand precisely what fills our worldview.

## METAPHYSICS

The prefix "meta" can mean "with," "after," "between," or "beyond." In this case the "meta" has reference to "beyond." So "meta"-"physics" addresses that which goes beyond the physical. Metaphysics is the study of reality. In metaphysics we explore and seek to explain answers to questions like: What is real? What is the nature of reality? Is reality only physical or are their nonphysical realities? If so, how do the physical realities relate to the nonphysical realities? Is reality only "natural," or are there "supernatural" realities? What might we even mean by "natural" and "supernatural"? What is the nature of time and space? Is the universe eternal? What is the origin of all reality? How do we access knowledge of reality? Is there a reality beyond our earthly life?

## EPISTEMOLOGY

Epistemology is the study of knowledge. In epistemology we explore and seek to explain answers to questions like: What is knowledge? How can we have knowledge? How do we know that we know? What is the role of human reason in knowledge? What are the limits of human knowledge? If there are "supernatural" realities, how can humans know them? What is the role of faith or trust in human knowledge? What role do our five senses play in our knowledge? How does the knowledge we gain through

19. Sire, *Universe Next Door*.

our five senses relate to knowledge of "supernatural" realities, if there are such things? Are there particular things that everyone can know, or does know? If so, what are they and how do people know them? What is meant by objectivity and subjectivity in knowledge claims? How does the objective aspect of knowledge relate to the subjective aspect? Is there such a thing as "pure" objectivity or "pure" subjectivity?

## THEOLOGY

Theology, in its broadest sense, is the study of God. There are more precise and better definitions then that, but for now this broad definition is sufficient. In theology we explore answers to questions like: Is there a God? If so, what is he like? How can humans know God? What characterizes the relationship between God and (1) the material world and (2) humans? What has God done? Is God doing anything currently? If so, what is he doing? What is the relationship between God and the Bible, and other "holy books" from religions other than Christianity? Who is Jesus? What characterizes Jesus's relationship to God?

## ETHICS

Ethics is the study of right and wrong, good and evil in human thinking and behavior. In ethics we are concerned with "ought" and "should." In ethics we explore and seek to explain answers to questions like: Is there one standard of right and wrong for all people, for all times and places? If so, what is it, and how can humans know it? What characteristics should humans possess? What ought humans believe or think? What should humans do? Should all human societies seek to uphold a particular standard of right and wrong? What is justice? Does the Bible require that all people conform to a particular standard of ethics? Is it possible to have ethical standards for things like art? How should humans relate to plant and animal life? Is it right or morally permissible to try and clone humans? What does a morally right use of technology look like?

## ANTHROPOLOGY

Anthropology is the study of humans. In anthropology we explore and seek to explain answers to questions like: What is a human being? Do humans have a soul? If so, what is the relationship between the soul and the body? What is the human mind? What is the relationship between the body and the mind? What is the origin of humans? What is the purpose of human life? Do all humans share particular things in common, and if so, what? Can humans know God? Under what conditions do human beings flourish? Is there such a thing as gender, and if so, what is it? Can people actually change their gender or biological sex?

## ANALYZING NASH'S DEFINITION OF A WORLDVIEW

Ronald Nash's definition of a worldview seems helpful because it brings clarity to the term and the concept it communicates by identifying the precise way in which it is and is not useful to use the term. Let's explore and explain Nash's definition of the term and how we can use it in a way that is consistent with things that God's word affirms as true.

### "A CONCEPTUAL SCHEME . . . EVERYTHING WE BELIEVE"

First, everyone thinks. That is, everyone has a conceptual scheme with which they function, and it is not possible for people to not have beliefs in the five subject areas that we just covered. In everything we claim to know, and in everything we think about, all five subjects are touched upon. Whether people recognize it or not, they possess some sort of system of thinking. It is *their system*. It makes sense to them at some level, or they would not possess it. We cannot think about one of the subjects in our worldview without thinking about the other four. Again, people do not have to be *aware of how* the subjects are related in order for the subjects to *be* related. Which means that people may not recognize that they are actually thinking about all five subjects even while they are. We can take a simple example of our thinking about ourselves to demonstrate this.

If I am thinking about myself, I am unavoidably, in some way, thinking about who I am. This not only means I am thinking about an *anthropological* issue, but a *metaphysical* one as well, because thoughts about what a thing is involve the nature of reality. In particular, they address a branch of metaphysics called ontology, which is the study of being. Further, as I think about myself, I invariably believe that I know some true things about myself. My thinking cannot even get started unless I embrace beliefs that I think are true. In other words, I think I know something. So, *epistemology* is touched upon. Yet, as I consider these things that I think are true, I am also unavoidably affirming that it is either good or bad for me and others to think such thoughts. As I think and affirm something to be either true or false, right or wrong, good or bad, I am engaging in an *ethical* activity. We can simply ask ourselves this question: Are there particular things that I, and all people, ought to think? No matter how we answer that question, our answer is *ethical* in nature. Of course, it is probably safe to say that most people think they are obligated to believe what is true. Yet, even if someone says they believe people ought to believe lies, this too is an ethical belief. Still further, even the person that says humans are not obligated to believe a particular set of beliefs, is to still embrace a belief that is the expression of an ought. In this case the person is saying, "Humans ought not to think that they are obligated to embrace a particular set of beliefs regarding anything." Of course, if you are really thinking, you will recognize such a thought to be a contradiction.

Finally, such thinking unavoidably touches upon *theology*. One of the ways we can see this is in recognizing that our standard of *ethics* cannot simply come from ourselves. If we allow that we can simply create and operate according to our standard of ethics, then we have a recipe for disaster. Human society cannot function according to such a principle, because there would be no basis other than sheer power to establish a standard of ethics. In believing that the individual can simply determine for him or herself what is good, I would be giving license to every form of perversion that could possibly interest and delight people. Further, there would be no means by which we could judge conflicts between individuals. We would have total anarchy. So we know we have a need for an ethical system. Put another way, we all recognize a "good" and an "evil" and yet, whether we recognize it or not, such a standard does not come from us, yet we must submit to it. This is simply another way of saying that such a standard is our "God." It is what captures our ultimate allegiance and invariably guides our thinking, whether we know it or not. Biblically speaking, it reveals what we worship. In other words, *ethics* is unavoidably connected to our *theology*.

Maybe you noticed that I explained *ethics* in relation to *theology* in a way that does not require someone to admit that they have thoughts about a God in order for them to actually possess such thoughts. It is most likely that you will not have to do this with people. Research has shown for decades that the vast majority of people willingly admit that they believe there is a God. In your conversations with people, you might, at some point, simply ask them, "What do you believe about God?" When you demonstrate that you are genuinely interested in knowing what they think, you are likely to not only hear some definite beliefs they possess, but also have a wonderful opportunity to discuss these matters with them.

### "We consciously or unconsciously place or fit everything we believe"

Second, this does not mean that people are necessarily aware that they are thinking about these five subjects, or what they are thinking about regarding the subjects. In fact, it is probably safe to conclude that most people are unaware of much of what they think about regarding these five subjects, or that they are even thinking about them. One might do an informal survey to note what people know about metaphysics and epistemology in order to see that many people are unaware of the character of their thinking. People, however, do not have to be aware that they have a worldview in order to have a worldview. Yet, people are actively engaged at some level in changing their worldview: in accepting new beliefs, modifying their existing ones, and getting rid of those they no longer believe are true. All of this is another way of affirming what philosophers and theologians have affirmed for thousands of years—that we cannot avoid thinking both deductively and inductively simultaneously.

Deductive reasoning is when we use broad or general beliefs and from them draw conclusions and arrive at other beliefs. Inductive reasoning is when we receive specific information or data from our experiences and then move to general conclusions from them. Both processes are dependent on each other. Our deductive reasoning is unavoidably built upon millions of sensory experiences that have comprised our life. Our reasoning apparatus, in effect, grows as we do. Sometimes, if not perhaps often, people consciously and actively engage in this reasoning process and the growth or changing of their worldview. This is why Nash stated that our worldview is "a conceptual scheme in which we consciously or unconsciously place or fit everything we believe."[20] This is why it is, in some sense, illegitimate to fault those who have functioned with the worldview concept in the past of functioning with a "large framework" by which they are interpreting either Scripture or any other experience. It is also why it is illegitimate to affirm that worldview should not be the

20. Cf. 4n.

means to a Christian education, but instead the end or goal of it. It is both simultaneously, and it could not be otherwise (cf. 42n). The issue is not whether we will engage in deductive or inductive reasoning, or whether our worldview will be operative as we instruct others or not. People do not choose in these matters! Instead, the questions with respects to our reasoning is whether we are allowing what we experience moment by moment to inform and possibly change our large deductive framework or whether we stubbornly impose our large framework of thinking upon our experiences so that we deny the reality that is mediated to us in that sensory experience. If I stubbornly insist that all girls named "Jane" are mean and should not be my friend, then when I meet a girl named "Jane" who is in fact kind, polite, and friendly, I will end up ignoring or distorting my experience of that "Jane's" kindness, politeness, and friendliness.

What Nash's definition gives credence to is the basic human experience of both having a large conceptual scheme by which we have to try and make sense of our individual experiences and at the same time allowing our individual experiences to inform and possibly change our large conceptual scheme that we bring to our individual experiences. This already get us into the next phrase in Nash's definition.

### "BY WHICH WE INTERPRET OR JUDGE ALL REALITY"

Third, our worldview is not only a conceptual scheme that we are adding beliefs to, but also the means through which we interpret and evaluate the reality we encounter. By "interpret," I mean that we decide or discern the significance or meaning of something. People will interpret reality differently. This is the result of people screening such reality through their different beliefs that comprise their worldview. If I have in my worldview the thought that real Christians vote for Republican candidates, and then I encounter a thoughtful and committed Christian that doesn't, then my interpretation and evaluation of such a person is going to be affected by the way I think real Christians vote. Of course, such an experience also might serve to cause me to evaluate my worldview and change it in some way.

By way of summary let's remind ourselves that (1) everyone possesses a worldview and people do not need to be aware that they have one in order to have one; (2) everyone's worldview *can* be properly analyzed as possessing five subjects: metaphysics, epistemology, theology, ethics, and anthropology; (3) those five subjects are unavoidably related to each other, and therefore our worldview is an elaborate system of beliefs; and (4) we are actively involved in using and modifying our worldview.

The great calling of God's people is that they are to think and live in accordance with God's word, or in obedience to it. Yet, the great challenge with which God's people are confronted is great because of their fallen condition as sinners, and the sin of the people that surround them. God's people will always be prone, to one degree or another, to embrace ways of thinking and living that do not conform to God's word (Deut 12:28–32; Rom 12:1–2). Put another way, there is always the need to reevaluate and revise our worldview. Repentance, in other words, is the lifelong activity of the true disciple of Jesus. And, yes, if you are thinking, you will recognize that this, once again, reveals the union of the five subjects. But in thinking about these five subjects and their union we need to recognize a vitally important truth—the union of these five subjects is not merely or even primarily best characterized as a conceptual union, but rather an *organic* one. That is, metaphysics, epistemology, theology, ethics, and anthropology are not merely or even primarily existing in a union that can be rationally explained and understood, but rather a union that we experience in our soul, shapes us, and is lived out. This is so because the Lord Jesus Christ, the Second Person of the Trinity, is the one who created, currently sustains, and embodies the truth regarding all five subjects. It is Jesus who *is* the truth. Jesus does not merely rationally or intellectually know truth; he is the truth. And this is the distinguishing feature that makes Christianity and the Christian worldview fundamentally different from every other worldview or belief system. This is another way of saying that if Christians are going to use the term "worldview" to express Christianity, they better be clear that their use of the term is quite different from how non-Christians will be using it.

## THERE ARE ULTIMATELY ONLY TWO CATEGORIES OF WORLDVIEWS

One of the great things about the Bible is that it communicates a truth many ways. We can see this revealed even with respects to the truth that there really are only two categories of worldviews from which to choose. Both the Old and New Testament teach this with respects to worshiping or obeying God (Josh 24:15; Rom 1:23). When we sin, we are rejecting the worship or obedience of the one true living God and deciding to worship a god of our imagination, or an idol. But the number of idols to choose from are numerous, and yet there is still one fundamental choice between the one true living God and all substitutes to him. While addressing the sin of rejecting God in favor of worshiping money, Jesus said, "No one can serve two masters. Either he will hate the one or love the other, or he will be devoted to the one and despise the other. You cannot serve both God and money" (Matt 6:24). While addressing the nature of sin in general, Paul wrote, "For although they knew God, they neither glorified him as God, nor gave thanks to him, but their thinking became futile and their foolish hearts were darkened. Professing to be wise, they became fools and exchanged the glory of the immortal God for images made to look like mortal man and birds and animals and reptiles" (Rom 1:23). Notice the plurality of images versus the singularity of God. Within both Jesus's and Paul's statements we have the acknowledgment that life is, in a sense, one great "Either/Or." Either we will repent and worship God, or we will fail to repent and worship a god of our imagination. Of course, it is precisely because we are sinners that we often do not see our lives as characterized by such a clear choice. Further, rather than there being only one "god of our imagination" there are a multitude of false gods to serve. We might express it this way: There are a lot of ways to go wrong, and only one way to go right. This was demonstrated in the life of God's people as they prepared to live in the land he promised them during the Old Testament era.

## IDOLATRY: A CASE OF CHOICE OVERLOAD

Near the end of the book of Joshua, we read of Joshua's closing words to God's people. They had just seen God give particular people and cities into their possession, and now Joshua was warning and encouraging them. He was warning them of the possibility of their turning away from God. Yet, if they turned away from the one true living God, then they would have a choice to make. They would have to choose which false god they would serve. As Joshua said, "Now fear the Lord and serve him with all faithfulness. Throw away the gods your forefathers worshiped beyond the river and in Egypt, and serve the Lord. But if serving the Lord seems undesirable to you, then choose for yourselves this day whom you will serve, whether the gods your forefathers served beyond the river, or the gods of the Amorites, in whose land you are living, but as for me and my household, we will serve the Lord" (Josh 24:14–15). Contrary to how this text is sometimes handled, Joshua's main point in telling them to choose is not merely to highlight the choice of either serving God or not. Oh, we do have to choose to follow God, and Joshua was calling upon the people to obey and worship the one true living God. But, when Joshua said "choose for yourselves this day whom you will serve," he was highlighting that if one rejects the one true living God, then the choice has to be made regarding which false god one will serve. There are thousands of false gods, but only one true living God.

One of the implications of all this is that there is a particular kind of simplicity that marks the truly Christian life that does not characterize the life of the one who rebels against God. The one who rebels against God has to constantly decide which god will be served. Have you ever had an experience in which you had "choice overload"? Maybe it was the restaurant menu, the possible colors for a dress, the cereal aisle at the grocery store, or simply which channel to watch on TV. An abundance of choices can be emotionally and psychologically draining. This reality greatly characterizes American life. And because we were not created for such an abundance of choices, this choice overload weighs heavy upon our souls. Even many non-Christian psychologists have identified this overload of choices in our own time as the source of much of the anxiety that afflicts people. Yet no single society created such a phenomenon. Rather, it is part of the character of human sin. When we reject the one true God, then we have many false gods from which to choose. This is not to say that an abundance of choices is necessarily bad. We may have an abundance of choices simply because there is a variety of a particular thing. Being able to choose or having to choose between alternatives is not in itself sinful. That is not the point. The point is with respects to the topic of whether we will or will not worship the one true God.

All of this simply testifies to the truth that we really only have two general categories of worldviews from which to make an "ultimate" choice. Either we choose to think and live in accordance with God's word—the Scriptures of the Old and New Testament—or we choose to think and live according to our reasoning and what seems wise to us. This is made clear in Rom 1:21–23, when Paul explains that sin is our refusal to glorify God as God and to give him thanks. This in turn leads to futile thinking and darkened hearts. Even though we profess to be wise, we actually become fools. In other words, we either live by God's word or we live by our "wisdom." We either live by "right reason"—reason, or thinking, that is brought into submission to God's word—or we live by "wrong reason"—reason or thinking that is in rebellion to God's word. Such thinking or reasoning is unavoidably united to our way of living. Perhaps this can help us to also see that there is a sense in which, because all non-Christian worldviews are really about how a person who is not trusting in Jesus for their salvation actually lives or gives expression to their way of thinking, and because this does not manifest itself in precisely the same way in all non-Christians, then we are right to affirm that there is a sense in which there are as many different non-Christian worldviews as there are people. But wait—does this not apply in some sense to Christians? Indeed it does. No Christian perfectly thinks and lives in harmony with what Scripture teaches. The Christian's growth or sanctification consists in them becoming more and more conformed to the image of Jesus, or to be more like him (Rom 8:29), which means, among other things, that their thoughts and actions become more and more obedient, or in line with, God's word. So when we use the term "right reason" we ought to recognize that it is not identifying Christianity as simply or only a way of thinking disconnected from living. It is simply one legitimate way among several regarding how we can describe the Christian faith or life.[21]

Still, what is contained in this "right reason," or this right way of thinking about the five subjects in our worldview? We've explored the definition of a worldview, the five subjects in everyone's worldview, and what generally characterizes everyone's worldview, but we are still in need of exploring and explaining what qualifies as a "biblical" or "Christian" worldview. That is what we will turn to next.

21. "Right reason" was one of the ways in which Warfield referred to the thinking of the redeemed sinner when it was conforming to biblical truth. Unfortunately, this has either been misunderstood and/or misrepresented by scholars over the past several decades. See Warfield, "Apologetics," in *Works* 9:3–15. For a helpful article explaining how Warfield used the term "right reason" see Helseth, "B. B. Warfield's Apologetical Appeal," 156–77. See also Johnson, *B. B. Warfield* for another helpful resource in becoming acquainted with Warfield's thought. For a misanalysis of Warfield's use of "right reason" see Van Til, *Defense of the Faith*. Van Til's misanalysis appears to have been quite influential in leading many astray in their understanding of Warfield's thought. See my fuller treatment of these matters in *B. B. Warfield's Scientifically Constructive*.

# 8

# Exploring and Explaining Apologetics and a Christian Worldview

"The truth is that a man's opinions on matters of historical fact or of metaphysical truth—call them opinions on minute details or not, as you choose—are absolutely determinative of his whole life. It is a matter of metaphysical opinion whether there is a God or not; or whether there is such a thing as right or such a thing as wrong. We cannot adopt even so simple a maxim as David Crockett's famous, 'Be sure you are right and then go ahead,' without having committed ourselves to many very deeply cutting metaphysical opinions, and many of these are capable of being represented as opinions on very minute details."[1]

B. B. Warfield

"We do not possess the separate truths of religion in the abstract: we possess them only in their relations, and we do not properly know any of them—nor can it have its full effect on our life—except as we know it in its relation to other truths, that is, as systematized. What we do not know, in this sense, systematically, we rob of half its power on our conduct; unless, indeed, we are prepared to argue that a truth has effect on us in proportion as it is unknown rather than in proportion as it is known. To which may be added that when we do not know a body of doctrine

1. Warfield, "Faith and Life," 365–66.

systematically, we are sure to misconceive the nature of more or fewer of its separate elements."[2]

B. B. Warfield

## INTRODUCTION

In the previous chapter, we defined the term "worldview" and noted that it had some use in helping us understand what people claim they believe about the most important matters of life. Yet, we dare not overlook that term "claim." Herein lies a window into seeing one of the weaknesses of trying to use the worldview concept as a way of speaking of Christianity, or of any of the other religions of the world, which amount to anyone's life commitments. What people claim to believe and what they actually believe are not necessarily the same thing. We have already observed that Scripture teaches that every Christian stands in need of believing the gospel more faithfully and consistently; even the Christian is evangelized. It is why Paul was eager to preach the gospel to the Roman Christians, who were already trusting Jesus for their salvation. Still further, Christianity is not merely a set of beliefs, but a way of life that expresses what the true Christian believes. When commending the gospel to others, our ultimate concern ought not to be simply trying to get people to adopt a certain set of beliefs. Nor can we accurately assess where someone stands in relation to the Lord Jesus merely by listening to them tell us what they claim to believe, even as helpful as that might be. The gospel call of repentance demands a changed life that, while intimately and organically joined to our beliefs, cannot be reduced to mere beliefs or thinking. Since the worldview concept focuses on what we believe and how we use our beliefs to interpret and judge reality, and since Christianity cannot be reduced to this, we need to be careful about how much importance we place on treating Christianity as a worldview. Still, what we and others believe is a vital part of our lives, and so the worldview concept has some usefulness in identifying what Christianity is and therefore has some usefulness for apologetics.

In this chapter, then, we explore some of what Scripture teaches that we ought to believe about the five subjects that comprise everyone's worldview.

2. Warfield, "Idea of Systematic Theology," in *Works* 9:83.

## A CHRISTIAN WORLDVIEW

While it is important to understand the limitations that come with regarding Christianity as a worldview, the concept is not without its advantages. The good news of what Jesus accomplished in his life, death, resurrection, and ascension impacts all reality because Jesus is the creator and sustainer of all reality and the redeemer of creation, and of all those who put their trust in him. In other words, Jesus affects all things in heaven and on earth precisely because he is God and Lord of heaven and earth (Col 1:15–20). The covenant that Jesus fulfills is not simply between God and his people, but also between him and all creation (Gen 9; Jer 33:20–26; Rom 8:17–25). God created humans in his image to be fruitful, multiply, fill the earth, and subdue it; we were created to rule the earth on God's behalf. Such ruling, of course, is not a license to exploit creation for our narrow self-gratification. Nor does human dominion over the earth automatically lead to exploitation. One of the things this doctrine teaches is that all of what humans were intended to do is impacted by human sin. Therefore, the redemption from sin secured by Jesus results in consequences that reach as far as the original creation mandate, and the rebellion against it reached. The eighteenth-century hymn writer Isaac Watts was correct: Jesus came "to make his blessings flow far as the curse is found."[3] This means that biblical Christianity touches upon every subject matter of life. This is why the worldview concept can sometimes be helpful in expressing biblical Christianity. In turn, such a worldview analysis can sometimes help us show people that Christianity does not merely touch upon one or a few aspects of life, but impacts all of life, just as everyone's worldview does.

Since we have seen that one of the ways of analyzing a person's worldview is according to what they believe about metaphysics, epistemology, theology, ethics, and anthropology, let's explore some of what the Bible directs us to believe within each of these five subjects. Keep in mind that what follows is not intended to completely cover all of what Christians necessarily ought to believe regarding these five subjects. Rather, it is meant to express those beliefs that ought to be believed, and which then serve to direct our thinking about that subject and those matters related to it.

3. See Watts's hymn "Joy to the World."

## METAPHYSICS

The God of the Bible (the Old and New Testament) is the creator who has created all realities or allowed them to come into being. I phrase it this way because, while sin currently exists within God's creation, God is not the creator or author of sin, but he has allowed it to be in his creation for a time. God is life (Gen 1; John 1). God created by speaking his word (Gen 1; Ps 33; John 1; Col 1; Heb 1). Genesis 1 tells us that the Spirit of God was present at creation, and so we are correct to understand life as a joint effort of God's Word and Spirit. All reality has existence only by the will of God. God sustains all reality. Or, as Col 1 expresses it, "In him all things hold together," or as Heb 1 states, "He upholds all things by the word of his power." The Creator and creation are distinct, but not separated. God is not dependent on the creation for his being, or his purposes being fulfilled, but every aspect of the creation is dependent on God for its existence, for what it can do, or what it is allowed to do (Acts 17:22–28). The invisible God is known through the visible creation that he created, yet that knowledge of God that is only accessible through the visible creation can only give humans enough knowledge to make them accountable for their sin against God. All humans have this kind of knowledge of God (Rom 1:19–21).

There is a physical and a spiritual "realm" of, or to, reality. These realms are distinct, but not separated, and so there is an inseparable union between the physical and spiritual "realms" of reality. This is seen perhaps most clearly in that Jesus is God's Word made flesh (John 1:1–5; Heb 1:1–4; Matt 1:18–25; Luke 1:26–38). There are particular spiritual realities that are demonstrated in analogous and typological ways by physical realities. We learn of these analogies and typologies in God's written word (see Gen 1–3; 1 Tim 2:13–15; Gen 12:1–3; Heb 11:8–16; Rom 4:13; Rev 21:1–4; Gen 15, 17; Rom 9:6–9 and Heb 11:11–12; Gen 22:1–19; Heb 11:17–18). There was a beginning point to created realities. The only reality that does not have a starting point is the Trinitarian God. All created realities were originally good according to God's standard of goodness, which is, ultimately speaking, the only true or right standard. Sin or evil is not a created reality for which God is morally culpable, and its "origin" is not made exactly clear in the Bible, though we do know that its "presence" in human history is the result of the work of Satan. God allows evil to exist for a time, but there will come a time when Satan, evil, and all its consequences will be destroyed. Human language at some points limits us in what we can explain regarding these realities.

The creation fell under God's curse through the sin of Adam (Gen 3). Through Jesus, who is both God and man, the creation has been, is being, and will be rescued from the corruption of and bondage to sin (Rom 8:17–25; 1 John 3:8). History, or the time/space realm in which humans live, had a beginning, is the outworking of God's purposes, and will have a stopping point, at which time Jesus will render a final judgment on the living and the dead (Gen 1; Heb 1; Matt 24). All of history is characterized by a conflict, set in place, governed, and won by God. This conflict is ultimately between God and Satan and incorporates realities that are visible and invisible to humans. All people are involved in this conflict, as they either consciously side with God or consciously or unconsciously side with Satan.

What a thing or person is (what God created it to be or has allowed it to become) determines what it, or he or she, does. What a thing or person does reveals what they are (Matt 7:15–20; John 8:43–47). Thus, being comes before doing, which also includes knowing, and God is the source and sustainer of all being.

## EPISTEMOLOGY

All humans are able to possess true knowledge of God, themselves, and visible and invisible realities, because they are created in God's image and God enables them to truly know (Gen 1:26–28; Rom 1:18–25). Only those who place their faith in the Lord Jesus Christ for salvation are able to rightly know. Christians are able to consciously know that what they know, they know in relation to the Triune God, and it leads them to place their trust in Jesus for their salvation from sin (Ps 25:1–5; Prov 3:5–8; John 8:31–32; 2 Thess 2:13). All knowledge claims are made on the basis of faith in some authority. The faith that non-Christians exercise in their knowing process differs from the faith that the Christian exercises for salvation in at least two discernible ways—its object and its detectability. First, the non-Christian's faith, though having an object, namely themselves, does not result in the same thing as the Christian's faith. Second, even though there is a difference in object and results, the non-Christian is still exercising a religious and epistemological faith, whether or not they are consciously aware that they are exercising faith. Since God created all the objects of human knowledge, and human beings in his image, all human knowing is a theological or religious matter. God is the source of all knowledge, for he is either the source of all reality or its providential governor that allows it to exist. God knows everything. He is omniscient. God's knowledge of all things is for us a necessary correlate of his creating, sustaining, judging, and redeeming activities. In other words, it is right for us to infer that because God created, sustains, judges, and redeems, he must be all-knowing or omniscient. The Bible, however, does not simply imply that God knows all things, but also states it (Ps 147:5; John 21:17; Heb 4:12–13; 1 John 3:20). Humans know truly because God truly reveals knowledge. God's Word, written and made flesh, and his Spirit are the means through which God reveals knowledge because it is through God's Word and Spirit that he (1) creates the objects or subjects known, and (2) by which he reveals the truth about these objects and subjects. God is not only the means by which we know, but also is *that* which we know, because all creation truly reveals God, is the means through which humans serve God, and it finds its fulfillment in God (Rom 11:33–36). Since God is the creator and redeemer, all things serve his purposes and are only rightly known in relation to him. Thus, a Christian epistemology recognizes theology as "the Queen of the Sciences."

All human knowledge is inherently systematic because it is ultimately about knowing the Triune God. That is, because God is Triune, three persons in one being, we only know him in his Trinitarian relations. Thus, unity and diversity is an inherent aspect of who God is. The divine nature of God as three-in-one is seen in the creation. Part of what this means is that we know in relationships. That is, we only know one reality as it relates to other realities (Gen 1–2). All our knowledge is marked by us relating one object of knowledge to other objects of our knowledge. Human knowledge is the expression of a systematic theology. This systematic theology can be evaluated as to its accuracy to what Scripture reveals as true. To the degree that we learn the Scriptures and think and act in accordance with what they reveal as true, then to that degree our systematic theology and all our knowledge will be in accord with the Scriptures. Only biblical Christianity possesses and teaches the biblical doctrine of the Trinity, and therefore, only biblical Christianity can give a credible answer for how humans can know and answer the question of how there can be true unity and true diversity simultaneously.

Unregenerate humans do have some true knowledge of God and created realities (Ps 19:1–6; Rom 1:18–32; 2:1–16). The visible realities reveal God's invisible attributes. However, this knowledge does not reach its "proper" resting point (the glory of God) in non-Christians in the same way that it does in the Christian, because the non-Christian both refuses and is unable to acknowledge the origin and proper resting point of this knowledge (Rom 1:18–25; Eph 4:17–19). The means by which anyone knows anything is rooted in, or based on, God. Humans both deny and distort truth because of their sin (Rom 1:18–32; Eph 4:17–19). God must overcome sin in order for humans to have true knowledge, and he must redeem fallen sinners if that knowledge is to be properly understood in relation to the Trinitarian God (John 1:1–18; 2:29; 3:1–21; 5:30–47; 8:31–47). As such, the knowledge the unregenerate possesses simply makes them accountable for their sin; it does not lead them to be redeemed from it (Rom 1:18–25). Unregenerate humans are able to attain a significant degree of knowledge, and some have and do. There is only one reality for humans to live in, and in order to live in it humans must possess some true knowledge of it.

Saving knowledge of God is mediated through God's Word, written and made flesh (John 1; Col 1; Heb 1). The term "knowledge" in Scripture refers most fully to not only a cognitive comprehension that results in the ability to express correct propositions about something—statements that correspond to what actually is—but also results in the ability to exercise one's being in obedience to God's law. Knowing, then, is ultimately an activity that encompasses the whole person. Knowledge is a moral and intellectual issue since morality and the intellect can never be separated in a Christian view of God, humans, and knowledge. Repentance leads to the knowledge of the truth (2 Tim 2:25). Many knowledge claims can be empirically evaluated because reality does not originate with humans, and is not what it is by virtue of human apprehension or affirmation of it. Yet, reality can be accurately perceived through a person's five senses and rightly reasoned about through the illuminating work of the Holy Spirit governing our interpretation of it by God's word. There is a place for not only a test of rational coherence, but also a test of empirical correspondence with people's knowledge claims, because the Triune God is the creator and providential governor of his creation and overcomes the noetic effects of sin (sin's effect on our thinking and knowing) through his word and Spirit. In the end, then, there is both an objective and subjective aspect to all knowledge claims. There is no such thing as either "pure" objectivity or "pure" subjectivity, because as both finite and sinfully fallen creatures created in the image of God, all humans possess some true knowledge, but this knowledge is always from our finite or limited perspective as we, the knowing subject, experience it. The Triune God alone is the absolute personal being in whom there is a complete and totally true objective and subjective knowledge.

## THEOLOGY

In what follows, I have cited some Scripture texts that support the points I make. I do not try and cite a Scripture text for every sentence. Many of the texts I cite support multiple statements. Many of the texts are taken straight from the citations given in the Westminster Confession of Faith. By doing this I do not mean to imply that the Confession of Faith is the last word in theology to which nothing need be added. Instead, my point is that I believe that the Westminster divines got things correct regarding the doctrine of God. In turn, that previous sentence does not imply that they got anything wrong regarding any of the other doctrines. It does not imply anything regarding the other parts of the Confession of Faith at all. I am dealing in this section with what is sometimes called "theology proper" and, thus, the doctrine of God. My statement is about the Westminster Confession of Faith regarding its doctrine of God. Please do not read into it something that is not there.

There is only one God and he is Trinitarian. This means that the one and only God is three persons in one being. These three persons are God the Father, God the Son—Jesus—and God the Holy Spirit. Humans do not possess the capacity to fully comprehend God. The three persons of the Trinity are of the same substance, equal in power and glory. The Triune God is creator of all that is, is in covenant with his creation, must sustain it if it is to continue to exist, and must redeem it if it is to be redeemed (Gen 3; 6–9; Deut 4:26; 30:19; Jer 33:19–26; Col 1:15–20). God calls his relationship to all things "his covenant" (Gen 6:18; 9; 15; 17: Jer 33:19–26). God is the judge of the living and the dead and will judge all most perfectly and righteously in accordance with his perfect law on "the last day." God is "infinite, eternal, and unchangeable in his being, wisdom, power, holiness, justice, goodness and truth" (Westminster Confession of Faith, Shorter Catechism A. #5; Deut 4:15–19; 33:27; John 1:18; 4:24; 1 Kgs 8:27; Ps 90:2; 139:7–10; 145:3; 147:5; Jer 23:24; Heb 6:17–18; Jas 1:17).

God is the only completely and truly free or independent being. This means that nothing outside of God forces him to do anything.

God has no needs (see especially Isa 40–45). There is nothing outside of God that meets some need or deficit in him. God has all life within himself, and is therefore the only truly self-sufficient being (Gen 1–3). God works all things according to the counsel of his own unchangeable and righteous will for his own glory (Eph 1). God is slow to anger and abounding in lovingkindness; patient, gracious, merciful, and abundant in goodness and truth, forgiving iniquity, transgression and sin; rewards those who diligently seek him; just, hates all sin, and will "by no means clear the guilty" (WCF 2.1).[4] God's knowledge is "infinite, infallible, and independent" (WCF 2.2). It is "independent" in that there is no means outside of himself upon which God relies in order to know the things that are distinct from him, i.e., his creation. God requires and deserves all obedience, service, and worship from his creatures (Exod 20:1–17; Deut 5:1–20). He has by the counsel of his own will foreordained whatsoever comes to pass, yet so that he is neither the author of sin, nor has he violated the will of the creatures, "nor is the liberty or contingency of second causes taken away, but rather established" (WCF 3.1).[5] "Although God knows whatsoever may or can come to pass upon all supposed conditions, yet he has not decreed anything because he foresaw it as future, or as that which would come to pass upon such conditions" (WCF 3.2). In other words, no aspect of creation is operating outside of the personal governing control of God.

God directs, disposes, and governs "all creatures, actions, and things, from the greatest even to the least, by his most wise and holy providence" (WCF 5.1; cf. Isa 40–45: Matt 5:45; 6:26–34. Notice that it is the doctrine of God that Jesus applies to the most practical matters of human life.). God may act in his creation directly apart from means or indirectly through the use of means. By the decree of God, for the manifestation of his own glory, some people and angels are predestined to everlasting life, and others foreordained to everlasting death (WCF 3.3). Such "people and angels are particularly and unchangeably designed, and their number is so certain and definite, that it cannot be either increased or diminished" (WCF 3.4). Those predestined to life were chosen in Christ before the foundation of the world out of God's "mere free grace" (Eph 1:3–14;

4. WCF stands for the Westminster Confession of Faith. Puritan pastors and theologians produced this document from 1643–47.

5. To say that God is not the "author" of sin is to say that he is not blameworthy for it. He still governs it, and has allowed it to exist (another controversial thought about sin) for a time in his creation.

2:1–10; Rom 9; WCF 3.5) "without any foresight of faith, or good works, or perseverance in either of them, or any other thing in the creature, as conditions, or causes moving him thereunto; and all to the praise of his glorious grace" (Eph 1:3–14; 2:1–10; WCF 3.5). God obligates himself to save particular people from sin, but he is not obligated to save anyone from sin past what he has obligated himself to do.

God has also appointed and sovereignly disposes those means by which his elect and the unregenerate reach the goal he has for them. Both those elect, or born again to a living hope, and the unregenerate are recipients of God's mercy and justice, yet in different ways. The difference between the two groups is in the degree to which they receive God's mercy and justice, and what results from what they have received. God would be perfectly just and glorified in condemning all humans to hell, but does not, simply out of his mercy and grace. A standard of justice that we devise cannot be used against God, because God *is* the standard of justice.

God became a man at a particular place and time through the miraculous work of the Holy Spirit overshadowing the Virgin Mary bringing about the birth of the baby Jesus (Matt 1; Luke 1–2). Jesus, as fully God and fully man, perfectly obeyed the law of God, paid the God-appointed death penalty for disobedience to his law by being crucified on a cross (the curse of his covenant), was buried, rose bodily and victoriously over the grave, walked and taught among his disciples for forty days after his bodily resurrection, ascended into heaven, and intercedes for his sheep, or people, at the right hand of the throne of God.

Jesus is king and head of the church, his body, which he purchased with his own blood, and continuously intercedes for those who are his. Jesus has all authority in heaven and on earth, and is exercising his royal authority to build his church and kingdom. The Father and Son sent the Holy Spirit to take that which belongs to Jesus on account of his perfect righteousness, sacrificial death, and victorious resurrection and apply it to those for whom Jesus died (John 10:15, 26; 15:26; 16:5–15) and chose before the foundation of the world (Eph 1:3–14). The Holy Spirit must make God's word known to people, or illuminate them, and regenerate them in order for them to repent and place their faith in Jesus (1 Cor 2:1–16; Titus 3:3–7). The work of bringing the new birth is also attributed to God the Father and the word of God (1 Cor 1:30; 1 Pet 1:3, 23; Jas 1:18).

God is bringing his created order to the goal he always had for it. God's covenant that Jesus fulfills is with all creation, as well as his covenant people (Gen 9:1–17; Deut 4:26; 30:19; Jer 33:19–26; Rom 8:17–25; Rev 21:1–8). Central to this fulfillment is the preaching of God's word through the church by the men gifted and called by God to do it (John 8:31–36; Rom 1:16–17; 10:14–17; 2 Tim 3:16—4:2). God uses means, often referred to as the "means of grace," to fulfill his promises to and through his people.

## ETHICS

God is good and is therefore the standard of all goodness. God determines what constitutes the good. We know the good through God's general revelation in creation and special revelation in his written word and Word made flesh—Jesus. Both God's creational revelation (that which only comes from the creation, also known as general revelation) and saving revelation are sources of knowledge of God's goodness, but God's creational revelation can only give enough knowledge of God's goodness that leads sinners to be accountable for their sin (Rom 1:18–25). In other words, people do not know God's good will through general or creational revelation alone, nor can people possess the ability to do God's good will that leads to salvation through general or creational revelation alone.

All humans, after the sin of Adam, are, in their nature, not good; that is, we are sinners; that is, we fall short of God's glory or the ideal that God designed for us (Rom 3:9–20, 23). Though by nature we have some knowledge of the good, even this knowledge is thoroughly corrupted by us (we are the sinner) so that apart from a merciful act of God we remain ignorant of much of what is ultimately, and sometimes immediately, good. Ultimately, we neither desire nor do what is ultimately good. This is not to say that unregenerate people, or those not resurrected from the spiritual dead, cannot possess some knowledge of what is good. They in fact do possess some knowledge of it, but that knowledge remains so corrupted by their sin that, in the final analysis, Scripture characterizes their thoughts and deeds as "not good" or sinful. Every sin, or failure to conform to and practice God's law, is worthy of death (Rom 6:23). As we come to know the good that is centered in and on Jesus and obey God's word, we grow in our understanding or knowledge of what is good.

All people ought to be like God, which is to say that we all ought to be like Jesus in that we ought to possess his moral character traits. God's children—those who have salvation—are commanded to imitate God (Eph 5:1; Rom 8:29), but it is by no means self-evident what this means. Since God is unique, there is a definite sense in which we are not like him. This means we cannot simply think that the question "What would Jesus do?" fully captures our ethical situation and directs us properly. What something *is* determines what it does. Since we are sinners, and never totally lose that identity or nature in this life, we can never perfectly imitate God. Moreover, we would have no desire to do so were it not for the sovereign redeeming work of God in us by his word and through the Holy Spirit. This means that for Christian living, ethical imperatives (what we are to do) are always preceded by the electing indicative (what is) of the Father, Son, and Holy Spirit (Exod 20:1–17). All that we think, do, and say ought to be for the glory of God (1 Cor 6:19–20; 10:31). Though all people are sinners, they are still created in God's image, and should be treated with dignity and respect. What is most fundamental about humans is not sin, but that they are created in God's image. Jesus is fully human and is without sin. Christians are not to identify themselves, or refer to themselves, by highlighting their sin or any particular sins.

Understanding what is good is dependent on our recognizing that the term is used in the creation account to refer to the reality that all God originally created did all he intended for it to do. This meant that all things occupied their proper place and performed their intended function in God's created order. If we are to begin to think biblically about what is good in situations not explicitly addressed in Scripture, we must have a right understanding from Gen 1–2 of the order God created. Our understanding of the created order is aided when we understand what sin did to that order, as revealed in Gen 3. The three creation realities, or what some refer to as ordinances, that form the order in which humans are to live are: sabbath, work, and marriage/family. There are at least three fundamental questions in ethics: (1) What sort of person ought we be? (2) What goals ought we pursue? (3) What practices ought we do?[6] It is the law of God, which is summarized in the Ten Commandments, that is good, and ought to be obeyed. Those who have been truly born again, or regenerated by God, seek to obey God's commands through the Holy Spirit who works in them enabling them to obey.

The biblical idea of goodness is united to its idea of beauty. In both the Hebrew Old Testament and Greek New Testament, the terms most

6. Jones, *Biblical Christian Ethics*.

often used for "good" are sometimes translated "beautiful" or "beauty." The other terms are, in other places, translated "splendor," "attractive," or "pleasant," depending upon the context. The notion that something or someone is beautiful or possesses beauty communicates that they are attractive or appealing in some way, that there is something good about them, or something good about it, as the term *good* is defined by God's word. This beauty can be either physical or spiritual, that is, either external or internal, or both. When addressing a person's spiritual or internal beauty, Scripture is referring to moral character. As a result, there is a moral component to even beauty, so that we can say that people ought to have particular responses to what is in fact beautiful—namely, they should give God praise for it in some way.

One of the most common Hebrew terms used for "good" is the word *tov* or *tob*. It is this term that is used throughout Gen 1 and is used in 1:31, when it tells us that God saw all that he had made and, behold, it was very good. It is also this term that is often translated "beautiful." Part of the profundity of the creation account in Gen 1 is that it establishes for us an organic union between the physical external world that God created and the spiritual and internal world of morality. God, who is invisible to us except in the God-Man Jesus, has moral attributes; he is holy, righteous, just, merciful, good, and kind. Romans 1 tells us that in creation God's internal power and divine nature are seen. That is, the beauty of God's moral character is seen in the physical beauty of creation.

## ANTHROPOLOGY

Humans, both male and female, are created in the image of God, were originally sinless, and had perfect communion with God, each other, and exercised dominion over the creation. Now, after Adam's fall into sin, all people are "by nature children of wrath" (Eph 2:3), or sinners, who fall short of the glory of God. This means we have a communion with God and each other that is corrupted and distorted, not obliterated, and are without hope of salvation, or fulfilling our intended purpose, except for the sovereign mercy and grace of God in Jesus Christ through his Holy Spirit. Since humans are finite creatures, they have always existed in a relationship with God based on faith. This is true for all humans whether they recognize it or not. Humans are most accurately described as being comprised of body and soul. The terms in the New Testament for "soul," "spirit," "mind," and "heart" do not, in the end, refer to different parts or aspects of our being, but are different ways of referring to the same fundamental reality. Humans can be thought of as performing three basic functions—we think, feel, and act—and these three functions are inseparably and organically united. Thus, there is an intellectual, affective, and volitional component to everything we do.

When summarizing the gospel, Scripture (Rom 1) categorizes all people as either true or false worshipers. All of human life can be understood as worship, and if we are to think about the communication of the gospel to humans, in accordance with how Scripture teaches us to think of them, then one of the chief ways in which we are to do this is from the subject, or perspective, of worship. Human worship is expressed in the thoughts humans believe are true, the desires that they believe are satisfying or fulfilling, and actions they believe are good. Humans are identified as being sinful, and this means that it is the whole person, in the entirety of their being, who is corrupted and ruined by sin. We are sinners. Humans are, therefore, described as being both unable and unwilling to worship God correctly or able to please him (Rom 8:5–8). We do not exercise our will apart from the condition of our heart or soul. Humans, like plants (Matt 7:15–20), do that which proceeds from what they are.

Unregenerate or non-Christian people, though knowing and doing some of God's righteous standard, nevertheless embrace thinking and living that is corrupted by their sin (Rom 2:15). Therefore, we ought to question to what degree truth, wisdom, and beauty can be discerned and experienced in the lives of those in rebellion against Jesus (Rom 12:1–2; 1 John 2:15–17). This is not to say that non-Christians won't seek to embrace some of God's truth or wisdom. Nor is it to say that we cannot experience God's truth, wisdom, and beauty outside of the church. The non-Christian must embrace some of God's truth, wisdom, and beauty in order to live, because God is life. Yet, the primary place from which all people will discern and experience God's truth, wisdom, and beauty is in God's written word, in the lives of God's redeemed people, and through the visible church. Truly, the created order reveals the invisible attributes of God, yet this creation must be interpreted in light of God's written word. It is therefore within the covenant community of God—the church—where truth is to be found and ought to be sought (Matt 16:16–19; Eph 4:1–16; 1 Tim 3:1–15). Because all people live in the one creation that is being redeemed by God, all people must experience God's grace to some degree. The church of the living God is the eternal community he created in order to dispense his grace and mercy in word and deed for the regeneration and renewal of people.

The life of a human is ordered according to three primary relationships: our relationships to God, other humans, and the creation. These three relationships correspond to the creation realities or ordinances of sabbath, marriage/family, and work (Gen 1–2). All of humanity can be categorized according to the great conflict set in place, governed, and won by God between the seed of the woman and the seed of the serpent (Gen 3:15). All humans ultimately, therefore, receive either God's covenant blessing or curse. All humans possess some true knowledge of God that causes them to be held accountable for their sin, but only those to whom God chooses to reveal himself in a saving way have enough true knowledge of God to save them from their sin (Matt 11:25–27). All sin has consequences that affect humans and their several relations in a variety of ways. No person is as sinful as they possibly could be because of the restraining grace of God preventing them from fully following their sinful condition.

The foundation of all social relations between humans is the family. A family is the marriage of one male (man) to one female (woman) and any children God chooses to bless them with, either through physical birth of children to the husband and wife or adoption. The marriage of one woman to one man is an analogy of Christ's relationship to the church (Eph 5). A male cannot be married to another male or a female married to another female, because they cannot be united to become one flesh as designated in Gen 2. Humans find their fulfillment as they receive salvation in Christ, and thereby become members of his church or family. Salvation in Christ, in other words, is a profoundly social matter that involves one's participation in God's family. When a husband conducts himself in relation to his wife and whatever children they may have in obedience to the Scriptures, he reveals his fitness for leadership in the church.

When humans die, their soul is separated from their body, and their soul either goes to be in the presence of the Lord or is banished to Hades, and awaits the resurrection on the last day, when their body and soul will once again be reunited, and they will forever with the Lord. The saved will pass out of judgment and enter into the glorious kingdom of the Lord Jesus in the new heavens and new earth, while the unrepentant will have both body and soul destroyed in hell for eternity (Matt 25:31–46; Luke 23:43; Phil 1:23; Rev 20:11–15; 21:1–8).

## CONCLUSION

Needless to say, there is much more that could be said about each of these five subjects. Countless books have been written about simply one seemingly small aspect of some of them. These five summary statements, however, are meant to present the basic structure of what constitutes Christian thought and belief about each of the five subjects. Yes, of course, there is disagreement among Christians regarding these matters. We do not conclude from the presence of a disagreement, however, that we are without any truth or correct answers, or that we have no way of knowing which answers are correct. Jesus said that if we abide in his word, we are truly his disciples, and then we would know the truth, and the truth would set us free (John 8:31–32). In other words, knowledge of the truth that sets us free from sin is a *process* that personally confronts us with God or Jesus, who is the truth.

As we keep reading God's word, listening to it preached and taught, and repent of our sin that is uncovered as a result of our reading and listening, we come to knowledge of the truth. Eternal life, according to Jesus (John 17:3), is knowledge of God. Yet, we have already seen that every knowledge claim is intimately related to God because God is the creator, sustainer, and redeemer. It is this matter of epistemology and its union with theology that is perhaps *the* central concern of every worldview, not simply a Christian one. It is certainly at the heart of Christian apologetics, discipleship, and evangelism. Only Christianity gives a credible explanation for what human knowledge is and how it can be possessed. It is to the exploration and explanation of this that we now turn.

# 9

# Exploring and Explaining God's Revelation and a Credible Basis for Knowing

"As all nature, whether mental or material, may be conceived of as only the mode in which God manifests Himself, every science which investigates nature and ascertains its laws is occupied with the discovery of the modes of the divine action, and as such might be considered a branch of theology. And, as on the other hand, as all nature, whether mental or material, owes its existence to God, every science which investigates nature and ascertains its laws, depends for its foundation upon that science which would make known what God is and what the relations are in which He stands to the works of His hands and in which they stand in Him; and must borrow from it those conceptions through which alone the material with which it deals can find its explanation or receive its proper significance."[1]

B. B. Warfield

"It was not without reason that Augustine renounced the knowledge of all else but God and the soul; and that Calvin declares the knowledge of God and ourselves the sum of all useful knowledge. Without the knowledge of God it is not too much to say we know nothing rightly, so that the renunciation of the

1. Warfield, "Idea of Systematic Theology," in *Works* 9:69. For a similar point regarding the theological nature and foundation of human knowledge see Bavinck, *Reformed Dogmatics* 1:209–10.

knowledge of God carries with it renunciation of all right knowledge."[2]

B. B. Warfield

"When we seek to know God obediently, we assume the fundamental point that Christian knowledge is a knowledge under authority, that our quest for knowledge is not autonomous but subject to Scripture. And if that is true, it follows that the truth (and to some extent the content) of Scripture must be regarded as the most certain knowledge that we have. If this knowledge is to be the criterion for all other knowledge, if it is to govern our acceptance or rejection of other propositions, then there is no proposition that can call it into question. Thus, when we know God, we know Him more certainly, more surely than we know anything else. When He speaks to us, our understanding of His Word must govern our understanding of everything else. This is a difficult point because, after all, our understanding of Scripture is fallible and may sometimes need to be corrected. But those corrections may be made only on the basis of a deeper understanding of Scripture, not on the basis of some other kind of knowledge."[3]

John M. Frame

## INTRODUCTION

We have already explained that the Scriptures of the Old and New Testament are the ultimate authority for the truth claims that a disciple of the Lord Jesus makes. Of course, there are other authorities upon which we base truth claims. Yet, all of them are dependent upon the Trinitarian God's existence. In other words, it is the Bible that warrants us relying upon what we might call secondary authorities for knowledge or truth claims. Furthermore, it is not merely the Christian who has God and Scripture for their ultimate authority for knowledge but also the non-Christian, despite denials to the contrary. In this chapter we explore and explain not only some of the relationship between these secondary authorities, but also their relationship to the Triune God. Thus, we will explore and explain how only Christianity gives us the explanation for how

2. Warfield, "Task and Method of Systematic Theology," in *Works* 9:97.

3. Frame, *Doctrine of the Knowledge of God*, 44–45.

people can possess true knowledge. Along the way, we will address some of the more basic matters involved in making claims to true knowledge.

## AUTHORITY, KNOWLEDGE, AND TRUST

If someone wanted to know the outcome of any Major League Baseball World Series over the past several decades, they could rely upon the official records of Major League Baseball, or they could rely upon the testimony of eyewitness accounts from those who watched those games. In either case, epistemologically speaking, the authority upon which the person would be receiving the knowledge claim would still be considered *secondary*. It is secondary because one still trusts an authority that is actually dependent upon another authority for the knowledge. So, even if I trust my personal experience to give me true knowledge, then I am still trusting that my senses did not deceive me and that my reasoning about what I perceived through my senses was able to allow me to arrive at true knowledge. Or, consider the fact that there are some people who do not believe that men ever landed on the moon. They do not believe that what was being transmitted to them through the TV was actually taking place on the moon. Well, whatever we might think of that conclusion, we should at least give such people credit for recognizing that one had to trust that what was coming through the TV was actually taking place on the moon. More recently, we have seen this phenomenon emerge with those who deny that the Holocaust (Hitler's overseeing the killing of six million Jews during World War II) ever took place.

What these matters reveal, among other things, is that everyone has to trust some authorities in order to know. *Every claim to knowledge or truth is involved in an intricate web of many related authorities*. Yet, ultimately, this network of interrelated authorities must rest upon one ultimate authority. According to Christianity, that one ultimate authority is the Triune God. Among other things, this reveals that all secondary authorities can only be considered legitimate to the degree that they correspond to what Scripture reveals about human knowledge, and matters related to it.

Biblical apologetics, and the whole Christian faith, can be thought of from the perspective of what you know and the basis upon which you know it. Of course, in the Christian conception of knowledge the "*what*" is ultimately a "*who*," namely God. John 1:1–5 speaks to this latter point.

> In the beginning was the word, and the word was with God, and the word was God. He was in the beginning with God. By him all things were made, and apart from him nothing was made that has been made. In him was life, and the life was the light of men; and the light shines in the darkness, and the darkness has not overcome it.

Of course, it is no accident that John began his Gospel in a way similar to the way the Old Testament begins.

> In the beginning God created the heavens and the earth, and the earth was formless and void, darkness covered the surface of the deep and the spirit of God hovered over the surface of the water. And God said, "Let there be light." And there was light. God saw that the light was good, and he separated the light from the darkness. God called the light "day," and the darkness he called "night." And there was evening and there was morning, the first day. (Gen 1:1–3)

John reveals that the one who spoke creation into being is none other than the Lord Jesus. God took physical flesh and became a man. He took up space in one place, for a time, in his own creation, and was seen and heard and touched, as well as whipped, beaten, crucified, and he rose from the dead. The Christian account of Jesus is that he is the creator who became a creature. Yet, just as he brought life where there was no life, in his original act of creating, because he is life itself, he also rose from the dead, bodily. The organic union between us and God has been manifested most clearly and vibrantly in the Lord Jesus Christ. We have union with God through the Lord Jesus Christ. So, John wrote his Gospel that we might believe that Jesus is the Christ (the Messiah), and that by believing we might have life in his name (John 20:31). We have knowledge of God through Jesus, and this has profound implications for our knowledge of anything and everything.

According to Scripture, any knowledge claim in any branch of knowledge is ultimately related to Jesus and theology, because Jesus is God, the creator of all reality who is present and revealed in it. As we explore more precisely the character of human knowledge, we discover that there are seven essential aspects to it, and that only Christianity can account for all seven, because only Christianity affirms the biblical doctrine of the Trinity—that God is the Father, the Son, and the Holy Spirit, who is the creator and redeemer. Let's explore this thesis in greater detail.

## EXPLAINING THE SEVEN NECESSARY ASPECTS OF EVERYONE'S KNOWLEDGE

There are seven aspects of human knowledge that are part of one organic whole. Unavoidably, this means that each of the seven are constituent parts of one another. They are listed in no particular order. They are:

1. Authority
2. Trust or Faith
3. Objective or Empirical Data
4. Subjective Personal Experience
5. Reasoning
6. Witness
7. Exhaustive Knowledge

Only the biblically Christian worldview provides an intelligible basis for being able to say that humans possess true knowledge, because it alone can account for all seven aspects of everyone's knowledge claims, although every worldview makes claims to knowledge! This is a glaring inconsistency possessed by all non-Christians. A Christian perspective on knowledge teaches that knowledge is present because God, who knows all things (exhaustive knowledge), has made himself known through the creation, the Old and New Testament, and Jesus (Gen 1–3; Ps 19; 44:21; 135:6; 139; Job 38–42; John 1:1–5; Heb 1:1–4; Col 1:15–20; Rom 1:18–32; 11:33–36). A true understanding of God's revelation leading to salvation comes through the work of the Holy Spirit (Matt 13:1–23; John 14:15–31; 16:7–16; 1 Cor 2:6–16). It is only the Christian who has a credible basis for being able to say that he or she truly knows because his or her knowledge rests on the self-attesting God who knows all things, brings all reality into being, and reveals himself to whom he chooses, in accordance with his own will (Matt 11:25–27; John 1:1–13; 5:18–47). This means that it is God's Word (remember Jesus and the Bible are both referred to as "God's Word") that is the basis or authority upon which the Christian has knowledge of anything. In the end, it is also why God's Word is the basis or authority upon which anyone has knowledge.

God's Word is also the basis or authority upon which the non-Christian knows anything, although the non-Christian does not acknowledge this. Everyone knows what he or she knows by virtue of God's revelation.

In fact, it is God's revelation of himself that is known when people know anything, because everything, in some way, reveals God or his attributes (Ps 19; Rom 1). Even sin is only truly known in relation to God, because it is a violation of God's will and a lack of conformity to his glory (Gen 3; Rom 2, 3). Therefore, it takes knowledge of God's law in order to rightly understand sin. The Triune God of Scripture has all knowledge, or exhaustive knowledge, and is able to reveal knowledge to people. One of the things God knows is how to make you and I know. He makes us know by revealing himself in and through what he creates (Ps 19:1–7; Rom 1:20), and speaking and interpreting his written word to us through the power of his Spirit (John 1; Heb 1; Col 1; 1 Cor 2:6–16). It is one of the Holy Spirit's functions to reveal truth to those whom God chooses to reveal it (John 14–16).

This means that all aspects of everyone's epistemology are defined and intelligible, or understandable, by the Scriptures of the Old and New Testament. Of course, some might quickly object and claim that this is to "argue in a circle," because the basis of my reasoning is God's word and I am arriving at the conclusion that God's word is trustworthy as my source of truth. All correct. But this is where we must explain to people that ultimately everyone argues in a circle; we have no other choice. As finite beings we must place our faith or trust in some authority by which we make knowledge claims and by which we reason. The real question with respects to our knowledge claims is not whether we ultimately argue in a circle, but whether the authority upon which we rest our knowledge claims can account for all the factors that must be accounted for in order for us to possess true knowledge. Only Christianity can account for all these factors, because Christianity alone rests on the self-attesting Triune God, who knows everything and can thereby make humans know.

Since Jesus is God, he is authoritative, for he has all authority (Ps 22:28; 24:1–2; Matt 28:16–20). God the Father bears witness to himself through his Son and Spirit (Matt 16:17; 1 John 5:8) and raised up men to witness to Jesus both in the old and new covenant eras (Gen 12:1–3; Exod 2:23—3:10; John 5:37–49; Acts 3:18–26; Rom 3:21–26; Gal 3:6–14; 1 Pet 1:10–12; 2 Pet 1:16–21). Here we ought to note what the New Testament reveals about the relationship of the apostolic witness regarding Jesus to the written and preached word of God. See Acts 13:16–52; 1 Thess 2:13; 2 Thess 2:2, 13–15; 2 Pet 3:14–16; Jas 1:18; Rev 1:1–3, 11, 19. This conforms, also, to how God revealed himself to his people in the old covenant era, and the need for God's people to listen and read (see

Exod 17:14; 20:1; Deut 1:1, 9; 4:1; 6:4–9; 18:9–22). This witness, because it takes place within the created realm of time and space, entails empirical data accessed and understood through a personal, subjective experience (Exod 19:18–20; 20:18–19; Luke 1:1–4; John 1:19–51; 8:31–47; 14:1–15; 1 John 1:1–5; 2:3–6, 25–29). Because the non-Christian's personal experience can only take place within God's creation, and because every person is created in the image of God, the non-Christian cannot help but know some truth about God and his creation. The non-Christian knows such truth because God has made those things known to him or her (Acts 14:15–17; Rom 1:18–25). The non-Christian still reasons rightly to some degree regarding reality, because he or she is created in the image of God and carries within him or her some true knowledge of God. Yet this reasoning, though still dependent on a faith commitment, does not lead the non-Christian to repent of his or her sin, because his or her faith commitment does not rest upon the Lord Jesus.

Because only God has exhaustive knowledge (knows all things), all people must exercise faith or trust in their knowing. As finite, dependent, time-and-space-bound creatures, we receive knowledge by placing our faith or trust in our abilities to make sense of our experience through our reason. Furthermore, we must place our faith or trust in the reason of others and their testimony, or their authority. We see and experience this phenomenon every time we read a book, access a website, or listen to another person's testimony about something they experienced in order to learn something. This faith or trust always extends to the witnesses that we receive and the reasoning behind that witness or testimony. To have a saving knowledge of God, we are called to believe "in" or "on" the Lord Jesus Christ or the Scriptures, God's written word about Jesus. Or, to put it another way, we are called upon to believe God's prophets and apostles to whom God revealed his message concerning Jesus (Matt 7:24–28; John 5:33–47; Rom 10:1–21). The Old Testament prophets and New Testament apostles who wrote Scripture were the primary witnesses who have given us the right interpretation of Jesus and therefore God and upon whom we are to depend for our knowledge of God. It is upon the prophets and apostles or their testimony upon which God builds his church (Matt 16:13–18; Eph 2:19–22). In all of this, we see that the Bible gives the only credible explanation for how people are able to know anything truly, and how a saving knowledge of God that frees us from sin is given to whom God chooses to give it.

## CONCERNS, QUESTIONS, AND OBJECTIONS

Sadly, we live in a skeptical age in which people have many questions about the ability to possess true knowledge, especially of God and eternal matters, and have doubts about how they or anyone can be certain of such knowledge. Yet, this is nothing new. We are under the same burden that B. B. Warfield and those of his time were under over a hundred years ago. Warfield addressed this, in part, regarding the work of Immanuel Kant (1724–1804) and Friedrich Schleiermacher (1768–1834) in relation to his own beliefs about the gospel and apologetics:

> In the wake of the subjectivism introduced by Schleiermacher, it has become very common to speak of such an apologetic [Warfield's] as has just been outlined with no little scorn. . . . The subjective experience of faith is conceived to be the ultimate fact; and the only legitimate apologetic, just the self-justification of this faith itself. For faith, it seems, after Kant, can no longer be looked upon as a matter of reasoning and does not rest on rational grounds, but is an affair of the heart, and manifests itself most powerfully when it has no reason out of itself.[4]

The idea that people's knowledge claims should be accepted as legitimate merely because they believed themselves to be justified in them was already present in Warfield's lifetime. The result was that some Christians well over a hundred years ago believed that you can't "reason people into the kingdom of God." We who live a full century after Warfield's death have seen further maturation of Kant and Schleiermacher's subjectivism. It is not merely thought that reasoning with people is a waste of time, but rather that people can live in their own privately constructed reality. After all, we have people denying the most basic and fundamental realities marking human beings as male and female. We do well, then, to explore some of the concerns, questions, and objections common to all people that arise around the issue of true knowledge.

## THE BIBLE: TRUE TO WHAT IS

The great twentieth-century Christian apologist Francis Schaeffer (1912–84) was known to have stated that there are two primary ways in which a person knows the Bible is true: (1) because God has revealed it as true,

4. Warfield, "Apologetics," in *Works* 9:14.

and (2) because it is true to what is, or it corresponds to what is. In other words, God can immediately act upon a person through his Holy Spirit and cause them to know the Bible is true, or people can know the Bible is true by comparing its truth claims to reality and seeing that they match up. Of course, some Christians object and say that unless God intervenes and changes the presuppositions by which people are interpreting reality, then they will not acknowledge the Bible's truthfulness. True enough. But this does not then mean that the Bible does not correspond to reality or vice versa. The non-Christian's blindness to the truth of Scripture and the truth of reality does not render either the Scriptures or the reality they are experiencing something other than what they are. In other words, the subjective experience of a person does not alter the objectivity of reality. I am afraid that too many professing Christians who may have rightly understood the importance of a person's presuppositions for interpreting Scripture and their life experience have failed to rightly understand the organic relationship between a person's subjective experience and objective reality. In turn, misunderstanding this relationship inevitably influences how one thinks of and engages in apologetics, discipleship, and evangelism.

We are called by God to reason with people, to press the claims of Scripture upon people's intellect or their reasoning. This addresses the process of knowing. Confusion arises when we do not keep the reality of being (that something is) distinct from the process of knowing (how someone comes to know what is). These are organically related but they are not the same exact thing. Part of what we need to recognize is that, in large measure, because of Kant's philosophy, Schleiermacher's theology, and the developments of them, we have seen the dissolving of the reality of being into the process of knowing. Part of the result of this is the disappearance of the true objectivity of reality from our thinking. One of the casualties of this among professing Christians has been the neglect and disparaging of explanations of the rational validity of the Christian faith. Warfield, at the beginning of the twentieth century, expressed the point. I quote him at length because both he and this point have been significantly misunderstood, especially over the past several decades.

> It is equally easy to say that Christianity is attained, not by demonstrations, but by a new birth. Nothing could be more true. But neither could anything be more unjustified than the inferences that are drawn from this truth for the discrediting of Apologetics. It is certainly not in the power of all the demonstrations in the world to make a Christian. Paul may plant and Apollos

> water; it is God alone who gives the increase. But it does not seem to follow that the faith God gives is an irrational faith, that is, a faith without grounds in right reason. It is beyond all question only the prepared heart that can fitly respond to the "reasons"; but how can even a prepared heart respond, when there are no "reasons" to draw out its actions? One might as well say that photography is independent of light, because no light can make an impression unless the plate is prepared to receive it. The Holy Spirit does not work a blind, an ungrounded faith in the heart. What is supplied by his creative energy in working faith is not a ready-made faith, rooted in nothing and clinging without reason to its object; nor yet new grounds of belief in the object presented; but just a new ability of the heart to respond to the grounds of faith, sufficient in themselves, already present to the understanding. We believe in Christ because it is rational to believe in him, not though it be irrational.[5]

When we defend and commend the Christian faith, we are not merely saying that we like it, it makes sense to us, and it may prove helpful to others as they get along in life. This would be to tilt the matter too far in the subjective realm. While the Christian faith is truly the only subjectively satisfying system of belief and way of life, it is just that precisely because it is objectively true for all people, for all times and all places. How people come to know the truthfulness of Christianity is certainly fused with all kinds of subjective experiences in which they are unavoidably involved, but the Bile's truthfulness and that of the Christian faith and life is not determined by those subjective experiences, but rather confirmed by them. So, the subjective confirmation does not create the gospel or the Christian faith and life, nor give it its essential character. Fundamentally, this is why there are arguments to be made and presented to non-Christians, even while these arguments, by themselves, cannot create a Christian.

Whether God causes people to know what is true through the various means he created, sustains, and in which he is present, or bypasses

5. Warfield, "Introduction to Beattie's *Apologetics*," in *Selected Shorter Works* 2:98–99. Perhaps the great irony in this quote is that it is part of Warfield criticizing Abraham Kuyper's organizing of Christian theology that left only a marginal place for apologetics. The irony is found in the fact that so many in the world of Reformed theology in particular have for many years praised Kuyper for inspiring the development of a Christian worldview in the service of Christian apologetics. Yet, in his organization of Christian theology, Kuyper relegated apologetics to a fringe spot and role. While Kuyper has been lauded for having affirmed that there is not one inch of the cosmos over which God in Christ does not declare his ownership of it, he did not, at least according to Warfield, understand very well the implications of this truth for Christian theology as a whole and apologetics in particular.

those means and acts directly upon a person, in both instances it is ultimately the only living Triune God who causes people to know truth. But just because God is the ultimate cause of people coming to know and trust him as their Lord and Savior does not render the explanations by those already regenerated of no consequence for others coming to saving faith in Jesus. It is God's written word, the Old and New Testament, that reveal and confirm these truths. This is revealed even in these seven aspects of everyone's epistemology. As we have seen, the Bible reveals these seven aspects as comprising the Christian's system of knowledge. Yet, these seven aspects are not simply part of the Christian's way of knowing. Everyone operates with these elements, because every person is part of the created order. Thus, there is an objective validity to the gospel and the Christian faith and life. We can see this in the very way in which we normally functioning humans begin to acquire knowledge.[6]

## THE NORMAL HUMAN EXPERIENCE OF ACQUIRING KNOWLEDGE[7]

A little child first begins to acquire knowledge by trusting both their senses and the one raising the child. The child learns to trust the testimony about reality that he or she is given. Gradually, the child's reasoning capacity is developed through this personal subjective experience that the child has with empirically verifiable objects and the testimony of others. Gradually, the child learns that some sources of authority provide reliable knowledge and others do not. Moreover, there are some times

6. By "normally functioning" I do mean to imply that there are humans, due to various birth abnormalities or earthly experiences, for whom the given explanation will not be fully true to varying degrees depending on the abnormality.

7. This is what philosophers and theologians identify as a realist epistemology. For a clear explanation of a realist epistemology see Bavinck, *Reformed Dogmatics* 1:223–33. As Bavinck stated (1:223) endorsing the observation of the early church father Tertullian: "One must first live, then philosophize (*Primium vivere, deinde philosophari*). Natural certainty is the indispensable foundation of science. Scientific knowledge is not a destruction but a purification, expansion, and completion of ordinary knowledge. Every human, after all, accepts the reliability of the senses and the existence of the external world, not by a logical inference from the effect, in this case the representation in his consciousness, to the cause outside of himself, nor by reasoning from the resistance his will encounters to an objective reality that generates this resistance. Prior to all reflection and reasoning, everyone is in fact fully assured of the real existence of the world." Warfield endorsed the same view as can be seen in his essay "Right of Systematic Theology," in *Selected Shorter Writings* 2:219–79.

when an authority is trustworthy to provide reliable knowledge and other times, or circumstances, when that authority is not reliable. Some people, books, institutions, etc., provide reliable knowledge about only particular subjects. If I want to learn about the Civil War, I don't make my primary source of knowledge a grammar of the Greek language. Yet, even with the sources we rely upon for knowledge, we must place our faith or trust in those sources to provide us truth. There is always, however, some related issue to any object of knowledge that could be explored further that might change what I think I know. Yet, none of us can know everything that is possible to know, though we all still make knowledge claims. The only basis upon which we can claim to know, then, requires that somewhere someone must know everything and we must trust that this all-knowing Being communicates true knowledge. This means that both our experience in the world and the Bible teach us that authority, witness, trust or faith, reason, objectively or empirically verifiable data, our subjective experience, and exhaustive knowledge are part of everyone's system of knowing. Only Christianity can account for all seven.

## "SCIENTIFIC" OR RELIGIOUS KNOWLEDGE? ADDRESSING THE FACT/VALUE SPLIT

With any analysis of human knowledge there has to be a recognition of the distinction between the objects that we know and the knowing subject who knows. This distinction has been basic to the exploration of human knowledge and been recognized by all the influential thinkers in the history of human thought. We see this distinction made all the way from the ancient Greek philosophers to the present.[8] This distinction between the objective and subjective aspects to human knowledge is also addressed from the topics of facts and values. Typically, facts are identified with the objective realm and values identified with the subjective realm. As we saw previously, however, we in Western culture are living under the cloud of the philosophy of Immanuel Kant and the theology of Friedrich Schleiermacher that significantly contributed to imposing upon us what has come to be called the "Fact/Value Split or Divide." The following chart shows which topics are placed in each category. As you can see from the chart, particular subjects (topics) and experiences are thought to belong

8. Any reputable history of philosophy reveals this point. For an excellent concise summary of the history of philosophy see Stumpf, *From Socrates to Sartre*.

to one of the two spheres of reality. The biblical metaphysic and epistemology mandates that we think of these as organically united, even while they are able to be distinguished from each other. The two dangers we need to avoid are either (1) disconnecting these realities from each other so that they are conceived as having no meaningful influence upon each other and do not condition one another, or (2) dissolving them into each other so that everything disappears as it were into the individual knower and his or her private experience. Let us remind ourselves of the "Fact/Value Divide" that we looked at previously, as it has been conceived in Western thought as a result of the influence of Kant and Schleiermacher.

## "THE FACT/VALUE DIVIDE": TERMINOLOGY AND CONCEPTS

| **Facts** | **Values** |
|---|---|
| Empirical Data | Personal Experience |
| Objects and Objectivity | Subjective and Subjectivity |
| Reason and Rational Discourse | Faith and Feelings |
| Science, Knowledge, and the Intellect | Spirituality |
| Education and Scholarship | Religion and Theology |
| Politics | Worship |
| Public Policy | Ethics |
| Government and Laws | Interpretation |
| Public | Private |

While the table presents the categories of facts and values as possessing particular subject matters that are divided into two columns, the biblical way to think of the two categories and all of the subject matters is from the perspective of them all residing in a circle in which they mutually affect one another. In other words, they exist in an organic union to each other. In part, this means that there is no such thing as knowledge that is purely or only objective or purely or only subjective. Instead, every knowledge claim and every true bit of knowledge has both an objective and subjective character to it. The real question with respect to any true knowledge becomes: How do the objective and subjective aspects to knowledge relate to each other in my possession of that knowledge?

One cannot live without knowing and claiming to know something. Still further, when we claim to know, we also have some means by which we think we are able to know what we know. Sometimes we even go through a series of tests in order to know, or gain certainty that we know what we think we know. This is true not only for those who are seeking knowledge of objects that can be measured in some immediately empirical way, but also true of those who seek knowledge of objects or subjects that are not so readily empirically verifiable.

For example, if I want to know what happens when I mix two parts hydrogen with one part oxygen, I can mix the elements and observe what happens. Such an experiment can usually be measured rather easily. However, if I want to know the true identity of Jesus of Nazareth, written about in the Gospels, then the method by which I arrive at this knowledge is not so obviously empirical. Yet, it does have an empirical character to it. Knowing the true identity of the Jesus referred to in Scripture involves us in accessing and evaluating empirical data. In the end, though, engaging in a scientific experiment appears to be one type of knowledge and knowledge of Jesus another type. The difference, however, lies not in terms of their being different kinds or types of knowledge per se, but rather in the way all the elements in everyone's epistemology is used in order to gain access to the specific knowledge. In addition, there is also a difference in how these pieces of knowledge appear to us. Because they seem or appear to be different in *kind*, some people make the mistake of believing that they are. When we understand, however, that everyone must rely upon seven distinct factors when making any knowledge claims, and we know what those factors are, then we are better able to see the similarities in all knowledge claims.

## DEFINING "KNOWLEDGE" OR "KNOW"

Most of us probably take for granted what is meant by the terms *know* and *knowledge*, and yet these are often difficult words to define. Since our ultimate authority is Scripture, we need to rely upon it for our definition. Unfortunately, the Bible rarely provides us with what we could call a formal definition of a term. Scripture is certainly not a dictionary in that sense. Most of the time, in order to understand the definitions of particular words given by the Bible, one has to piece together how the term is used in it. This is made more difficult by the fact that a single term can be used in different ways, not only by two or more of the human authors, but also within the writings of one author. For example, one of the reasons why it is difficult to interpret the apostle Paul's writings is that Paul often uses one term in a variety of ways, even within the same passage or verse! This is one reason why word studies can be dangerous, and the conclusions derived from them misleading. Words have meaning in accordance with how an author or speaker uses the word. This does not mean that words do not have a history or have what we might call a common cultural usage. They do. Still, we should not lose sight of the fact that authors and speakers choose words and use words to communicate their intended meaning. Furthermore, even the issue of intended meaning can be slippery, because the ultimate meaning of a term in Scripture is determined by God. We actually might not be able to pin down exactly what the human author had in mind when he wrote, but, in the end, this does not prevent us from arriving at the meaning of the text, because the text's meaning was not, in the final analysis, determined by the human author, but by God. All that to say that we need to exercise caution when trying to acquire *the* definition of a word from the Bible.

## TERMS FOR "KNOW" OR "KNOWLEDGE"

There are a number of words in the original Hebrew and Greek that are translated into English as "knowledge" or "know." Sometimes the Hebrew term *yadah* that can be translated "know" is also used to refer to someone choosing something or someone, or even having sexual relations. Again, we need to be careful that we do not think that every time the term *yadah* was used in the Old Testament that all of what it possibly could mean was in the mind of the human author, or the speaker. In other words, just because *yadah* can mean to have sexual relations does not mean that every use of it carried with it this meaning. So how should we think, in general, about the whole range of meaning of the terms used in the Bible to communicate the concept of knowledge?

The biblical concept of human knowledge is along the following lines: Human knowledge is the acquisition of a cognitive and experiential understanding of a person, object, or concept that corresponds to what God made that person or thing to be and do, or what that concept means within God's revelation, and that leads to at least partial obedience to God.

As a result, the acquisition of this understanding can never be divorced from the person's choices or subjective experience—objectivity and subjectivity are unavoidably and organically joined in human knowledge. This means that as we make choices in life, these choices either move us toward or away from understanding God and what he has created.

## GOD AND THE "FOUNDATIONS" OF KNOWLEDGE

From one perspective, the biblical conception of knowledge is fairly simple: God has all knowledge and he, ultimately, reveals all knowledge that we possess.[9] This knowledge, no matter which way we categorize it, is ultimately theological because it is both from God and reveals God in some way. So, all human knowledge is a subset of God's knowledge, a knowledge that is perfectly comprehensive. God knows everything. As Warfield put it: "Only in God's mind, of course, does science lie perfect—the perfect comprehension of all that is, in its organic completeness."[10]

9. Despite Mark A. Noll's attempt to regard such simplicity as somehow avoidable and even uncharacteristic of the view held by Warfield and the other Old Princeton theologians, the fact is the biblical epistemology is simple and has been affirmed as such by many in the church for centuries, including those at Princeton in the nineteenth century. The problem is that this simplicity offends sinful people who want to avoid its claims on their lives. Those in academic institutions that are not only indifferent, but also often hostile to the lordship of Christ, have a sinful bias that prevents them from admitting the truth about the biblical epistemology. That bias is known as the noetic effects of sin. Scripture speaks clearly to it. The great irony in all this is that Warfield and the other Old Princetonians repeatedly highlighted these noetic effects of sin, and yet have been routinely accused of not doing so. A more accurate account of the historiography on Old Princeton recognizes that the moral clarity with which Warfield spoke of the insufficiency and immorality of the humanistic epistemology of Western academia did not give room for those who had a vested interest in the life of that academy to justify their own position. Needless to say, the historiography regarding the Old Princetonians by much of Western academia has been unwilling to tell the story accurately. Noll's original contention was that Warfield was a product of the teaching of John Witherspoon, and because he believed Witherspoon's beliefs were corrupted by non-Reformed beliefs, so too were Warfield's. This assertion and the link that Noll alleges on various grounds has not merely been refuted by Gideon Mailer and Kevin DeYoung, as Noll is willing to concede (cf. "Afterword," 215–31), but, in various ways, by David B. Calhoun, W. Andrew Hoffecker, Peter Hicks, Jaroslav Pelikan, Paul Helseth, John Woodbridge, Jeff Stivason, Fred Zaspel, and Richard Muller, to name a few, and all prior to Mailer and DeYoung's work. Noll, thankfully, has acknowledged at least some of his inaccuracies. For a more thorough treatment of the historiography on Old Princeton in general and Warfield in particular see Smith, *B. B. Warfield's Scientifically Constructive*, 15–46.

10. Warfield, "Review of *De Zekerheid Des Geloofs*," in *Selected Shorter Writings* 2:119.

This is what theologians for centuries have referred to as *archetypal* knowledge, that God's knowledge is the archetype or supreme example or pattern for human knowledge. Still further, faithful Christian theologians have affirmed that human knowledge should be regarded as *ectypal*, that is, derived from, and in some sense a reflection of, God's knowledge. In the history of Christian theology the way this has been analyzed and categorized is that God's knowledge has been regarded as the archetype of human knowledge, and our knowledge as ectypal of God's knowledge.[11] Since every kind of knowledge is ultimately about God, every kind of knowledge was identified as theological, which in turn highlights the foundational role that the Bible has for human knowledge. All the aspects of epistemology that are needed for anyone to be able to *truly* know anything are *only* met by the biblical epistemology. As we have already seen, those who think they know anything apart from Jesus actually have no credible basis or foundation for their knowledge claim. Some, however, are not comfortable with using this term *foundation* when referring to knowledge claims, because they believe it is rooted in and a reflection of the humanistic and atheistic Enlightenment in Europe in the seventeenth and eighteenth centuries. But, we need not be hesitant to use it.

Much has been written about foundationalism in epistemology. Many faithful Christian philosophers and theologians believe that thinking about knowledge in terms of it having a "foundation" is misguided. In the end, it depends on what you mean by "foundation." Many of the difficulties regarding this matter of foundations in knowledge stem from the intricate relationship between "belief" and "knowledge." When I use the terms "foundation" or "basis" with respects to knowledge, I have in mind one of two things: either (1) those beliefs, or (2) that personal being that makes knowledge a reality. By this, I do not mean to suggest that our beliefs and God are the same. Far from it! This is why I have designated them as two different things. It is important to recognize, however, that either one can legitimately be referred to when speaking of "the basis or foundation of our knowledge." Everyone bases their knowledge claims on something or someone. It was not Descartes or any Enlightenment philosophers who produced this way of thinking about knowledge. The Bible teaches that we are dependent creatures who are part of a creation that is what it is by virtue

11. See Muller, *Post-Reformation Reformed Dogmatics*, 233–38, especially, for the distinction between archetypal theology that God alone possesses and the only possible knowledge of God that humans are capable of as ectypal theology. Both Warfield and Bavinck affirmed these points.

of what God created or allows it to be. We cannot escape the reality that our knowledge, though apprehended by us, and therefore having a subjective element to it, is ultimately rooted in God and his activities, and therefore has an objective element to it as well. Do note that in a biblically Christian epistemology the objective element is an all-knowing subject—God. Thus, biblical Christianity teaches a radical and organic union between the objective and subjective elements in knowledge.

## OUR BELIEFS AND GOD

Our beliefs are an unavoidable part of our entire system of knowledge. If we hold to some beliefs, we will be shut off from knowing particular realities. This is part of the apostle's point in Rom 1. When we fail to believe the truth, we proceed down a path marked by a darkened understanding, twisted desires, and foolish choices (Eph 4:17–19; Rom 1:18–25). On the other hand, if we believe the truth, namely God's word, then this opens us to an experience where we come to a clearer understanding of who people are (including ourselves), what things are, and who God is. From a Christian perspective, however, our whole being, including the way we perceive reality and our beliefs about it, is part of the entire creation. The whole creation is what it is based on what God made it and maintains it to be. Everyone's claims to knowledge in this sense rests on some *foundation* or *basis*. That foundation is the Trinitarian God of the Bible. In fact, God is not only the foundation, but the means and goal of all knowledge claims. That should not be a surprise to those of us who recognize Jesus as the Alpha and Omega; the Beginning and the End; the First and the Last (Rev 1:8). The apostle Paul wrote, "For from him and through him and to him are all things. To him be the glory forever and ever, Amen" (Rom 11:36). Or, as he expressed it in Col 1:15–20:

> He [Jesus] is the image of the invisible God, the firstborn[12] of all creation. For by him all things were created, in the heavens and on the earth, visible and invisible, whether thrones or dominions or rulers or authorities—all things have been created by him and for him. And he is before all things, and in him all

12. The biblical term "firstborn" does not communicate that Jesus is a created being, but rather, as this passage communicates, possessed a position of prominence, and was entitled to certain privileges. The "firstborn" son of a Jewish family, during the time of the Old Testament or covenant, was the one in position to receive the inheritance, or the best part of it.

> things hold together. He is also head of the body, the church; and he is the beginning, the first-born from among the dead; so that he himself might come to have first place in everything. For God was pleased to have all his fullness dwell in him, and through him to reconcile all things to himself, having made peace through his blood shed on the cross, whether things on earth or things in heaven.

## BELIEVING IT DOESN'T MAKE IT SO

Stating that no one knows anything apart from Jesus, though, is not to say that a person must be aware of this truth, or believe it, in order for it to be true. There is an important distinction to make between the *order of being* (that something is) and the *order of knowing* (how anyone comes to know what is). Certainly many people make true knowledge claims every day without acknowledging or understanding the role that Jesus fulfills in making knowledge a reality. The point is not that others have to first acknowledge the function of Jesus in knowledge claims before Jesus is able to have that function. Jesus is who he is, has done what he has done, does what he does, and will do what he will do regardless of what we or anyone else think about him. This is to affirm that there is a fundamental objectivity to human knowledge. In order, however, to better understand anyone's knowledge claims, including our own, we must understand the function Jesus fulfills in human knowledge. Before we explore and explain this in detail, we should clear up some likely common misconceptions regarding the acquisition of and claims to human knowledge.

## RELATIVISM AND AGNOSTICISM

In American culture in particular, and Western (Europe and North America) culture in general, knowledge is generally thought of in relativistic ways. By "relativistic," I mean thinking that knowledge is the individual's perceptions about their relationship to the object that is known. In other words, people think that what they know is largely, if not sometimes completely, determined by their perceptions of what characterizes their relationship to the object that is known. Because this is the primary way in which people think about knowledge, there are at least two realities that often emerge with people in respects to knowledge. Because relativ*ism* denies in significant ways the reality God created, it cannot help but lead the person to contradict themselves in what they affirm and deny. We see this with two important realities that emerge when a person embraces relativism in knowledge.

## CERTAIN OF MY UNCERTAINTY

First, it is often assumed that a person's denial or affirmation of a knowledge claim removes virtually all possibility of the denial or affirmation being questioned. I see this reality express itself when some of my students are completely thwarted by a person's denial of a particular biblical truth. Some of them report matters to me as if the person's denial is the end of the issue. So, it probably bears repeating: a person's denial or affirmation of a knowledge claim does not remove all possibility of the denial or affirmation being questioned. The second reality that emerges in knowledge claims in a culture of relativism is that most people live with a significant amount of uncertainty regarding knowledge claims. One would think that if a person's denial or affirmation of a knowledge claim simply settled the matter, then people would have no sense of uncertainty. Yet, this is often not the case. Depending on the person and subject matter, various degrees of uncertainty will be expressed regarding knowledge claims. Some people appear certain, when in reality they are not. It is pretty apparent from the content of many popular songs, movies, and TV shows in America that uncertainty regarding knowledge claims is rampant in American culture. The late 1990s and early 2000s TV show *The X-Files* ("The truth is out there somewhere." In the meantime we haven't seemed to have acquired it—but we truly know it's out there!) and the late 1990s movie *The Truman Show* are two expressions of this uncertainty in knowledge. Both are the ripened fruit of reducing knowledge to the limited experience of finite individuals within a vast cosmos. A strong dose of agnosticism has affected many people in the West for several decades.

The word *agnosticism* comes from the Greek word *gnosis*, which means "knowledge." When you put the Greek letter alpha or our "a" before it, this gives you the opposite of the term. So *gnosis* means "knowledge" and *agnosis* means "a lack of knowledge," or "ignorance." A theist is someone who believes in a god, while an "a"theist is someone who does not believe in a god. Of course, most thinking people can detect the inherent contradiction in an absolute agnosticism. After all, in the end, the agnostic is saying that he is certain that he knows that he is uncertain! OK, say that slowly, and out loud! So, there isn't only uncertainty in knowledge. We can be certain that we know we are uncertain. So true knowledge of something is possible, and now the agnostic is open to being questioned: How can you embrace with certainty an absolute or radical principle of uncertainty in knowledge? Of course, the answer is: You can't. This is not to say that we are certain of all of our knowledge claims. But agnosticism as an entire epistemological position, which attempts to embrace the idea that we cannot be certain of possessing any true knowledge, is a contradiction. Despite some people's claims to "embrace contradiction" and pass it off as sophisticated, we need to recognize that when someone contradicts themselves, they have said nothing. Saying nothing, by definition, is to have no credible intellectual position of any kind. Yet, some people who want to embrace this radical relativism still want to make knowledge claims. We must reveal to people the contradictory nature of a radical relativism. Furthermore, we must reveal to them every person's knowledge predicament that requires us all to exercise faith as we seek to know or reason about anything.

## KNOWING EVERYTHING OR ANYTHING?

Much of the agnosticism within our culture is the result of people recognizing, at some level of understanding, that in order to know anything truly there must be exhaustive knowledge somewhere, and we must have access to it in some way. Yet, since Western culture makes humans the measure of all things (expressed by Protagoras in the fifth century BC) it sits on an epistemological foundation that caves in. When humans and their experiences are considered the final authority or ultimate foundation for knowledge, skepticism is the result. Humans are obviously limited in their capacities and range of experiences and therefore cannot know all things. Under such a system, the possibility exists that there is still a piece of knowledge "out there" somewhere that would radically alter our understanding of everything that we think we know. So, one of the unspoken creeds of Western culture is: "Since I do not know everything, I cannot know anything." Of course, people cannot and do not truly live based on such a principle, because the statement is a lie and does not correspond to who we actually are, or what actually exists in reality.

## TRUE VS. EXHAUSTIVE KNOWLEDGE

Just because we do not know everything does not mean we do not know anything. Our knowledge of another person is a perfect example of this point. Just because we do not know everything that could possibly be known about another person is no indication that we do not know anything about them. One need not know everything in order to be able to know something. The fact that much of Western culture seeks to operate on the belief that "since I do not know everything, I cannot know anything," and at the same time does not actually live consistently with this belief, serves to illustrate that the non-Christian is inconsistent with his or her principles, and must be inconsistent with them in order to live. In other words, the non-Christian must live on "borrowed capital." That is, the non-Christian must borrow from the biblically Christian belief system in order to actually think and live. This is precisely the case because the Triune God does exist and his whole creation reveals him. Everyone makes knowledge claims and possesses some true knowledge, and we cannot help but do this, because we are created in God's image (Gen 1:26–28; Rom 1).

## THE SEARCH FOR CERTAINTY: THE GOOD, THE BAD, THE NECESSARY

In Western culture, one of the fundamental principles or beliefs regarding knowledge is that knowledge is primarily my perception or interpretation of the things I experience. When held to consistently, this leads to disillusionment and despair, and leads people to try and find meaning in whatever or wherever they choose to find it.[13] Despair and disillusionment follow from thinking that knowledge is primarily, if not completely, my perceptions of the things I experience, because on this basis I can never be certain of anything other than the fact that I had a particular experience. Even then, "knowledge" simply based on my experience, with no governing reference point outside of my experience to direct my

13. This idea of simply choosing the meaning you want your life to have is called existentialism. It is reflected in people thinking that their philosophy to life is supremely justified if they can say, "It works for me." In this we can see the relationship between existentialism (man must choose what meaning there will be to his existence) and pragmatism (good and evil are determined by whether the results we want are achieved).

thinking or interpretation of it, does not allow me to reliably interpret my experience.

Contrary to what many philosophers, theologians, and historians may argue, people can only live when they have some significant degree of certainty regarding their knowledge claims. We could say, "People need some ground to stand on." It is simply a historical, anthropological, and theological mistake to think that certainty in knowledge was simply Rene Descartes's (French philosopher of the seventeenth century) search, or the goal of pre-Enlightenment or Enlightenment thinkers. The search for certainty is part of what it means to be human precisely because we are finite creatures who must live by faith. The problem with respects to certainty is with regards to (1) how much we attempt to acquire and (2) where, or in whom, we try and acquire certainty.

## THE QUEST TO BE GOD

One of the ways we can summarize what it means to be a sinner is that we want to be God. We reveal that we want to be God when we seek to be able to do that which only God can do, or possess those characteristics that only God possesses. One of the ways this desire shows itself is in our attempts to attain a level of certainty that removes the element of faith from our knowledge. God does not operate on faith. God created all things, is the source of all things, knows all things, and interprets all things exhaustively because he created them. God is not dependent on anyone or anything at any time for anything. He is self-sufficient. We, on the other hand, are dependent creatures who are limited in our capacities. We must exercise faith or trust in our quest for knowledge. Yet, like Adam and Eve in the garden, we want to operate without depending on God; we want to operate without having to exercise faith in God. One of the ways this shows itself is through our quest to possess absolute certainty, to remove all doubts. This is a quest to be God. It is chasing after the wind. One might as well try and drink all the oceans. In reality, even the non-Christian has to admit that he or she must exercise faith in someone or something outside of himself or herself in order to know and live. This means faith and reason, for humans, are forever united in this lifetime. Scripture reveals these points as true (Gen 1–3; Jer 17:9–10; Ps 14:1–3; 53:1–3; Rom 1:18–32; 3:9–18; Eph 4:17–19).

## FAITH AND REASON: THEIR INSEPARABLE UNION

A very popular yet misguided understanding of the relationship between faith and reason that is taught within Roman Catholicism, but also embraced by some Protestants, goes like this: God gave us reason by which to know particular realities, but our reasoning can only take us so far. Where reason stops, faith begins or "kicks in." Hence, it is thought that there are truths beyond human reason that can only be accessed by faith. Like all falsehoods, this has a certain amount of truth to it. Unfortunately, it gravely obscures the reality that human reason, by its very nature, entails trust or faith. As finite creatures, we know nothing exhaustively, not even ourselves. There is no time or experience in which our reasoning is not operating on faith commitments. This is the important insight of those who emphasize the need to examine and call into question people's presuppositions that they use to interpret reality. "Faith" does not "kick in" where or when our reasoning takes us "as far as we can go." Human reasoning is an exercise in trusting. As humans seek to reason about any reality, they automatically rely upon faith commitments. It is not otherwise. This is why it is an extremely vital truth to reveal to people that it is not simply the Christian who operates on "faith." Everyone operates on faith all of the time, for all their knowledge claims. When we and others recognize this reality, certain types of questions about everyone's knowledge claims begin to emerge. Some of those questions address the relationship between the object of our faith, our degree of certainty, and our life experiences, which unavoidably involve suffering.

## BIBLICALLY CHRISTIAN CERTAINTY AND SUFFERING

When the apostle Paul wrote, "For I know whom I have believed, and am persuaded that he is able to keep that which I have committed unto him against that day" (2 Tim 1:12), he was writing a confession regarding not only the certainty of his faith in the Lord Jesus Christ as the one and only Savior, who would deliver him from sin, but also why he was not ashamed of his sufferings. Often, people will interpret the experiences of suffering as meaning that the one enduring the suffering had directly caused it by something he or she had done. This way of thinking was expressed by the disciples in John 9 when they encountered a blind man, and asked Jesus, "Rabbi, who sinned, this man or his parents that he was born blind?"

Jesus's response was, "Neither this man nor his parents sinned, but this happened that the work of God might be displayed in his life."

Not all human suffering is the direct result of the sufferer's sin. Yet, this is a common way people think about suffering. The Scriptures teach us that everyone suffers in this lifetime and all suffering is ultimately the result of Adam's sin, even as some suffering is the result of the sufferer's sin. The true disciple of the Lord Jesus will certainly suffer, and one of the results of these sufferings will be that they will bring the true disciple into more intimate fellowship with God. This often brings with it a greater certainty about God. This is directly related, of course, to biblically Christian apologetics because suffering and the submission to authority are the primary topics addressed by Peter in 1 Pet 3, where we find the classic text for apologetics. More specifically, it is faith in, or submission to, God's authority that brings with it true knowledge, and ever-increasing knowledge that produces greater conviction of the truth. Part of our suffering, then, means we must relate to God on God's terms. This means, among other things, accepting what God reveals through his written word and creation regarding how we acquire knowledge.

## CONCLUSION

There have been many movies and TV shows over the past several years that have tackled the subjects of metaphysics and epistemology. Oh, to be certain, they do not announce that this is what they are doing. TV and movie writers and producers, as well as the people that market those shows and movies, are much too shrewd to do that. Instead, they weave a tale using an intriguing or suspenseful narrative and the latest in technology to raise questions about what people think they know, how they think they know it, and how knowledge claims of any kind are fragile at best. One such movie, which is now quite dated (1998), was *The Truman Show*. The movie communicates something profound about how TV and movies, and even technology in general, mediate our perceptions of reality, and direct our lives. It teaches that our perceptions of what we believe is real, grounded in the video image and other technologies, determine for us what we claim to know and what we think is possible. In many ways it is an adaptation of Neil Postman's early 1980s book *Amusing Ourselves to Death*, both of which seem rather old, given the explosion in technological developments. Still, the movie's basic message is still as relevant today as it was then. Indeed, in many ways it has proven to be very prophetic.

The movie ends in a rather provocative way. In the end, Truman breaks out of his TV world that had been created for him while millions of viewers cheer his revolutionary and rebellious act. One is seemingly left with the great moral that humans can also achieve these boundary-breaking acts and live in the reality they choose. Yet, the final scene, after one is caught up in the euphoria experienced by the TV viewers rejoicing with Truman, is the sight of two rather dull-witted fellows staring at a TV, changing the channel from *The Truman Show* and wondering what else there is to watch as the screen goes blank. Truman supposedly broke out of his technologically engineered world, but did he? What real hope do we actually have of breaking free from our human-engineered lives and limitations?

What a tragic and depressing view of people and life. *The Truman Show*, however, helps us see more vividly how one's metaphysical and epistemological beliefs are unavoidably related to one's anthropology. Our beliefs about what humans are, the purpose of human life, and how one can achieve such a purpose are unavoidably connected to what we believe is real and to what (content) and how (methods) we know. *The Truman Show* certainly declares that message, at least in part, but long before it did, God revealed the fully accurate truth about these things in his written word. Only by exploring God's written word and submitting to it will we know the only hope of salvation, be equipped to explain it to others, and, by God's grace, see it established both in others, and even further in ourselves. Only then will we and others know the truth as it is in Jesus that sets sinners free from our greatest limitation—sin.

Apart from the only living and true Triune God revealed in the Old and New Testament, we can have no genuine certainty that what we believe or claim to know is true, because we are simply confined to our own limited perceptions of what we think is a reasonable interpretation of what we experience, even while constantly subjected to a vast universe full of new things to learn that regularly undermine our assured conclusions. But with the Triune Creator and Redeemer of the Old and New Testament we have access to the one who knows everything and can make us know truth. He, and he alone, is the only basis upon which we can have a sure and certain hope through his Son, the Lord Jesus Christ, and by the power of his Holy Spirit.

# 10

# Conclusion

"It is not, strictly speaking, even faith in Christ that saves, but Christ that saves through faith. The saving power resides exclusively, not in the act of faith or the attitude of faith or the nature of faith, but in the object of faith; and in this the whole biblical representation centres, so that we could not more radically misconceive it than by transferring to faith even the smallest fraction of that saving energy which is attributed in the Scriptures solely to Christ Himself."[1]

B. B. Warfield

"Now it would seem a grave mistake to separate the men of the palingenesis from the race, a part of which they are, and which is itself the object of the palingenesis. And no mistake could be greater than to lead them to decline to bring their principles into conflict with those of the unregenerate in the prosecution of the common task of man. They will meet with dull opposition, with active scorn, with decisive rejection at the hands of the world: but thereby they shall win the victory."[2]

B. B. Warfield

1. Warfield, "Biblical Doctrine of Faith," in *Works* 2:504.

2. Warfield, "Review of *De Zekerheid des Geloofs,*" in *Selected Shorter Writings* 2:119. "Palingenesis" is a term that literally means "again born" or, as we would say in English, "born-again," or "regenerated," or the "new birth."

## A REVIEW: APOLOGETICS, DISCIPLESHIP, AND EVANGELISM

Christian apologetics is the defense of the Christian gospel, and that gospel is the good news that the Lord Jesus Christ, by his life, death, resurrection, and ascension, saves his covenant people and physical creation from sin. As the prophet Jonah stated it: "Salvation belongs to the Lord" (Jonah 2:9). King David stated it as well: "Blessed be the Lord, who daily bears us up; God is our salvation. Our God is a God of salvation, and to God, the Lord, belong deliverances from death" (Ps 68:19–20). This salvation is eternal life, or knowledge of God (John 17:3), and therefore is nothing less than the revelation of God, from God, by God, and about God (Matt 11:28–30; Rom 11:33–36) that brings God's kingdom to the whole earth. Just as God brought the creation into being by his Word and Spirit, so too has God re-created deadened sinners by his Word and Spirit (Gen 1:1–2:3; John 1:1–4; Eph 2:1–10; Col 1:15–20; Heb 1:1–4; 2 Cor 4:6; Titus 3:3–7). And precisely because salvation is eternal life or knowledge of the Triune God, we must recognize its comprehensively organic character. Because our salvation is eternal life, we only rightly think of it as that which grows or matures deadened and finite sinners through the historical process that is their physical life, and is organically joined to the historical process of the entire creation. This eternal life is that which progressively causes people to be freed from sin (Gal 3:6–9; Phil 2:12–13; Rom 6:1–15; 8:28–30; Heb 4:1–16; 6:1–3; 10:19–39; 1 Pet 2:14–18; 1 John 1:6–10). Salvation is both definitive and progressive. God in Christ Jesus through the power of the Holy Spirit has won, is winning, and will win the battle against sin and death and the devil.

To believe or trust in the Triune God for salvation is to trust in what he has done, is doing, and will do to "destroy the works of the devil" (1 John 3:8). To evangelize someone to this gospel is to proclaim these truths or this One who alone saves from sin, so that they turn from their sin or repent of their rebellion or disbelief in God, and turn to this God to give them eternal life. Sinners who genuinely do this only do so because this eternal life has already been given to them, enabling them to trust in Christ for salvation. Yet, no sinner who ever does this merely does this once, but rather throughout their life because this initial act of repentance is to be repeated as they continue to "walk in the newness of life" (Rom 6:4; 1 John 1:6–10) and live in the freedom that belongs to the children of God, because "no one born of God makes a practice of sinning" (1 John 3:9). Thus, there is a sense in which everyone who has been evangelized to the gospel continues to be evangelized to it throughout their life, which is why Paul was eager to preach the gospel to the Romans, and other Christians in many other Mediterranean cities (Rom 1:1–15). This experience is nothing less than the powerful call of God to discipleship, to a life of learning about the Triune God, of who he is and what he does as both Creator and Redeemer, of who he is as Lord. Thus, the Christian's discipleship is their perpetual evangelization to the gospel, and, by the very nature of the case, it means them regarding Jesus as Lord, or growing in their recognition of him as Lord, as the one who is holy, so that they are able and ready to explain the reason for their hope in him (1 Pet 3:15). Evangelism is discipleship is apologetics.

But we dare not overlook the obvious. If we are to defend the gospel, then we must know it, and the biblical gospel is, first and foremost, about who God is and what he does, not who the Christian is and what the Christian is doing. Thus, defending the gospel is about the Christian growing in their understanding of how God saves from sin. That it is God and God alone who saves from sin is Warfield's point in the quote about saving faith that begins this chapter. That, strictly speaking, we are not saved by faith likely comes as a startling claim to many faithful Christians, and perhaps especially in the conservatively Reformed and Presbyterian communities that stand fast on the five solas of the Reformation. It seems like a direct contradiction of *sola fides*—by faith alone. It is not. As Warfield went on to say, the most accurate way to speak of our salvation is that we are saved by Jesus through faith in him. The difference between the two statements is simply that the first places too much stress on the person's faith in Jesus and not enough stress on Jesus for the believer's faith. The first places too much (notice the emphasis) stress on what pertains to the individual and not enough stress on what is true of Jesus. Precision matters. According to Warfield, a right interpretation of the Old and New Testaments, and indeed the Westminster Confession of Faith, affirms that sinners are saved by Jesus on account of who he is and what he does. Who the sinner is and what the sinner does must be thought of as subordinate to, and an aspect of, who Jesus is and what he does.[3] It is why Paul wrote the following in Eph 2:10 regarding the Christian's relationship to the Triune God: "We are his workmanship, created

3. I am therefore delighted to see that Kapic, *Christian Life*, has adopted this perspective in his presentation of this biblical doctrine.

in Christ Jesus for good works, which God prepared beforehand, that we might walk in them."

As we have seen, central to correctly understanding the biblical gospel and having any hope of rightly defending it is to recognize its organic and unitary character. Like the DNA that runs throughout every aspect of a living organism and that can be used to identify that organism, so too Christianity has a DNA. This DNA is the gospel, or who Jesus is and what he does. Because of who he is and what he does, three simultaneous actions are produced in the person in whom he has made to become a partaker of his divine nature (2 Pet 1:4)—evangelism, discipleship, and apologetics. Not only should the Christian know that these three activities will mark their life, but also that the organic nature of the gospel means that all the doctrine of the Christian faith and life is united in a living system, not merely a rational one. Indeed, we need to give full weight to the reality that the rational character of the Christian faith and life is only rightly understood as part of a living system. Among other things, this means that the doctrines that the Christian is to set their mind upon nourishes the soul and grows him or her in the grace and knowledge of the Lord Jesus. This spiritual growth, like physical growth, is not always easy to detect, but it eventually works through the individual, changing them so that they improve in their faithful obedience to God's law and demonstrate more of the fruit of God's Spirit. What exactly this will look like in any given person will vary just as the physical features and maturation of people differs, even while marking them as humans. Yet, one of its indispensable aspects is an increasingly improved intellectual understanding of the Christian faith and life that enables that person to be a more faithful apologist for the Christian faith and life.

But this organic growth is not confined to individual Christians, but marks the entire body of Christ, the church. The Christian faith does not merely have an individualized growth component, but a communal one. It is not just individual Christians who grow, but the church and the kingdom of God as well. This growth is both quantitative and qualitative. That is, people are added to the church and kingdom (quantitative) and the people added are nourished, matured, and eventually perfected, and the reign of God over every aspect of human life on earth spreads and develops. God does all this. He acts upon people. He works *in* them and then *through* them. The Christian faith is radically God-centered and therefore God-glorifying. This is why Jesus said that his "yoke is easy" and his "burden is light" (Matt 11:30). This is also why what the

Christian does as Jesus's disciple is to bear witness to who the Triune God is and what he does, or, more specifically, what he has done, is doing, and will do. Ironically, then, the focus in Christian living or in Christian evangelism, discipleship, and apologetics is not on the Christian, nor the church, but on God. As the apostle Paul wrote, "All this is from God, who through Christ reconciled us [his covenant people] to himself and gave us the ministry of reconciliation; that is, in Christ God was reconciling the world to himself, not counting their trespasses against them [those he has and will birth again by his Spirit], and entrusting to us the message of reconciliation" (2 Cor 5:18–19).

This message of reconciliation is the gospel that is the power of God for salvation to all who believe it, and therefore the message of the life, death, resurrection, and ascension of Jesus is also the means to salvation. Thus, the explanation of the gospel is part of the gospel. There is an authoritative interpretation of Jesus given by Jesus, and this is what we have with the New Testament. Jesus chose the men to whom he would explain, and through whom he would establish, God's kingdom on earth. The root of our knowledge of truth (epistemology) is organically joined to a correct theology, and in turn unavoidably joined to our understanding of all reality (metaphysics), since the Triune God is the creator. In addition, our ethics and anthropology are united to these matters, since Jesus is the God-Man who is not only, or even primarily, our example to follow but also, and chiefly, the one who enables us to have saving fellowship with God the Father. Thus, Christianity can and should be regarded as a comprehensive worldview that can be compared to other worldviews that also address these subject matters.

All other worldviews, however, are unable to account for knowledge of truth, because they do not rely upon the Triune God, who is the all-knowing creator and redeemer, who gives knowledge of himself in his rescue of sinners from sin. Thus, only faithful biblical Christianity gives us a credible basis for knowledge. These things not only can be explained, but also must be in order for the Christian faith and life, or the kingdom of God, to be established on earth as it is in heaven. This explanation has been given by the apostles Jesus chose, and has been proclaimed by their preaching it and writing it down. As we are faithful to their message, we become a means of its spreading in accordance with God's sovereign will.

## APOLOGETICS: THE DNA OF CHRISTIAN LIVING AND THEOLOGY

All this is why, at the turn of the twentieth century, B. B. Warfield was a bit perplexed over the Dutch Reformed churchman, statesman, and theologian Abraham Kuyper, along with his compatriot, Herman Bavinck, organizing theology in such a way that they gave a rather subordinate place to apologetics. Despite affirming that every square inch of the cosmos belonged to Christ and over which Christ declared "Mine!" Kuyper and Bavinck placed apologetics in a minor role within Christian theology.[4] But for Warfield, apologetics is central to Christianity, because it is in the world "to *reason* its way to the dominion of the world."[5] Christianity presents itself as "the only reasonable religion" that has as its task "to *reason* the world into the acceptance of the 'truth.'"[6] Just because people denied the rational validity of the Christian faith or refused to use their reasoning to either defend it or listen to its defense did not then mean that the true Christian should concede pressing rational argumentation.[7] The expressed declaration of God's word regarding what the apostle Paul did in Acts 17 and 18 clarifies that reasoning with the unregenerate and calling them to repentance is what the Christian ought to do. This was nothing less or more than what John the Baptist and Jesus were said to have done in preaching, "Repent, for the kingdom of heaven is at hand" (Matt 3:2; 4:17). The statement is a concise summation of what sinners must do (throughout their lives) and the reason why they must and can do it.

Warfield, therefore, regarded apologetics as an unavoidable aspect of the entire Christian faith and life, because Jesus had come to destroy the works of the devil (1 John 3:8). These diabolical works encompassed the totality of who we are as humans and the purpose for which God created man as male and female in his image to be fruitful, multiply, fill the earth, and subdue it (Gen 1:26–28). In other words, God created humans to fulfill an earth-wide purpose and Satan's work was not confined to the human soul or some narrow sphere of spirituality divorced from the

4. See, for instance, Kuyper, *Principles of Sacred Theology*, 150–76.

5. Warfield, "Review of De *Zekerheid Geloofs*," in *Selected Shorter Writings* 2:120. Italics Warfield's.

6. Warfield, "Christianity the Truth," in *Selected Shorter Writings* 2:213. Italics Warfield's.

7. Warfield, "Right of Systematic Theology," in *Selected Shorter Writings* 2:228.

physical material realm in which people were given to live, form societies, and subdue the whole earth. For Warfield, the Christian faith and life entailed every aspect of creation, because God is both the creator and redeemer who is engaged in a re-creation in his work of redemption that emphasizes the organic union of people not merely to God in the narrowest sense, but also to the creation itself in the widest sense. These emphases can be seen, in part, in numerous essays that Warfield wrote. What follows is a brief sketch of some of Warfield's more prominent essays that might aid the reader in gaining a better grasp of his apologetical insights and approach.

## A BRIEF BIBLIOGRAPHICAL ESSAY

Warfield specifically addresses the nature and function of apologetics in his essay "Apologetics" in volume 9 of the edition of his *Works*. There he states that it is

> the function of apologetics to investigate, explicate, and establish the grounds on which a theology—a science, or systematized knowledge of God—is possible; and on the basis of which every science which has God for its object must rest, if it be a true science with claims to a place within the circle of the sciences. It necessarily takes its place, therefore, at the head of the departments of theological science and finds its task in the establishment of the validity of the knowledge of God which forms the subject-matter of these departments; that we may then proceed through the succeeding departments of exegetical, historical systematic, and practical theology, to explicate, appreciate, systematize and propagate it in the world.[8]

Throughout the essay, Warfield explains the nature and function of apologetics that is consistent with the quote above. He explicitly denies that the Christian apologist makes his or her primary appeal to the reasoning of the non-Christian. As he wrote:

> It is certainly not the business of apologetics to take up each tenet of Christianity in turn and seek to establish its truth by a direct appeal to reason. Any attempt to do this, no matter on what philosophical basis the work of demonstration be begun or by what methods it be pursued, would transfer us at once into the atmosphere and betray us into the devious devices of the old vulgar rationalism,

8. Warfield, "Apologetics," in *Works* 9:4.

> the primary fault of which was that it asked for a direct rational demonstration of the truth of each Christian teaching in turn.[9]

Yet, it would be incorrect, according to Warfield, to think that just because a direct appeal to human reason by itself was not in accord with Christian apologetics that this meant that there was no place for reasoning with the non-Christian. In part, the Christian can understand the role of reasoning with the non-Christian by understanding the very nature of saving faith itself. While he agreed that saving faith is "a moral act and the gift of God, it is yet formally conviction passing into confidence; and that all forms of conviction must rest on evidence as their ground." Yet, "it is not faith but reason which investigates the nature and validity of this ground." By this, Warfield was not affirming that human reason is not an exercise in trust or faith, but rather that the Christian's saving faith in Jesus did not come about apart from the individual rationally considering whether such faith was actually rationally valid. In other words, "the faith which God gives" in salvation is not "an irrational faith" or "a faith without cognizable ground in right reason." After all, the Christian believes in God "because it is rational to believe in Him, not even though it be irrational." This does not mean that "mere reasoning" can make someone a Christian, but this "is not because faith is not the result of evidence, but because a dead soul cannot respond to the evidence." Warfield believed that the "action of the Holy Spirit in giving faith is not apart from evidence, but along with evidence; and in the first instance consists in preparing the soul for the reception of the evidence."[10] Warfield rejected both rationalism (human reasoning is the supreme authority for knowledge claims) and fideism (faith requires no other justification than itself).

While his essay "Apologetics" reveals Warfield's understanding of the nature and function of apologetics, it is precisely because Warfield saw apologetics as foundational to all theology that we grasp more clearly his views on the subject by reading other essays where he addressed the nature of systematic theology, and the biblical doctrines of revelation and salvation.

In his essays "The Biblical Idea of Revelation," "Christianity and Revelation," and "The Idea of Revelation and Theories of Revelation," Warfield explained the Christian doctrine of revelation.[11] He used the

9. Warfield, "Apologetics," in *Works* 9:8–9.

10. Warfield, "Apologetics," in *Works* 9:15.

11. Warfield, "Biblical Idea of Revelation," in *Works* 1:3–34; "Christianity and

common categories of general and special revelation, but also identified the term *general* with *natural* or *cosmical* and the term *special* with *supernatural* or *soteriological.* For Warfield, it was vital to understand that the two types of revelation existed in an organic union, and this is the key to his analysis of each type of revelation in itself, and the relationship the two have to each other. Since the two types of revelation are actually not disconnected, there is a sense in which we ought to affirm that there is a supernatural character to natural revelation and a natural aspect to supernatural revelation. Of course, humans are both the recipients of this revelation and in various ways a part of both. So, Warfield not only goes into great depth in explaining the intricacies of these relationships, but helps reveal how all the doctrines of the Christian faith and life are organically related to the biblical doctrine of revelation. Warfield did this on the basis of his knowledge of and adherence to the Westminster Confession of Faith, the Shorter Catechism, which he had memorized by the age of six, and the Larger Catechism, which he had memorized as a teenager. Anyone wishing to understand what wielded the greatest influence upon Warfield's thought would do well to start by placing proper weight to this historical fact.

Unavoidably related to Warfield's view of Scripture's doctrine of revelation is his understanding of the theological nature of all knowledge. In his essays "The Idea of Systematic Theology," "The Task and Method of Systematic Theology," "The Right of Systematic Theology," "Theology a Science," and "Indispensableness of Systematic Theology,"[12] we discover him explaining the union between human knowledge (epistemology)

---

Revelation," in *Selected Shorter Writings* 1:23–30; "Idea of Revelation," in *Works* 1:37–48.

12. Warfield, "Idea of Systematic Theology," in *Works* 9:49–87; "Task and Method of Systematic Theology," in *Works* 9:91–109; "Right of Systematic Theology," in *Selected Shorter Writings* 2:219–79; "Theology a Science," in *Selected Shorter Writings* 2:207–12; "Indispensableness of Systematic Theology," 280–88. This quote from "Task and Method of Systematic Theology" (*Works* 9:97) gets to the heart of Warfield's position: "We cannot thus lightly renounce the knowledge of the most important object of knowledge in the whole compass of knowledge. Over against the world and all that is in the world . . . stands God; and He—He Himself, not our thought about Him or our beliefs concerning Him, but He Himself—is the object of our highest knowledge. And to know Him is not merely the highest exercise of the human intellect; it is the indispensable complement of the circle of human science, which, without the knowledge of God, is fatally incomplete. It was not without reason that Augustine renounced the knowledge of all else but God and the soul; and that Calvin declares the knowledge of God and ourselves the sum of all useful knowledge. Without the knowledge of God it is not too much to say we know nothing rightly, so that the renunciation of the knowledge of God carries with it renunciation of all right knowledge."

and theology. It all revolves around understanding God as the creator and redeemer. Through these essays one can see Warfield, the Presbyterian, devoted to the Westminster Confession of Faith, giving expression to its doctrine of God as the creator and providential redeemer.[13]

Complementing these essays that specifically and explicitly explore and explain the Christian view regarding the most central features of the relationships between epistemology, theology, and anthropology are volumes 3 and 4 in Warfield's *Works* on perhaps the two most influential theologians in the history of the church—Augustine and Calvin. In these we have illuminating evidence of Warfield, the historical theologian, unpacking how Augustine and Calvin understood the doctrine of the knowledge of God. Richard A. Muller's assessment that Warfield's work "on Calvin's doctrines of the knowledge of God and of the Trinity . . . constitutes a major monographic effort still to be reckoned with" should fuel further reading of Warfield on these two theological giants.[14]

In numerous other essays in the *Selected Shorter Writings* volumes, not to mention lengthier academic essays in the *Works* volumes and sermons he preached that are found in *Faith and Life* and *The Saviour of the World*, one discovers Warfield explaining the various doctrines of the Christian faith as he proclaims the gospel of the Lord Jesus.[15] All of them give expression to his view that all the doctrines of the Christian faith and life are organically united, so to rightly apprehend and comprehend one of them, one cannot help but grasp, to some degree, all the others. In

13. For a concise treatment of Warfield's theological epistemology see Smith, "'Circle of the Sciences,'" 165–81.

14. Smith, *B. B. Warfield's Scientifically Constructive*, 40; cf. 141n; Muller, *Post Reformation Reformed Dogmatics* 3:28.

15. Warfield, *Faith and Life*; *Saviour of the World*. For representative examples beyond ones already mentioned cf. "Christian Supernaturalism," in *Works* 9:25–46; "On Faith in Its Psychological Aspects," in *Works* 9:313–42; "Latest Phase of Historical Rationalism," in *Works* 9:585–645; "Mysticism and Christianity," in *Works* 9:649–66; "God and Human Religion and Morals," in *Selected Shorter Writings* 1:41–45; "How to Get Rid of Christianity," in *Selected ShorterWritings* 1:51–60; "Significance of the Confessional Doctrine," in *Selected Shorter Writings* 1:93–102; "Some Thoughts on Predestination," in *Selected Shorter Writings* 1:103–09; "God's Providence Over All," in *Selected Shorter Writings* 1:110–15; "Jesus Christ the Propitiation," in *Selected Shorter Writings* 1:167–77; "Resurrection of Christ a Historical Fact," in *Selected Shorter Writings* 1:178–92; "Resurrection of Christ a Fundamental Doctrine," in *Selected Shorter Writings* 1:193–202; "What Is Calvinism," in *Selected Shorter Writings* 1:389–92; "Religious Life of Theological Students," in *Selected Shorter Writings* 1:411–25; "Westminster Doctrine of Holy Scripture," in *Selected Shorter Writings* 2:560–571; "Dogmatic Spirit," in *Selected Shorter Writings* 2:663–67; "Authority, Intellect, Heart," in *Selected Shorter Writings* 2:668–71; "Heresy and Concession," in *Selected Shorter Writings* 2:672–79.

turn, we learn that to grow or mature as a Christian means to improve one's understanding of the doctrines by improving one's understanding of their organic relation to each other that then produces greater love for and faithful obedience to the Lord Jesus. Thus, Christianity "is the power of a new life" and neither an ideology nor "program of conduct."[16] In all these we encounter Warfield's apologetic methodology: proclaim the gospel of the Lord Jesus Christ by explaining the doctrines of the Christian faith and life in their organic relations. By the very nature of the case, resistance to any one particular doctrine automatically becomes resistance to all the other doctrines united to it. In turn, the strength of the argument is experienced in the interconnectivity of all the doctrines. Warfield's perspective was that the gospel is "a perfect and perfectly consistent system of truth," so to seek to merely defend the minimum of what one could defend was to lose "the grandest scheme of thought ever propounded to the world." The one who did this would go far towards likely forfeiting "the testimony of the Holy Spirit." Thus, "it may well prove true that he who speaks boldly in God's name all the truth that has been entrusted to him will have cause to admire God's power."[17]

In part, this is how we can see that those who have tried to dismiss Warfield's scholarship in full, or in part, on the basis of its dependence on Scottish common sense realism, or any other philosophy they have deemed contrary to Scripture, have neither sufficiently reckoned with his exposition of Scripture or the Westminster Confession of Faith, nor grasped his most fundamental assertion regarding the nature, content, and function of Christian doctrine. It raises the question as to whether they have actually read him at all.

But, as this work has attempted to show, recognizing the organic nature of Christian doctrine not only allows us to grasp the fullness of the gospel, but also enables us to explain it more accurately to others, because it has been established in us, who have been willing to explore it and discovered what it actually is—the living truth of God in the man Christ Jesus, who saves humans from sin and the entire cosmos by the power of God's Spirit so that one day the knowledge of the Lord will cover the earth like the waters cover the sea (Isa 11:9; Hab 2:14). May we continue

16. Warfield, "Christianity and Our Times," in *Selected Shorter Writings* 1:47. That this power of new life came solely from Jesus, according to Warfield, could be seen, among other ways, in that in this same essay, he wrote: "Christianity is the cross; and he who makes the cross of Christ of none effect eviscerates Christianity" (1:47).

17. Warfield, "Heresy and Concession," in *Selected Shorter Writings* 2:678.

to explore it so that we are enlivened and equipped to explain it to others so that it is further established in we who already believe it, and afresh in those who have yet to believe it.

# Appendix

## "A Brief Explanation on Why We Can Trust the New Testament"

Christianity is a historical reality, and as a religious faith it is united to historical events. Thus, it is not first and foremost defined by the subjective experience of those who confess it, but by the empirically verifiable historical events that have established it. The four New Testament Gospels are historical documents that make truth claims about the life, death, resurrection, and ascension of Jesus. The truthfulness of Christianity is unavoidably united to the New Testament text and in particular the Gospel accounts. The following reasons briefly explain why we have valid reasons why we can trust the reliability of the Gospel accounts. Any one of these by itself might not be all that significant, although I would argue that number 9 is quite significant and even beyond a credible explanation apart from the resurrection of Jesus. Yet, we must be careful to remember that what is "reasonable" or a "credible explanation" to one person may not be to another. What an individual allows as a presupposition makes all the difference as to what one does with the evidence. But there are objective realities outside of us all that are what they are regardless of how we interpret them. Still, the fact remains that together all ten of these warrant our trusting that the Gospels are testifying to the truth—Jesus is the Christ, the Son of the living God, and there is salvation in no one other than him. They also raise the question: What argument can refute all ten of these truths?

## 1. THE EDUCATIONAL SYSTEM IN THE ANCIENT WORLD

Our educational method is almost always determined by *how* we think people access information. The first-century Mediterranean world was a heavily oral culture; information came primarily through speaking. Speaking and listening played dominant roles in the dissemination of information. Consequently, people were much more versed in *listening*. It ought not to surprise us that, in matters that they all report, Matthew, Mark, and Luke share 85 percent correspondence with respects to their wording.

## 2. THE CONCERN FOR PRESERVING WRITTEN RELIGIOUS TEXTS

Number 1 does not mean that there were not written texts. There certainly were and those that existed were highly valued. Yet, this was especially the character of the life of religious writings: writings believed to have been received from a deity for the purpose of imparting a blessing or a curse. Dr. Robert Vasholz's *The Old Testament Canon in the Old Testament Church* is an excellent resource on this matter. Vasholz states, "The idea of canonicity was a widely held practice and had a long history in biblical and pre-biblical times."[1] The result was that this was not only the ethos of the culture in which the New Testament documents were written, but also was a significant part of the Jewish culture that was itself part of the broader culture of the ancient Near East. The Jews were obsessed with the preservation of a religious text—the Old Testament. If we are knowledgeable about this characteristic of the ancient Near East and the Jewish culture of the first century, we should not be surprised that the written Gospels were preserved so that we have a faithful rendering of what the original authors wrote. In fact, the New Testament is by far the most well-attested document in ancient history. No other document even comes close. For example, consider the following data (dates are approximate):

1. Vasholz, *Old Testament Canon*, 8.

| Source | When Written | Earliest Copy | Span | Number of Copies |
|---|---|---|---|---|
| Aristotle | 384–322 BC | AD 1100 | 1,450 yrs. | 49* |
| Homer (*Iliad*) | 900 BC | 400 BC | 500 yrs. | 643 |
| NT | AD 40–100 | AD 125 | 25 yrs. | 24,000+[2] |
| *—of any one work | | | | |

## 3. JESUS TAUGHT IN A MEMORABLE WAY

Jesus was regularly using smaller overstatements (Matt 5:29–30; Luke 14:26), exaggerations (Matt 23:23–24—not capable of being done as opposed to the previous category), puns (Matt 23:23–24—the terms *gnat* and *camel* in Aramaic sound alike; Matt 16:18—Peter's name and the term "rock" are *petra* and *petros*), similes (Matt 10:16; 12:40), metaphors (Matt 5:13; Mark 8:15), proverbs (Matt 6:21, 34) riddles (not an easily understandable category given our cultural differences; nonetheless, see Matt 10:34; 13:52), paradoxes (things that only appear to be contradictory; Mark 10:43–44; Luke 14:11), particular types of arguments (Matt 6:28–30; 7:9–11), irony (Matt 16:2–3, Luke 12:16–20), questions (Mark 8:27–32; 10:36), parabolic actions (Luke 19:1–6; Mark 3:14–19), and poetry (this type does not necessarily rhyme, but it does have a particular rhythm to it; Matt 7:7–8; Mark 3:24–25; Luke 6:27–28) as means to get his point across.[3] All of these aided in memory. They also stirred interest in what Jesus taught. Mark 6:35–36 and 8:2–3 indicate that it was Jesus's teachings that brought the large crowd together. Matthew 7:28 tells us that the multitudes were amazed at his teachings.

## 4. MEMORABLE THINGS WERE TAKING PLACE AROUND JESUS

According to the Gospel accounts, Jesus healed the paralyzed, the leprous, the maimed, the deaf, the blind, the bleeding, fed thousands with a few loaves and fishes, turned water into wine, stopped a storm on the

2. Comfort, *Quest for the Original Text*. See also McDowell and McDowell, *Evidence That Demands a Verdict*, 52–56.

3. Stein, *Method and Message of Jesus' Teaching*, 7–33.

Sea of Galilee, even healed people when he wasn't even in their presence, and raised the dead. He was involved in some extremely controversial debates with the most powerful and learned people in the Jewish culture. If indeed these things took place, one probably would have had to work diligently at forgetting them in order not to remember them. One should also add to this that the first heresy regarding Jesus in the early church was Docetism—the belief that Jesus only seemed human, but really was not. Why would this have been likely for people to believe? One very reasonable answer is that people's perceptions of Jesus was that he wasn't exactly a normal human being precisely because of the astonishing things that he was credited with doing.

## 5. GOSPELS LACK TEACHING THAT LATER TROUBLED THE EARLY CHURCH

If the Gospels are indeed products (fabrications) of the second-century church as some of the unbelieving critical scholars propose, then why didn't they have Jesus say things that would have cleared up the problems that plagued the early church? Doesn't it make sense to suppose that they would have addressed in the Gospels the matters that were most pressing for them? If they would willingly fabricate the Gospel accounts, then why would they not continue such an elaborate hoax by clarifying these matters that caused great trouble in the early church? Yet the Gospels are strangely silent about the following matters that caused significant controversy in the early church—the role of woman; the Jew/gentile issue; spiritual gifts; the marriage relationship of a Christian to a non-Christian; the role of the ceremonial and even moral law in the Christian life and how it relates to the life, death, resurrection, and ascension of Jesus; the administration or government of the church; eating meat sacrificed to idols; and qualifications for church leaders. To be certain this is an argument from silence. An argument from silence can rarely lead to *a* particular conclusion. Nonetheless, some can raise unavoidable issues that create significant problems for one side in a debate. This is the case with respects to this argument.

## 6. THE BIBLICAL WRITERS DO NOT HIDE THEIR FAULTS OR THOSE OF GOD'S COVENANT PEOPLE

Ancient literature that was written in order to be a historical account of a person, a group, or event was often done with the intention of presenting that person, group, or event in a way that was favorable to either the author or the main subjects of the narrative. Repeatedly in the Gospel accounts, Jesus's disciples are not presented in a favorable light. They frequently do not understand Jesus and have to ask clarifying questions, and even then, Jesus's answers regularly elude their intellectual grasp. James, the half-brother of Jesus, is among those who thought Jesus was crazy (Mark 3:20; John 7:5). Peter, who is the leader of the group (Matt 16:13–23), is so confused at one point that Jesus calls him Satan for his profession of what he thinks it means that Jesus is the Christ. The apostle Paul confesses that he was the chief of sinners (1 Tim 1:12–16) because he had previously persecuted the church. And nowhere in either the Old or New Testament will you find any of the biblical writers crediting Old Testament Israel or the New Testament church with wonderful wisdom, great moral courage, or astute intellectual insight that they possessed or acquired by themselves. In other words, no part of the Bible reads like a slanted, fictitious account that praises the virtues of writers or the community they represent. There is a character of objectivity to the text that is unparalleled in all of human literature, not merely ancient literature.

## 7. WRITERS OF SCRIPTURE DISTINGUISH BETWEEN THEIR WORDS AND JESUS'S

Paul in 1 Cor 7:10 and 12 distinguishes between when he is giving his counsel and when he is actually speaking as a binding authority upon the church for all ages by the following phrases: "not I, but the Lord," and "I, not the Lord." This speaks to two very significant realities. First, the apostles did understand, contrary to even a significant number of allegedly conservative scholars, that they had the authority to represent Jesus through their speaking and writing (1 Thess 2:13), and when they did, their words were binding upon the covenant community or church. The apostles whom Jesus chose through the work of the Spirit were given a privileged authoritative interpretation of Jesus's life, death, resurrection, and ascension (see John 15:26–27; 16:13–15; Acts 1:1–3). The awareness of this uniqueness possessed by the apostles was part of the faith of the church from the very beginning (see 1 Thess 2:13). Later generations would have to wrestle with who wrote what, and therefore have to discern which written texts were and were not authoritative. But that simply highlights the *historical* reality of the Christian faith. It does not mean that the church decided or picked which books were in the canon or the Bible. Instead, it highlights the reality that the church discerned through the guidance of God's Spirit which books already were authoritative. No person in the church decides or picks what is God's word. God does that. God attests to himself. The apostles at some point understood this. Second, they made a distinction between themselves as men who were fallen sinners, prone to error in a variety of ways, and those who nonetheless were used by the Holy Spirit in a way that the Holy Spirit did not use others. In other words, when Paul says in 2 Tim 3:16–17 that "all Scripture is God-breathed and profitable for teaching, for reproof, for correction, for training in righteousness, that the man of God may be thoroughly equipped for every good work," he is *not* saying, contrary to Roman Catholic thought, that the apostles are inspired and are able to pass on this power and authority to others. Rather, it is the text that is God-breathed, and is the divine instrument used by God to equip God's people to do what God calls and equips them to do. We were dependent upon the prophets and apostles precisely because all of God's creatures (including the prophet and apostles) are always dependent upon God. God makes himself known. The apostles knew and explained this, and knew that they possessed an authority unique to them. Not only was this part of the church's faith from the beginning, but also the apostles distinguished between their words and statements that were binding upon the church and those that were not. In other words, they were fully aware when they were and were not exercising their apostolic authority to write and proclaim Scripture. Such a doctrine is touched on in a general way in the Gospels, but comes out in clearer exposition in the New Testament letters.

## 8. THE APOSTLES WILLINGLY DIED FOR HIM AND LED OTHERS TO THEIR DEATHS

In some ways this is an expansion on number 6 above. It is one thing for an individual, or even a group, to die for what they believe is the truth and yet are simply mistaken about. It is another thing to willingly fabricate a hoax, to persevere in that hoax, convince others to believe in it, and to do so all the way to your death and the death of others. Do people willingly die for what they *know* is a lie? How does one explain how the disciples changed from being fearful, distraught, and confused after the crucifixion to being courageous, overjoyed, and certain of what they should teach and do in Jesus's name? The teaching of the unbelieving critical scholars is simply that the disciples came to believe that Jesus's example and teachings inspired them (the disciples). That is what the Gospel documents disallow us from thinking that they thought. The disciples' depth of understanding of both Jesus's example and teachings were horribly inadequate. This is one of the main messages of the Gospel of Mark. The disciples rarely understood correctly, regularly needed to be told specifically what things meant, and, even then, still ended up leaving him in his time of greatest need. Peter, of course, denied that he ever knew Jesus. In other words, the disciples were selfish, cowardly liars who could hardly get anything correct, on top of being fearful, distraught, and confused after the crucifixion. The explanation by the unbelieving critical scholars is simply not adequate because it doesn't accurately handle all of the historical data.

## 9. THE ENTIRE BIBLE AND THE CHURCH

This flows out of the final question in number 8. These two always go together. The Westminster Confession of Faith 1.5 mentions the evidence for how the word of God demonstrates itself as the word of God. Can these evidences be explained any other way that does not lead us to conclude that the Scriptures are what they claim to be? In order to be a reputable historian one must give a credible explanation for what is. Is there a credible explanation for the persistence and growth of the church of the Lord Jesus Christ through all the centuries, across the entire world, in the midst of diverse cultures, in the face of repeated attempts to corrupt her from within and wage war on her from the outside?

## 10. DISPUTES OVER THE INTERPRETATION OF THE BIBLE AND NOT ITS RELIABILITY

The questions raised by the vast majority of non-Christian scholars throughout the history of biblical scholarship has never been whether we have the correct text or whether there are other texts of equal weight and authority regarding the Jesus of the Gospels. Rather, the place where most non-Christian scholars have levied their attacks is on the interpretation of the canonical books. Documents like the Gospel of Judas and the Gospel of Thomas were never accepted in the church simply because they do not read like anything else in Scripture. They are almost completely lacking any historical narrative (a characteristic that dominates much of the Bible), and present a picture of Jesus that is quite at odds with the New Testament. The definition of "gospel," according to the four canonical Gospels, is the acts of Jesus, and the message about those acts that save people from the penalty, presence, and pollution of sin. The Gospel of Judas and the Gospel of Thomas are lacking such a proclamation.[4] The majority of biblical scholars who attempt to undermine the authority of the Scriptures do so by trying to reinterpret the text the church uses.

Other arguments could be, and have been, advanced for the historical reliabilities of the New Testament Gospels. When one considers all ten of these, not to mention other relevant points made in the previous ten chapters, one has more than a sufficient basis for believing the testimony of the New Testament that Jesus of Nazareth from the first-century Mediterranean world not only lived a perfectly holy life, but also died a sacrificially substitutionary death on the cross, paying the God-appointed penalty for sin, rose bodily from the grave, ascended bodily into heaven, promising to return, and has, together with God the Father, sent the Holy Spirit so that his gospel might be proclaimed and believed, resulting in the salvation of sinners from their sin. By doing this, Jesus has also rescued the entire cosmos from misery and ruin of sin, and thus the gospel of the Lord Jesus Christ is about the organic union of redemption of God's covenant people with this rescue of the created order.

4. See fuller details and explanations on these other Gospels in McDowell and McDowell, *Evidence That Demands a Verdict*, 128–39.

# Bibliography


Baird, William. *From Deism to Tubingen*. Vol. 1 of *History of New Testament Research*. Minneapolis: Augsburg Fortress, 1992.

———. *From Jonathan Edwards to Rudolf Bultmann*. Vol. 2 of *History of New Testament Research*. Minneapolis: Augsburg Fortress, 2003.

Bavinck, Herman. *Reformed Dogmatics*. Edited by John Bolt. Translated by John Vriend. 4 vols. Grand Rapids: Baker Academic, 2003.

Bingham, Matthew. *A Heart Aflame for God: A Reformed Approach to Spiritual Formation*. Wheaton, IL: Crossway, 2025.

Brock, Corey C., and N. Gray Sutanto. *Neo-Calvinism: A Theological Introduction*. Bellingham, WA: Lexham, 2022.

Brown, Colin. *Jesus in European Protestant Thought: 1778–1860*. Studies in Historical Theology 1. Editor David C. Steinmetz. Durham, NC: Labyrinth, 1985.

Calhoun, David B. *Princeton Seminary*. 2 vols. Carlisle, PA: Banner of Truth Trust, 1994, 1996.

Carson, D. A. "The Dangers and Delights of Postmodernism." *Modern Reformation* (2003) 11–17.

———. *The Gospel According to John*. Grand Rapids: Eerdmans, 1990.

Cohen, Jonathan. "Rationality." In *A Companion to Epistemology*, edited by Jonathan Dancy and Ernest Sosa, 415–20. Cambridge, MA: Blackwell, 1993.

Comfort, Philip Wesley. *The Quest for the Original Text of the New Testament*. Grand Rapids: Baker, 1992.

Copleston, Frederick J. *A History of Philosophy* 4. NY: Doubleday, 1985.

Cragg, Gerald R. *The Church and the Age of Reason, 1648–1789*. New York: Penguin, 1976.

———. *Freedom and Authority: A Study of English Thought in the Early Seventeenth Century*. Philadelphia: Westminster, 1975.

Craigie, Peter C. *The Book of Deuteronomy*. The New International Commentary of the Old Testament. Grand Rapids: Eerdmans, 1976.

Curley, Edwin. "Rationalism." In *A Companion to Epistemology*, edited by Jonathan Dancy and Ernest Sosa, 411–15. Cambridge, MA: Blackwell, 1993.

DeYoung, Kevin, et al., eds. *New Perspectives on Old Princeton, 1812–1929*. Routledge Studies in Evangelicalism. London: Routledge, 2025.

Dorrien, Gary. *The Making of American Liberal Theology: Reimagining Progressive Religion, 1805–1900*. Louisville: Westminster John Knox, 2001.

Eglinton, James. *Trinity as Organism: Towards a New Reading of Herman Bavinck's Organic Motif*. London: T. & T. Clark, 2012.

Frame, John M. *The Doctrine of the Knowledge of God*. Phillipsburg, NJ: P. & R., 1987.

———. *A History of Western Philosophy and Theology*. Phillipsburg, NJ: P. & R., 2015.

Harrisville, Roy A., and Walter Sundberg. *The Bible in Modern Culture: Theology and Historical-Critical Method from Spinoza to Kasemann*. Grand Rapids: Eerdmans, 1995.

Hazard, Paul. *The European Mind, 1680–1715*. Cleveland: World Publishing, 1967.

Helseth, Paul Kjoss. "B. B. Warfield's Apologetical Appeal to 'Right Reason': Evidence of a Rather Bald Rationalism?" *The Scottish Bulletin of Evangelical Theology* 16 (1998) 156–77.

———. *"Right Reason" and the Princeton Mind: An Unorthodox Proposal*. Phillipsburg, NJ: P. & R., 2010.

Hoch, Ronald E., and David P. Smith. *Old School, New Clothes: The Cultural Blindness of Christian Education*. Eugene, OR: Wipf & Stock, 2011.

Hodge, Charles. "What Is Christianity?" *Biblical Repertory and Princeton Review* 32 (1860) 118–61.

Johnson, Gary L. W., ed. *B. B. Warfield: Essays on His Life and Thought*. Phillipsburg, NJ: P. & R., 2007.

Jones, David Clyde. *Biblical Christian Ethics*. Phillipsburg, NJ: P. & R., 1994.

Kapic, Kelly. *The Christian Life*. Grand Rapids: Zondervan, 2025.

Kennedy, Simon P. *Against Worldview: Reimagining Christian Formation as Growth in Wisdom*. Bellingham, WA: Lexham, 2024.

Knight, George W. III. *The Pastoral Epistles*. Vol. 5 of *The New International Greek Testament Commentary*, edited by I. Howard Marshall and W. Ward Gasque. Grand Rapids: Eerdmans, 1992.

Kuyper, Abraham. *Lectures on Calvinism*. Grand Rapids: Eerdmans, 1931.

———. *Principles of Sacred Theology*. Introduction by Benjamin B. Warfield. Translated by J. Hendrik DeVries. Reprint. Scarsdale, NY: Westminster Discount Book Services, n.d.

Linnemann, Eta. *Historical Criticism of the Bible: Methodology or Ideology?* Translated by Robert W. Yarborough. Grand Rapids: Baker, 1990.

———. *Is There a Synoptic Problem? Rethinking the Literary Dependence of the First Three Gospels*. Grand Rapids: Baker, 1992.

Lints, Richard. *The Fabric of Theology: A Prolegomena to Evangelical Theology*. Grand Rapids: Eerdmans, 1993.

Maier, Gerhard. *Biblical Hermeneutics*. Translated by Robert W. Yarbrough. Wheaton, IL: Crossway, 1994.

McDowell, Josh. *The New Evidence that Demands a Verdict*. Nashville: Thomas Nelson, 1999.

McGrath, Alistair. *The Making of Modern German Christology, 1775–1990*. 2nd ed. Grand Rapids: Zondervan, 1994.

Machen, J. Gresham. *What Is Faith?* Grand Rapids: Eerdmans, 1925.

Mathison, Keith A. *Toward a Reformed Apologetic: A Critique of the Thought of Cornelius Van Til*. United Kingdom: Mentor, 2024.

Muller Richard A. *Post-Reformation Reformed Dogmatics: The Rise and Development of Reformed Orthodoxy, ca. 1520 to ca. 1725*. 4 Vols. 2nd ed. Grand Rapids: Baker Academic, 2003.

Nash, Ronald. *Faith and Reason: Searching for a Rational Faith*. Grand Rapids: Zondervan, 1988.

Naugle, David. *Worldview: The History of a Concept*. Grand Rapids: Eerdmans, 2002.

Noll, Mark A. "Afterword: Old Princeton in History." In *New Perspectives on Old Princeton, 1812–1929*, edited by Kevin DeYoung et al., 215–31. Routledge Studies in Evangelicalism. London: Routledge, 2025.

Old, Hughes Oliphant. *The Reading and Preaching of the Scriptures in the Worship of the Christian Church, Volume 1: The Biblical Period*. Grand Rapids: Eerdmans, 1998.

Oliphint, Scott K. *Covenantal Apologetics*. Wheaton, IL: Crossway, 2013.

Peterson, David G. *The Acts of the Apostles*. The Pillar New Testament Commentary. Edited by D. A. Carson. Grand Rapids: Eerdmans, 2009.

Ridderbos, Herman N. *Redemptive History and the New Testament Scriptures*. Translated by H. De Jongste. Revised by Richard B. Gaffin Jr. 2nd rev. ed. Phillipsburg, NJ: P. & R., 1988.

Sire, James W. *The Universe Next Door: A Basic Worldview Catalog*. 6th ed. Wheaton, IL: IVP Academic, 2020.

Smith, David P. *B. B. Warfield's Scientifically Constructive Theological Scholarship*. Evangelical Theological Society Monograph Series. Eugene, OR: Wipf & Stock, 2011.

———. "The 'Circle of the Sciences' and the Theological Nature of All Knowledge." In *New Perspectives on Old Princeton, 1812–1929*, edited by Kevin DeYoung et al., 165–81. Routledge Studies in Evangelicalism. London: Routledge, 2025.

Stein, Robert H. *The Method and Message of Jesus' Teaching*. Philadelphia: Westminster, 1978.

Stumpf, Samuel Enoch. *Socrates to Sartre: A History of Philosophy*. 5th rev. ed. New York: McGraw-Hill, 1993.

Trueman, Carl R. "The Renaissance." In *Revolutions in Worldview: Understanding the Flow of Western Thought*, edited by Andrew W. Hoffecker, 178–205. Phillipsburg, NJ: P. & R., 2007.

———. *The Rise and Triumph of the Modern Self: Cultural Amnesia, Expressive Individualism, and the Road to Sexual Revolution*. Wheaton, IL: Crossway, 2020.

———. *Strange New World: How Thinkers and Activists Redefined Identity and Sparked the Sexual Revolution*. Wheaton, IL: Crossway, 2022.

Van Til, Cornelius. *The Defense of the Faith*. Grand Rapids: Baker, 1972.

Vasholz, Robert I. *The Old Testament Canon in the Old Testament Church: The Internal Rationale for Old Testament Canonicity*. New York: Edwin Mellen, 1990.

Warfield, Benjamin Breckinridge. *The Power of God Unto Salvation*. Vestavia, AL: Solid Ground Christian Books, 2004.

———. *The Saviour of the World*. Carlisle, PA: Banner of Truth Trust, 1991.

———. *Selected Shorter Writings*. Edited John E. Meeter. 2 vols. Phillipsburg, NJ: P. & R., 1970, 1973.

———. "The Summation of the Gospel." In *Faith and Life*. Carlisle, PA: Banner of Truth Trust, 1990.

———. *The Works of Benjamin B. Warfield*. Edited by Ethelbert D. Warfield et al. 10 vols. New York: Oxford University Press, 1927–32.

Wilkins, Michael J. "Disciples." In *Dictionary of Jesus and the Gospels*, edited by Joel B. Green et al., 176–82. Downers Grove, IL: IVP, 1992.

Wolterstorff, Nicholas. *Reason Within the Bounds of Religion*. 2nd ed. Grand Rapids: Zondervan, 1988.

Wright, Christopher J. H. *The Mission of God: Unlocking the Bible's Grand Narrative.* Downers Grove, IL: IVP Academic, 2018.

Zaspel, Fred. *The Theology of B. B. Warfield: A Systematic Summary.* Wheaton, IL: Crossway, 2010.

www.ingramcontent.com/pod-product-compliance
Lightning Source LLC
LaVergne TN
LVHW050624100826
845148LV00011B/1718